The Life and Turbulent Times of Clara Dorothea Rackham

This is the first critical study of Clara Dorothea Rackham née Tabor (1875–1966), a towering figure in the suffrage, labour, co-operative, peace, and adult education movements but virtually forgotten today.

This clearly written and engaging study is based on unpublished primary sources including Rackham's unpublished speeches, letters, diaries, and contemporary media coverage of her work in local and national archives. It reassesses this remarkable woman not only as a politician who changed the face of Cambridge, the university city in which she lived and worked, but also as a public intellectual whose feminist advocacy of a fair, just, and equal society helped pave the way to Britain's postwar settlement and Welfare State. Rackham came to prominence as Chairman of the National Union of Women's Suffrage Societies, as a government factory inspector, and championing the rights of unemployed women in the 1930s. An early broadcaster on BBC radio, and among the first women appointed magistrates and councillors, her name became synonymous with enlightened local government. The transformation of women's lives in Victorian and twentieth-century Britain is crucial to understanding Rackham's ideals, intellectual formation, and priorities as a Labour Party politician.

This book will be of interest to historians and students of gender, history, and women's lives.

Maroula Joannou is Emerita Professor at Anglia Ruskin University attached to the Labour History Research Unit. She has published over forty book chapters and articles in peer-reviewed journals. She is the author of *The Mobile Woman and the Migrant Voice* and editor of volume eight of the Palgrave *History of British Women's Writing*.

Routledge Research in Gender and History

41 **Deviant Maternity**
Illegitimacy in Wales, c. 1680–1800
Angela Joy Muir

42 **Gender, Generations, and Communism in Central and Eastern Europe and Beyond**
Edited by Anna Artwińska and Agnieszka Mrozik

43 **Fathers and Sons in the English Middle Class, c. 1870–1920**
Laura Ugolini

44 **Women and Scottish Society, 1700–2000**
W.W.J. Knox

45 **Cinematic Representations of Women in Modern Celebrity Culture, 1900–1950**
Edited by María Cristina C. Mabrey and Leticia Pérez Alonso

46 **Oral Histories of Tibetan Women**
Whispers from the Roof of the World
Lily Xiao Hong Lee

47 **Women in the French Enlightenment**
From *Femme Savante* to Mother of the Family
Anna Maria Marchini

48 **The Life and Turbulent Times of Clara Dorothea Rackham**
Suffragist, Socialist, and Social Reformer
Maroula Joannou

For more information about this series, please visit: https://www.routledge.com/Routledge-Research-in-Gender-and-History/book-series/SE0422

The Life and Turbulent Times of Clara Dorothea Rackham

Suffragist, Socialist, and Social Reformer

Maroula Joannou

Routledge
Taylor & Francis Group
NEW YORK AND LONDON

First published 2023
by Routledge
605 Third Avenue, New York, NY 10158

and by Routledge
4 Park Square, Milton Park, Abingdon, Oxon, OX14 4RN

Routledge is an imprint of the Taylor & Francis Group, an informa business

Library of Congress Cataloging-in-Publication Data
Names: Joannou, Maroula, author.
Title: The life and turbulent times of Clara Dorothea Rackham : suffragist, socialist, and social reformer / Maroula Joannou.
Description: New York, NY : Routledge, 2023. |
Series: Routledge research in gender and history |
Includes bibliographical references and index. |
Identifiers: LCCN 2022019938 (print) | LCCN 2022019939 (ebook) |
ISBN 9780367373924 (hardback) | ISBN 9780367373931 (paperback) |
ISBN 9780429353499 (ebook)
Classification: LCC HD8393.R33 J63 2023 (print) |
LCC HD8393.R33 (ebook) | DDC 331.88092 [B]—dc23/eng/20220727
LC record available at https://lccn.loc.gov/2022019938
LC ebook record available at https://lccn.loc.gov/2022019939

ISBN: 978-0-367-37392-4 (hbk)
ISBN: 978-0-367-37393-1 (pbk)
ISBN: 978-0-429-35349-9 (ebk)

DOI: 10.4324/9780429353499

Typeset in Sabon
by codeMantra

To the Memory of Allan Brigham (1951–2020).

Street sweeper, historian, author, educator and Blue Badge guide whose legendary walking tours, writings and reflections on the lives of ordinary people in Cambridge have been an inspiration.

Contents

Figures

Tables

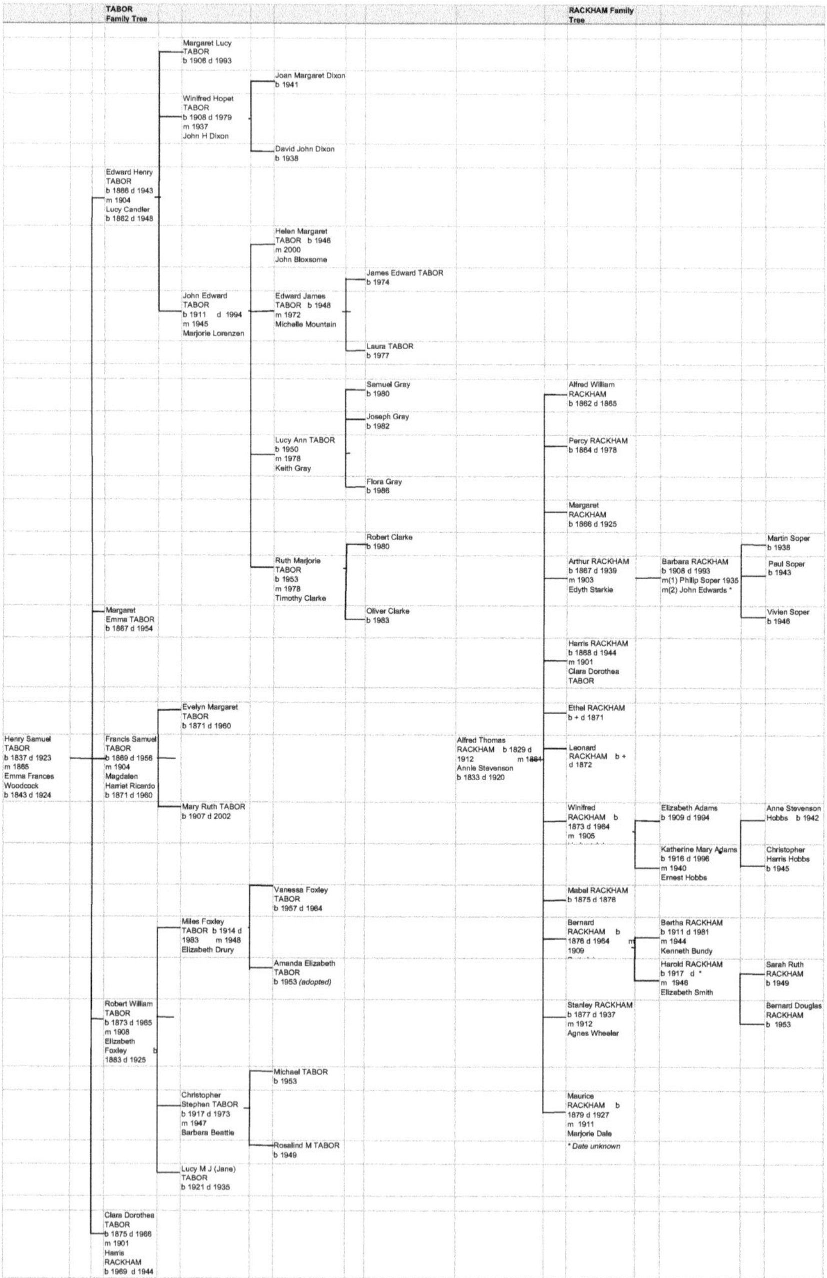

PLATE 1 Tabor and Rackham Family Trees. Courtesy of Helen and John Bloxsome and Lucy Tabor for the Tabor family tree and Sarah Rackham and Anne Stevenson Wright for the Rackham family tree.

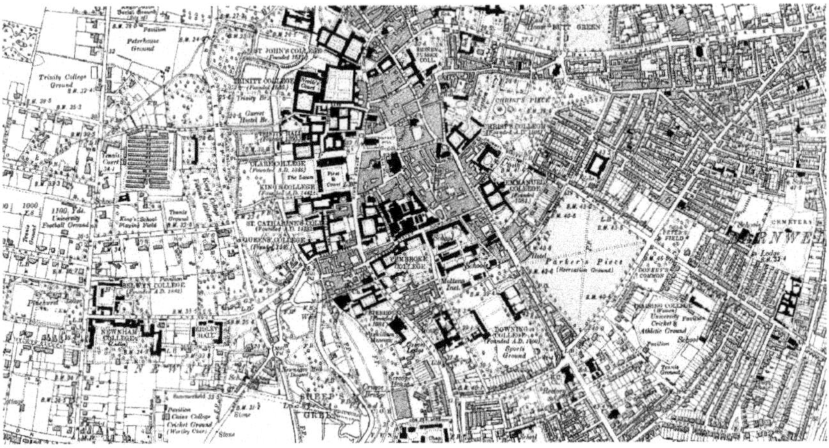

PLATE 2 Map of Cambridge in 1927. Courtesy of the Cambridgeshire Collection, Cambridge Central Library.

Acknowledgements

Access to archives and libraries was not possible for much of 2020 and 2021 and I thank Max Novick, my Commissioning Editor, and all at Routledge for their patience and understanding of the problems and delays that this has inevitably caused. In my own university, I thank Lucy Bland, Rohan McWilliam and the Anglia Ruskin Labour History Research Unit and Roderick Watkins, the Vice-Chancellor, for the financial support for the public event on Clara Rackham's life and work held in November, 2018. I deeply appreciate the invaluable archival research that Sue Kennedy was able to do for me in Hull after the Hull History Centre was re-opened to the public. I am very grateful to Lucy Bland, Sue Bruley, Peter Cunningham, Anne Logan, Angela V. John, Anne Summers, and Anne Stevenson Wright for generously setting aside their own work to read and comment helpfully on mine. The finished book has been immeasurably improved by virtue of their tact, acuity, and helpful revisions. In addition to his scholarly input on the history of education, Peter Cunningham has been efficient, reliable and good humoured whenever the need for practical help with computing and IT problems has arisen. I owe a huge debt to Carolyn Ferguson for her help with digital photography and the illustrations and for assisting me to transform a chaotic manuscript into a shape that was ready for submission.

I thank everyone whose interest and curiosity about Clara Rackham has made writing this book the pleasure it has been. They include my sister Androula, many good friends and neighbours, and all the groups, and organisations, local and national, which have invited me to speak. I acknowledge the support received from Frances Crook, Chief Executive of Howard League for Penal Reform and Claire McCarthy, who was then the General Secretary of the Co-operative Party.

On the Tabor side of Clara's family, I am deeply grateful to Lucy Tabor and Helen Bloxsome for their many insights into their great aunt's life and work and for showing me around Fennes, the beautiful north- Essex countryside, and the places where Clara grew up. Without their kindness, support and trust this book could not have been written. On the Rackham side of the family, my warm thanks go to Sarah Rackham and

Anne Stevenson Wright for their interest and encouragement, especially to Anne for the use of the reminiscences and anecdotes she has compiled on the extended Rackham family. I am indebted to former Cambridge city Councillor, Marie Thompson, for making available the materials that she had carefully assembled when she was planning to write her own biography of Clara.

My own thinking on Clara Rackham as a magistrate and penal reformer has been greatly influenced by the ground-breaking work of Anne Logan whom I thank for sharing both her published and unpublished research with me. I thank Sue Slack for her understanding of the women's suffrage movement in Cambridge, Gillian Sutherland for her encyclopaedic knowledge of the history of Newnham College, Deborah Thom for her expertise on the factory inspectorate, and Lucy Delap for her support for the project from the very beginning. The scholarship on the changing experience of women in the early twentieth century is rich, fascinating, and expansive. It is impossible to do full justice to this research in this book although I have tried my best to indicate how the work of feminist historians illuminates specific aspects of Clara's life and work within the main body of my text and through the use of references within the restricted word-limits available to me.

Archivists and librarians have been unfailingly helpful and I apologise to all whom I have been unable to mention individually by name. Special thanks must go to the librarians at Murray Edwards College, Cambridge, Anglia Ruskin University, and the Cambridge University Library Department of Manuscripts and University Archives, to Celia Tyler, Caroline Clifford, and Mary Burgess at the Cambridgeshire Collection at the Cambridge City Central Library, to Anne Thomson and Frieda Midgley, the archivists at Newnham College, Cambridge, and to John Wagstaff and Celia Varth in the library and archives of Christ's College, Cambridge.

Antony Carpen's lively and engaging 'Lost Cambridge' blog is a 'must' for anyone interested in Cambridge's pioneering women and has done much to introduce them to a new and younger audience. I thank Lucy Walker, Caro Wilson, Ila Chandavarkar, and everyone at the Mill Road History Society, Cambridge for many stimulating events over the years and for putting their research projects on line as well as all the town's enthusiastic 'kitchen-table historians', the contributors to Capturing Cambridge, and Helen Weinstein and Ironworks. This book is dedicated to Allan Brigham, Cambridge's much-loved and deeply missed people's historian who has taught many of us how the study of a city's past can underpin a vision of a more inclusive and democratic present and future.

Mary Joannou
Emerita Professor, Anglia Ruskin University, Cambridge.

Abbreviations

ASH	Anne Stevenson Wright formerly Hobbs (Family Reminiscences and Anecdotes)
BBC	British Broadcasting Corporation
CO	Conscientious Objector
COS	Charity Organisation Society
HLPF	Howard League for Penal Reform
JP	Justice of the Peace
LP	Labour Party
MA	Magistrates' Association
LSE	London School of Economics
MP	Member of Parliament
NUSEC	National Union of Societies for Equal Citizenship
NUWSS	National Union of Women's Suffrage Societies
NCW	National Council of Women
SJCIWO	Standing Joint Committee of Industrial Women's Organisations
TFP	Tabor Family Papers

Figure 0.1 Clara wearing necklace.
Courtesy of Helen Bloxsome and Lucy Tabor.

Introduction

This biography provides the first critical study of the suffragist, socialist, and social reformer, Clara Dorothea Rackham, née Tabor, known as Dorothea to her family. The commemorations of the centenary of women over thirty obtaining the vote in 2018 kindled some interest in Clara's achievements. Until then she was little-known outside Cambridge, the city which, with the exception of a few years spent as a factory inspector in London and in the North-West of England during the First World War, she loved and never left.

Who, then, was Clara Rackham? Her father, Henry Tabor, came from a long line of respected non-conformists who had farmed in north Essex for centuries. Clara's great-nieces Helen Bloxsome and Lucy Tabor continue the family tradition of responsible organic arable farming to this day. On her mother's side, the Woodcock family from Wigan in Lancashire was prominent in local affairs. Clara's sister, Margaret Tabor, after whom the Margaret Tabor Secondary Modern School for Girls, now the Tabor Academy in Braintree, is named, was an Alderman on Essex County Council and the first woman to be appointed a magistrate in Essex. Her niece, Mary Ruth Tabor, was a pioneering figure in the civic history of Stevenage, the first of the post-war New Towns.

The Rackham family into which Clara married were Unitarians who shared the Tabor family's socially progressive attitudes and dedication to public service, often combining the intellectual curiosity they fostered in all their children with a love of literature, music, and the arts. One brother-in-law, Arthur Rackham, was a leading artist in the golden age of book illustration. Another, Bernard Rackham, was a world authority on ceramics and their curator at the Victoria and Albert Museum in London. Clara's husband, Harris Rackham, a classical scholar at Christ's College, Cambridge, was a trustee of the Toynbee Hall settlement in the East End of London. He would, I think, have been bemused but not displeased had he known that the 'Lore Ipsum' placeholder text taken from his Loeb translation of Cicero's *De Finibus Bonorum et Malorum* is still used ubiquitously in modern typesetting and computer programming.

The transformation of the lives of women in late Victorian and early twentieth-century Britain is crucial to understanding Clara Rackham's

DOI: 10.4324/9780429353499-1

ideals, her intellectual formation, and her priorities as a Labour Party politician. Clara was born in 1875 at the height of Gladstonian Liberalism when bustles, flounces, and floor length dresses were *de rigueur*, and died in 1966 at the time of the first Wilson government when designer Mary Quant was manufacturing the mini-skirt six inches above the knee. She had witnessed, *inter-alia* two World Wars, the decline of the Liberal Party as a political force, the rise of Labour to power, and, like countless others, switched her allegiance from one party to the other. She had fought hard for, and lived to welcome, a veritable revolution in the status, rights, behaviour, and expectations of women. This, she cautioned her listeners in her last public speech read out to the National Association of Women in Cambridge in 1964 at the age of eighty-eight, still had far to go and should be regarded as unfinished business.

Clara Rackham's feminist ideas were shaped as an idealistic student in Newnham College, one of the two pioneering women's colleges at Cambridge University, and developed in the crucible of the women's suffrage movement. Alongside Jeannette Tawney, an alumna of Somerville College and the sister of William Beveridge, she was one of the first four women appointed as government factory inspectors during the First World War. Inspecting women in wartime factories gave her unique insights into the workplace and the nature of women's work that differed radically from the insights of the male leadership of the trade union movement. She was a recognised authority on the forty-hour week, unemployment, social security, and factory legislation. But for all her advocacy of workers' rights she was never a member of a trade union, and, in a male-dominated Labour Party where trade union membership mattered, was never given trade union support to fight a parliamentary seat.

As one of only two representatives of the Labour Party appointed to the Royal Commission on Unemployment Insurance, Clara led the hard-fought national battle against the National Government's attempts to reduce unemployment benefits ('the dole') and the extra-parliamentary opposition to the iniquitous Anomalies Act (1931) supported at the time by the bulk of trade unions and much of the Labour Party, whereby married women were prevented from claiming the benefits to which they had previously been entitled. An early broadcaster on BBC Radio, and among the first batch of women to be appointed magistrates and councillors in the 1920s, Clara served for thirty-one years on the borough council in Cambridge and twenty-eight years on the county council where her name became synonymous with enlightened local government.

My interest in Clara Rackham began around 2017 in the local archives, the Cambridgeshire Collection, housed in the Cambridge Central Library. As a specialist on the women's suffrage movement I knew a little about Clara as a leading suffragist and had a vague notion that 'she had done a lot for Cambridge' I wanted to find out more. An initial trawl of the local newspapers exceeded all expectations. As a public intellectual and a principled feminist, for whom political theory and practice were inseparable, Clara had applied her searching intellect to many of the important social questions of her day. The causes she championed had received extensive press coverage, particularly in *The Cambridge Independent* and *the Cambridge Daily News*. Some reforms transported one back to the days before the First World War, others to the middle of the twentieth century and the foundations of the Welfare State. Many struck me as timeless, 'modern', and advanced for their day.

The list was long and eclectic. The picture of Clara Rackham that was gradually taking shape in my mind was not of a garden variety local politician, albeit one with prodigious energy and commitment, but rather of a towering figure in the labour movement, the women's movement, the adult education movement, and in the worlds of local government and penal reform. So to write the biography that was taking shape in my mind I knew that I would have to search for information elsewhere. Preliminary enquiries revealed no manuscript sources, the *sine qua non* of any biography and ominous, if well-intentioned, warnings from friends along the lines of 'where angels fear to tread'. Moreover, I could find nobody in Cambridge who could remember Clara other than the late Lucy Munby, who furnished me with lively anecdotes but with no written documents until a fortuitous encounter with Marie Thompson. Marie is a former Cambridge city councillor who completed an MA at Ruskin College, Oxford in the 1980s with a final dissertation on women in local government. She had begun to assemble materials to write her own biography of Clara and was good enough to put them at my disposal. Marie had interviewed Mary Tabor, the daughter of Clara's brother, Francis and Magdalen Ricardo. Mary, who was at that point the custodian of Clara's personal papers and an impassioned defender of her aunt's legacy and reputation, had permitted Marie to read and photocopy documents from Clara's personal papers which were kept in a large suitcase. Marie Thompson did not know what had happened to the suitcase and was privately convinced that it had been lost or destroyed on Mary Tabor's death.

During the course of the centenary commemorations I made contact with Clara's great-niece by marriage, Sarah Rackham, and her cousins, Anne Stevenson Wright (née Hobbs) and Vivien Peto. Sarah proved to be immensely encouraging and supportive. Anne was in the process of compiling Rackham family reminiscences and anecdotes to which she very kindly allowed me access. Finally, an unforgettable telephone call from Lucy Tabor, Clara's great-niece, established the whereabouts of the missing manuscripts: Quite unexpectedly, Lucy had responded to a letter I had sent her and forgotten enquiring if she had any information about Clara. In the conversation that followed, Lucy explained that she had kept Clara's personal papers safely in storage in her own home, a beautiful old farmhouse Essex, quite unaware of their important to anyone other than the immediate family. It took a little while for this exciting news to sink in. Lucy and I very much wanted to meet in person and since l no longer drive a car l invited her and her sister, Helen Bloxsome, for morning coffee, cake and pastries in my own house in Newnham, Cambridge and then for lunch at nearby Newnham College. They offered to bring Clara's papers with them for me to see. Thanks to the amazing generosity of Helen and Lucy and their willingness to entrust their family documents to the care of a total stranger, I had the immense good fortune not only of being allowed to read Clara's, journals, diaries, letters, and papers but also to retain them in my home for reference purposes while this biography was being researched and written, from approximately March 2020 until the end of the covid-19 'lockdown' when I was virtually housebound and physical access to libraries and archives was impossible.

Like many biographers I was initially unsure how to address my biographical subject, wavering between Clara (overly familiar) and Rackham (overly severe). I decided on Clara, with Clara Rackham as a variant, a form I would have adopted had I been writing the biography of a man. Clara's family papers have yet to be catalogued and if the source of a statement is not indicated this can reasonably be assumed to be the Tabor family papers.

Winifred Holtby's novel, *South Riding* (1936) was written at the height of the Great Depression of the 1930s and is concerned with the municipal affairs of a fictional Yorkshire town. It is dedicated to Winifred's mother, Alice Holtby, who like Clara was among the first woman to be made a councillor and later an Alderman. In her prefatory letter Holtby makes an argument for the life-transforming potential of local government as the 'first-line of defence thrown up by the community against our common enemies – poverty, sickness, ignorance, isolation, mental derangement, and social maladjustment'.[1] Writing from the Olympian vantage point of half a century of public service in the Newnham College Roll Letter of 1958, in a piece specifically directed at Newnham College students and alumnae, Clara passionately reaffirmed her undimmed belief in the importance of local government 'in every department of life from the anti-natal clinic to the grave' It was, quite simply, 'the greatest safeguard of our liberties that we possess. It demands the best brains of the nation, drawn from the widest possible field, if it is to fulfil its functions in the community'.[2] 'The mere presence of women councillors has caused a change of attitude. Any return to the old attitude of indifference to the needs of children and old people is now quite impossible'.[3] The challenges facing Holtby as a novelist are similar those which face Clara's biographer today: how to make local government interesting? How to depict the idealism of the pioneering women for whom a voice in the council chamber represented not the tedium of innumerable committees and arcane procedures to be learnt but the precious opportunity to build a much needed new school, to place an abandoned child with a loving foster parent, to fight the never-ending battle against homelessness, malnutrition, child sexual abuse and child poverty?

The task of this biographer is complicated by the fact that the emotional and sexual dramas, that are the staples, the *res gestae*, of biography, are largely absent from Clara Rackham's life. There appears to have been no scandal, no great love affair, no dark hidden secrets, no abrupt reversal of fortune, no family ruptures, no tragic early death. Her courtship with Harris Rackham, seven years her senior and her tutor at Newham College, was conducted with the utmost propriety in contrast to the scandal surrounding the seduction of Amber Reeves by H. G. Wells within the walls of the college in 1909. It is necessary to read Clara's diary of her trip to Switzerland and Italy in March 1901 very carefully to check that this is indeed a record of her honeymoon and not one of her many foreign holidays abroad: she makes no mention of her wedding, and of her new husband by his initials, and then only once.

Clara chose not to confide in others about her intimate affairs. But without exception, those who knew her agree that the marriage was, happy, fulfilling, and companionate, bringing with it the pleasures of a large extended family and the nephews and nieces that she loved. If she had a contender for Harris's affections it was the writings of Aristotle, a rival that Clara understood and was happy to live with. Anne Logan (2010 and 2017) has highlighted the role that Clara played in the establishment of Criminology as an academic discipline, but Clara belonged to a cohort of middle-class married women who had no expectations of paid employment and was never to have a professional career in criminology, the social sciences, or in education for which she was eminently qualified. Neither the absence of the children that she once intimated to Mary Tabor she would have liked to have had,[4] nor the lack of opportunity to contest a winnable parliamentary seat, nor even the lack of a professional career, troubled her unduly. Clara Rackham was a sensible, level-headed woman who never allowed herself to forget the full extent of her own privilege, and who accepted whatever happened to her with equanimity. In the end the 'disappointments' mattered very little.

Clara did not take carbon copies of her own letters and all but very few of the hundreds she received are missing. The largest cache we have testifies to the collective outpouring of sadness and loss when the news of her retirement from public duties in Cambridge was announced. She was clearly moved by the response and pasted each letter carefully into a cheap red school exercise book marked 'Letters January, 1957'. Her diaries are extant as are the journals of holidays and prison visits in Eastern Europe, often written in separate exercise books. The diaries are legible, in clear, well-formed handwriting but they get smaller and smaller in size, amounting by the end to little more than the times and dates of appointments, the names of individuals and the places that she visited, and they contain nothing personal or very revealing.

Clara was capable of writing beautifully and with feeling as in her obituary of her friend, Susan Lawrence, in *The Fabian Quarterly* (1948). But most of the time she was preoccupied with journalism, drafting impersonal documents, dry business-like reports, and papers of a sociological nature. The notable exception is her unpublished account of growing up, 'Recollections of Childhood 1875–1891' consisting of sixteen handwritten pages which ends at the age of 16. We do not know when and why this was written, although it is probably late in life and purely for Clara's own satisfaction, and there must always be questions about the accuracy of recall and the effects of time on autobiographical subject matter recollected and written long after the events depicted. I have also made use of Margaret Tabor's autobiographical fragments (c.1949) also written for personal reasons and with no thought of possible publication. Clara's metier as a writer of discursive prose was the investigative report, including her reports as a government factory inspector, the survey of Cambridge for *Social Conditions in Provincial Towns* (1912) and the Minority Report on the Royal Commission on Unemployment Insurance (1933). Clara's reports were often not signed, or if signed, attributed to more than one person.

Within the category of women's writing non-fiction prose, and the report in particular, has been very much the 'poor relation' of the letter, the diary, autobiography, the journal, or the massive field of journalism in terms of the critical attention it has received. This is arguably because report-writing would appear to offer little scope for the imagination and indeed impersonality and objectivity lie at the very heart of the genre. Yet it is precisely because the report is a public document, and unlike the diary or the letter, written to identify the need for change and to persuade the reader of the need to act upon its findings and recommendations, that Clara was ineluctably drawn into writing investigative reports out of her sense of responsibility to the 'cause' or the 'movement'.

Clara considered her work to be of the utmost importance but she did not think of herself as a particularly interesting person. She was a modest, unassuming woman who valued her privacy and detested self-aggrandisement. Individuals who approached her wanting to write her biography – of whom there were several – were politely turned away. She also rejected the Freedom of the City of Cambridge and the OBE. Had she been asked how she wanted to be remembered she would almost certainly have replied that it was the reforms that mattered rather than the person, and that she did not wish to be remembered at all.

One significant expression of scholarly interest came from Brian Harrison, General Editor of *The Oxford Dictionary of National Biography* (ODNB), who thought Clara of sufficient importance to write her entry in the ODNB himself (2004). Harrison also conducted the taped oral history interviews with Clara's niece, Mary Tabor and Lucy Tabor, the daughter of Clara's brother, Edward and his wife, Lucy Margaret (née Candler), as part of a series on suffragists and suffragettes funded by the Social Science Research Council and deposited in the Fawcett Library, now the Women's Library at the LSE, in 1981.[5] He requested to see, and was shown, Clara's personal papers by Mary Tabor but decided against including her in his influential *Prudent Revolutionaries: Portraits of British Feminists between the Wars* (1987), concluding that 'there was insufficient manuscript material for a rounded biography'.[6] The paucity or absence of manuscript material has dogged Clara's would be biographers until this day.

With the exception of Jo Vellacott's *Pacifists, Patriots and the Votes* (2007) there is hardly a mention of Clara Rackham in any of the standard histories of the women's suffrage movement, even in those explicitly concerned with the non-violent suffragists rather than exclusively with the suffragettes. Elizabeth Crawford, author of *The Women's Suffrage Movement: A Reference Guide 1866–1928* (1988), an encyclopaedic work of reference containing 800 entries and 400 bibliographical entries on individual suffragists and suffragettes, came to Cambridge for her research but unfortunately did not write an entry on Clara Rackham. Since this magisterial work is often the first port of call for historians, archivists, librarians, 'kitchen table' historians, school children and college and university students researching women's suffrage at both a local and national level, the omission helps to explain why she is not better known today.

The Life and Turbulent Times of Clara Dorothea Rackham is predicated on an understanding that the life of an individual cannot be separated from the society and social movements to which that person belongs. I approach Clara through the lens of a feminist biographical study concerned with the retrieval of absent or silent women's voices, with collective as well as individual experience, and with what Julia Swindells called the 'voices on the other side of silence'.[7] I make no separation of the public and the personal aspects of Clara's life and focus on those who were nearest and closest to her: her husband, Harris, her sister, Margaret, her friend, Margery Fry, and others who knew and worked with her. Her life is discussed in relation to organisations such as the Labour Party, the Women's Co-operative Guild, the National Union of Women's Suffrage Societies, the Workers' Educational Association and the Howard League for Penal Reform, thus moving the reader beyond the life-story of the key individual to focus on a life lived not as a solitary individual but continuously in interaction and dialogue with others who shared her own vision and ideas, and on the changing social, historical and political context of her times.

Sifting through Clara Rackham's papers one becomes aware of the emotional intelligence that lies at the heart of her public work and the acute sensitivity to suffering that informed so much of what she wrote and did; her lifelong detestation of cruelty to animals, her awareness of the misery of the solitary prison cell, the terror of the unaccompanied child refugee or the petrified victim of sexual abuse. I lay no claims to expertise on questions of social policy and cannot began to do justice to the complexities of debates about unemployment, poverty and social security on which Clara was an authority nor to examine all the parliamentary legislation that she understood inside out. It is my hope that others will follow where I have left off.

The 'classic' criterion of what constitutes a good biography is that this should demonstrate and illuminate the subject's connections to the times in which they live. Clara Rackham first came to public prominence through her chairing of the National Union of Women's Suffrage Societies from 1909–1915. Its President, Millicent Garrett Fawcett, provided inspiration and leadership for supporters of the 'cause' but it was Clara who painstakingly worked to increase the number of NUWSS branches in Fawcett's home territory of the Eastern District. She also chaired the meetings of the National Executive Committee with consummate skill during the most turbulent moment in its history when the organisation was bitterly divided between the powerful anti-war lobby on the Executive Committee and those who accepted Fawcett's appeal for support of the women's war effort at the start of the First World War. After the war, Clara went on to take a leading editorial role on the journal of the National Union of Societies for Equal Citizenship (NUSEC), the successor of the NUWSS. As Eileen Price and Joyce Bellamy, authors of the excellent entry on Clara Rackham in the *Dictionary of Labour Bio*graphy, put it, 'the survival of the NUWSS was due as much to Clara Rackham as to any other single individual'.[8]

This biography enhances our understanding of the roles that women have played in the history of the Labour Party drawing upon the research of feminist historians such as June Hannam.[9] In contrast to her good friend, Margery Fry, also a Labour Party member, but one whose vast personal fortune insulated her from the day-to-day lives of ordinary people, Clara's loyalty to the Labour Party was unshakeable and deeply rooted in her knowledge of working-class communities. The railway workers and their families in 'Red Romsey', situated over the Mill Road Bridge in the east of Cambridge, whom Clara represented as a councillor, never allowed her to forget the importance of 'bread and butter issues' and the fight for decent housing, schools, hospitals, maternity care, wages, and working conditions. Romsey was a closely knit community 'with a heart' and it was there that she acquired a lifelong respect for traditional working-class values and moral codes based on the importance of family, group solidarity, fairness, mutual aid, co-operation, respectability, class loyalty, courage in adversity and community resilience. For forty years, on and off, Clara attended her local Women's Co-operative Guild on a weekly basis supporting working-class women to organise themselves, to campaign for the causes they believed in, to make their voices heard and to refuse to be cowered by men.

This biography draws attention to the importance of Clara's home in Cambridge as an 'open house'; an informal meeting place and discussion forum in which luminaries such as Hugh Dalton, Susan Lawrence, Leah Manning, Philippa Fawcett, R. H. Tawney and Henrietta Barnett were made welcome, and local teachers, Co-operators, and peace activists moved in and out. Through the groundbreaking research of Anne Logan (2008) and others we are beginning to understand more about how the feminist networks to which Clara belonged worked to bring about change in local government, the training of magistrates, and the criminal justice system, and the influence of pressure groups in shaping social policy between the wars.

Clara's network of friends and acquaintances was vast and acquired through Newnham College, her family connections, the women's suffrage movement, the Fabian Society, the Labour Party, the Co-operative movement, local government, the penal reform, and the adult education movements. Clara worked closely with Margery Fry on prison reform, with Clara Martineau of Birmingham City Council reporting to parliament on child sexual abuse, and with Leah Manning in support of improvements in education at the Ragged School and the experimental Open Air School in Cambridge. With Eva Hartree and Florence Ada Keynes she welcomed successive streams of refugees, political exiles and displaced persons from the Basque country, Fascist occupied Europe and Hungary after 1956, helping to establish the reputation of early twentieth-century Cambridge as a liberal, outward-looking city of sanctuary.

Local historians have often remarked on how strongly the civic history of Cambridge during the early and mid-twentieth century has been influenced by a remarkable cohort of women with humane, progressive social attitudes, for example, Eva Hartree, Florence Keynes, Jane Harrison, Edith Bethune-Baker, Lilian Mellish Clark, Rosamond Rootham, Agnes Ramsey, Freda Hardman, and Helen Pease, whose names are remembered for their tireless public service. *The Life and Turbulent Times of Clara Dorothea Rackham* pinpoints how women of all political affiliations and none, often associated with the Cambridge women's colleges, formed lasting friendships through feminist and women-centred organisations such as the Cambridge Family Planning Clinic and the National Council of Women, and were able to work together collaboratively to bring about change. The book illustrates the indefatigable commitment to improving the lives of ordinary townspeople demonstrated not only by Clara but also by many other women councillors, magistrates, school governors, and teachers, particularly in relation to the safeguarding of vulnerable women and children. It throws into question the familiar dichotomies between 'town and gown' in which the history of Cambridge is often framed.

In mapping out the full extent of Clara Rackham's achievements in Cambridge, and her influence far beyond, I bring together the national, the regional, and the local not only to make the case for Clara Rackham as an enlighted local politician who helped to change the face of modern Cambridge, but also as a public intellectual whose feminist advocacy of a fair, just, and equal and inclusive society helped to pave the foundations of the post-war settlement and the establishment of the modern democratic Welfare State.

Notes

1 Winifred Holtby, prefatory letter to Alderman Mrs Holtby, *South Riding* (1936) (London: Fontana, 1974), 5–6.
2 Clara Rackham, 'Old Students and Local Government', Newnham College Roll Letter, (January 1958), 19–23, 22–3.
3 Ibid., 19.
4 Brian Harrison oral history suffrage interviews, Miss Mary Tabor, interviewed, November 25, 1975, Ref 8SUF/BO62, Women's Library at the LSE.
5 Ibid., and also Miss Lucy Tabor, 8SUF/BO65, interviewed January 6, 1976.
6 Brian Harrison, *Prudent Revolutionaries: Portraits of British Feminists between the Wars* (Oxford: Oxford University Press, 1987), 12.
7 Julia Swindells, *Victorian Writing and Working Women: The Other Side of Silence* (Cambridge: Cambridge University Press, 1985).
8 Joyce M. Bellamy and Eileen Price, *Rackham, Clara Dorothea (1875–1966) Labour Alderman, Social Reformer and Educationalist*, in eds Joyce M. Bellamy and John Saville, *Dictionary of Labour Biography* ix, (1993), 232–8, 233.
9 June Hannam, 'Women as Paid Organisers and Propagandists for the British Labour Party Between the Wars'. *International and Working-Class History*, vol 77, issue 1, (spring 2010), 69–88.

1 Young Clara

One of Clara Tabor's earliest memories was of intense physical discomfort; of being made to sit bolt upright in a double three-wheeled perambulator in which it was impossible to lie down or sleep, alongside her brother, 'Willie'.[1] The Tabor children were taken by their nurse to Kensington Gardens; to see the fountains, the Speke Monument, and the Memorial to the Prince Consort. Clara loved watching grown men sailing their toy boats and racing them around the Round Pond. Sometimes they ventured further afield to Hammersmith Bridge or Kensal Green cemetery. When she was older Willie and Clara invented a game of counting their own names on the tombstone and, needless to say, Willie always won.[2]

Clara, known as Dorothea to her family, was born at 44 Lansdowne Road in the Notting Hill area of west London, on December 3, 1875. Clara's mother, Emma Frances (*née* Woodcock) was a solicitor's daughter from a family active in public life in Wigan in Lancashire. Clara's father, Henry Samuel Tabor, had relocated the family to this house earlier in the year from number 16 Lansdowne Road where Clara's four older siblings had been born. They were Edward Henry (Ned), b.1866, Margaret Emma, b.1867, Francis (Frank), b.1869, and Robert William (Willie), b.1873.

The Tabors' home in Lansdowne Road was a large, white mid-Victorian town house in a quiet, leafy residential street in fashionable Notting Hill. A single worn stone step joined the front garden to the garden square at the back where the siblings played games with other children whose houses backed on to theirs. There was a little garden where the children had their own special plot and they would plant seeds and watch their initials emerge from the ground in mustard and cress.[3]

Henry had purchased 16 Lansdowne Road (the 'wedding cake house') when he married and had given his rank or profession as gentleman' on his marriage certificate in 1865. He is remembered today as the author of a set of diaries chronicling aspects of contemporary life and current affairs in mid-Victorian England.[4] It was from her father that Clara was to develop her aptitude for close observation, diary-keeping and meticulous note-taking. Henry had grown up at Fennes (see Figure 2.2), the

DOI: 10.4324/9780429353499-2

family farm (now used as a popular venue for country weddings), surrounded by a patchworks of field and acres of rich rolling countryside, in the village of Bocking near Braintree in Essex. The name Tabor was an occupational one and originally denoted someone who played a small drum. The village of Bocking derived its name from a coarse wool once used for floor coverings and had been an important centre of the Essex woollen trade since the Middle Ages. A family called Tabor was living in north Essex at the time of Edward 111. The Puritan preacher, John Bunyan, was reputed to have written some of *Pilgrim's Progress* while staying with an ancestor, John Tabor, soon after his second imprisonment in 1675, and to have given sermons on one of the Tabor family farms. Generations of God-fearing Tabors had worked the rich clay soil honestly and had attended the chapel proudly, leaving the Church of England to others, often to 'incomers', families without their long years or rootedness in the land.

Henry's father, Samuel, Clara's grandfather, continued to live and work on the farm after the death of his wife, Margaret (*née* Silburn), rising at dawn to see to the animals until well into his eighties, hunched in his library over improving texts and agricultural manuals, until daylight faded. Whenever Henry and Emma had to be away the children were sent to Fennes to stay with Samuel and his housekeeper and Clara grew to love Fennes as her second home.

Clara's childhood experiences were liminal situating her on the borders of town and country and gentility and squalor. The Tabors' well-tended house in London had an aura of genteel respectability but there were pockets of great deprivation in the streets nearby including Pottery Lane at the heart of an infamous slum area known as the 'Potteries and the Piggeries'. Clara quickly came to recognise the signs of abject poverty around her. It was common to see drunken men in the street, to be hurried past brawls outside public houses, and for the children to be checked for fleas in their hair whenever they returned home. It was difficult to grow geraniums in window boxes. They were apt to be stolen in the night. Another telling sign of destitution was callers at the door enquiring after used tea leaves which they were glad to have for their own tea. In the Christmas holidays Clara was taken to serve cocoa for children from a poor neighbourhood at a play centre in Fetter Lane and to a night school where she felt proud to have taught a middle-aged domestic servant to read. Fees of a penny a week were charged by the elementary school and Henry would go to 'The Board' (the School Boards set up after the 1870 Education Act) once a week to speak on behalf of parents who could not pay the fee.

Henry and Emma took their large, close-knit family on long seaside holidays in August every other year: Hunstanton when Clara was five, Overstrand at seven, Felixtowe at nine, Teignmouth at eleven and Llanfairfechan when she was thirteen. Summer holidays in alternate years were spent on the family farm where the children were allowed to play all day outdoors in the woods and fields and Clara enjoyed a freedom that she could only dream of in her London life. They slid down straw stacks, climbed trees, rode in farm carts, worked in the garden, played croquet, and spent hours in the company of the farm hands. Clara remembered pushing open the cellar door at the age of three, tumbling down to the bottom of the stairs and sitting on Emma's knee at the kitchen table howling with shock although luckily no bones were broken. The children would come indoors when a large bell in the belfry rang to summon them for the frugal meals to which Samuel's was accustomed: nothing but bread and butter for breakfast and tea, milk, and cake brought in for them into the library the evening. There was, however, no way for Clara to avoid the sight of the farm labourers ringing pigs, cutting off lamb's tails or destroying nests when fledgelings were in them: 'These things', she wrote, in her Recollections of Childhood, 'caused me as much misery as the sufferings of the London horses'.

Clara's time on the farm imbued her with a remarkably confident way of seeing and judging the countryside which was to turn a clever, observant little girl into an adult woman expert on rural affairs in general, and the causes of rural poverty in particular. Her grandfather's bailiff, a man called Brewster, would come into the library at Fennes to discuss the running of the farm and she would hide in a corner and listen with intense interest and concentration.

Consequently, a working landscape was for the adult Clara almost never a 'view' but a matter of rents and power, of land that had to be worked responsibly, and of underlying economic relationships and systems. Crops had to be properly sewn, tilled, and irrigated, fences put in and ditches dug correctly to satisfy Clara's practised eye. Rural buses must be made to run on time, 'skivers' induced to attend school, insanitary cottages condemned, fair rents agreed, and ancient footpaths and rights of way unobstructed and properly signposted.

On Sunday mornings Clara and Willie would ride with their grandfather in the brougham to the Bocking Chapel with Clara vying with Willie as to who should sit in the box behind the coachman. But the 'old ways' were dying. The children preferred the fifteenth-century flint and limestone Anglican Deanery Church of St Mary the Virgin reached by a pleasant walk across the park to the austereness of the chapel. For as far back as she could remember, grandfather Samuel had seemed crotchety, older than his years. In 1890 Clara's grandfather died at the age of 91. She was fourteen. Grandfather had gone but Fennes remained in the family. Fennes was the one place that remained a fixed point of anchorage for her, where Clara knew that she could always return if she wanted, and be welcomed, until the very end of her own ninety-year life.

Henry and Emma took the children's early education into their own hands. There was a playroom with a wooden rocking horse in the basement, which was used as a schoolroom in the morning until each child was old enough to go to school at the age of ten.[5] Emma, taught the children to read and write before passing them on to their father. In the matter of their pre-school education Henry Tabor does not appear to have discriminated between his sons and daughters, demanding the same intellectual curiosity, rigour, and application from Margaret and Clara that he did from Francis, Willie, and Ned.

Margaret remembered that they learnt a great deal from dissected maps 'which were the jig-saw of our childhood', and enjoyed the Latin declensions, although she 'never forgot shed ding tears over a most confusing exercise about bad apple-trees (*mala mala*) which became a family joke'.[6] Astronomy, Botany, and Geology all interested Henry who transmitted his own enthusiasm to his children:

> We learned the names of the constellations and looked for Jupiter's moons with a telescope. We fathomed the mysteries of day and night, summer and winter, and always looked for meteors on the appropriate nights. We learned the names of flowers (even the Latin ones) and collected, dried and classified them. We shared in fact as far as we could all his scientific interests.[7]

When Henry and Emma detected signs of 'tomboyish behaviour' in their elder daughter, ten-year-old Margaret was sent to a finishing school for young ladies for two years before going to Notting Hill High School and from there to Newnham College. The finishing school reflected the middle-class obsession with genteel 'accomplishments'. Deportment was foremost in the curriculum and the girls were expected to attend piano lessons, and to learn drawing, painting, singing, and ballroom dancing which were the approved rites of passage into respectable Victorian womanhood. Margaret suffered agonies of embarrassment attempting to learn to waltz in the presence of her mother. French was spoken all day and every day, and so Margaret acquired a proficient grasp of the nuances and rhythms of the language and an impeccable French accent.[8]

The Tabors were loving but strict parents who practised an earnest and personal form of Christianity. Clara was taken along to a Temperance Organisation, the Juvenile Union, and entertained by old Bishop Temple at the annual fete in the grounds of Fulham Palace where she would play with his son, William, the future Archbishop of Canterbury. Margaret attended a Bible class run by a Dr John Gladstone, no relation to the Liberal politician, alongside his daughter, Margaret Ethel, who would one day marry the first Labour Prime Minister, Ramsay MacDonald. Emma and Henry believed in plain living, were wary of spoiling children, and quick to detect and eradicate the slightest intimation of Biblical sin, sloth, pride, greed, vanity, and conceit. It was a great fault to be proud of one's appearance. When a friend of Margaret's came to tea and wrote a letter of thanks referring to Clara as 'your pretty little sister', this was destroyed and the hapless friend never invited to the house again.

The Tabors were Sabbatarians adhering strictly to the belief that all trade and business should cease on the Sabbath which was set aside exclusively for religious worship. Memorably depicted by Dickens in *A Christmas Carol* (1843), Sabbatarianism was favoured by middle-class families like the Tabors with the wherewithal to maintain retinues of servants, but never successfully imposed either on the Victorian poor who deeply resented and resisted all attempts at legal enforcement or on the very rich with means of escape to private clubs.[9]

Sunday was always zealously observed. Willie, Frank, Margaret and Ned dressed in their best clothes would read missionary magazines until church attendance, usually at St Marks' at 11.00 am. Sunday lunch was always lentil soup and cold beef with a 'rather special' pudding. Then the Noah's Ark was brought out and more missionary magazines read until 3.00 pm at which time the children were dispatched to a Bible Class in a nearby house. While the children were away Emma entertained a class of girls from a Training Home for Young Servants in the dining room. There always had to be an interval before the family sat down to tea as all the windows had to be opened and the room thoroughly aired.

Bed times were rigidly adhered to and this was a cause of misery. Clara was a sensitive child with a strong imagination and was terrified of being left alone upstairs in bed. The infamous Whitechapel murders occurred when Clara was ten or eleven years old. The evening paper vendors shouted out the lurid headlines and she trembled in bed as she heard 'orrible Whitechapel murder' getting nearer and nearer the house.

Now and again Clara would refuse to eat meat but usually gave in when Emma made it clear that nothing else was to be put on her plate. Sweets were strictly forbidden so Clara developed a craving and made herself sick by eating too many. Anything 'rich' was bad for children's digestion and plain food good for their morals. This was not a question of economy: Clara emphasises that her parents did not hesitate to purchase the best milk from the Aylesbury Dairy, expensive though this was. She recalled watching a soft-boiled egg cut into two to be divided 'equally' between Willie and herself and the greater part of the yolk falling to her brother. It was much the same with oranges. They were cheap – her father used to buy them from street vendors in the city at six a penny – but the children were never allowed a whole orange only segments distributed 'fairly' between them according to the number of pips.

Henry took the children up and down the River Thames in penny steamers, to the Crystal Palace famed for its firework displays and, to the Zoo. There were visits to Hengler's Circus in the Christmas holidays and to the scientific exhibits and lectures at the Polytechnic in Regent's Street. They seldom went to the theatre as Emma disapproved (Henry did not), although an exception was made for Shakespeare. The pantomime in Drury Lane was forbidden because Emma considered it bad for children to see their favourite nursery tale characters 'all jumbled up'.[10] Henry was a great walker and fond of taking the family to Barnes Common, Hampstead Heath, Richmond and Kew. In 1887 Clara was taken to watch Queen Victoria's Golden Jubilee procession. Henry lifted the twelve-year-old on to his shoulders, giving her an unobscured view of the Queen.

Like many clever Victorian girls Clara deeply resented being treated unfairly because of her sex. What rankled was that the London open-top buses were reached by two or three widely spaced steps and the climb to the top considered only suitable for men and boys. 'The thought that I could never go on the top of a bus was one of the great sadnesses', she wrote in her 'Recollections of Childhood': 'It was a misery to see Frank and Willie climbing to the top' while the nursemaid and Clara, who sat on her knee to save the fare, got inside. The 'last straw' was when Willie, joining them below, enquired 'Was Dolly good?'

But the chief aspect of the London streets that shocked her was the cruelty to the horses. Anna Sewell's novel *Black Beauty* (1877) about the travails of a mistreated horse had left an indelible mark on her consciousness. It was an agony to see a crowd at the roadside because it often meant a horse had fallen and the driver was whipping it. Horses drawing buses up the slippery slope in Bayswater Road suffered badly. Cab horses were generally thin and in the quiet side streets their drivers whipped them into a gallop. But worse of all were the smart carriage horses with curb bits and tight bearing reigns, which never ceased to toss their heads in discomfort.

Clara was taken to the Royal Academy and quite unable to admire the fine pictures as she was so distressed by the carriage horses in the courtyard of Burlington House. Such early incidents installed a lifelong hatred of cruelty to animals and made her a strong supporter of the Royal Society for the Prevention of Cruelty to Animals after its foundation in 1895. It was always said that Clara 'took after' her mother, a kind-hearted Lancashire woman, in her 'fellow feeling' for suffering creatures, both animal and human.

Emma and Henry were both keen Liberal Party supporters. Clara remembered hearing of the death of General Gordon after the siege in Khartoum in 1884 and felt total incomprehension whenever she heard Gladstone being held responsible for Gordon's fate and vilified. A common quip was that his acronym GOM (Grand Old Man) should be transposed into MOG (Murderer of Gordon). When Gladstone's support for Irish Home Rule split the Liberal Party in 1885 and her parents declared themselves Liberal Unionists, Clara followed Gladstone's lead, proclaiming herself an Irish Home Ruler. Clara's earliest political activity was in 1889 canvassing with her mother at the first election in the newly formed London County Council. Emma did the talking while Clara held the leaflets. The two contending factions in North Kensington were 'Moderates' and 'Progressives'. Clara and Emma worked for the 'Progressive' candidate, a Mr Lloyd canvassing only the women on the voting register, who were either widows or single householders.

For all their enlightened social views, Henry and Emma were typical products of their time and social class. Like most monied Victorians (Henry had invested shrewdly in railway shares and land) they were committed to the public school system as an investment that would reliably turn out men fitted to run Britain, its industries, culture, legal institutions, and empire. Edward was sent to board at Rugby School and was exceedingly unhappy due to bullying by bigger boys who, unknown to the Masters, would throw his school books into the fire. He was frequently in trouble and would vent his anger in the holidays by bullying Willie. Edward wrote piteous letters beseeching to be removed from the school which Henry chose to ignore. The only occasion Clara ever recollected seeing her mother in tears was when she was reading Ned's missives home.[11] Emma would always blame any of Edward's personal shortcomings as an adult on his wretched experiences at school. Willie was dispatched to Haileybury public school in Hertfordshire which had a strong military ethos and was thoroughly miserable, resolving privately, as did Edward, that they would never send any of their own children to public school. The promise was kept. In contrast, Francis won a free place at St Paul's Day School and became one of 'Walker's Specials', selected for intensive tuition in Latin and Greek by the benign, scholarly headmaster Dr Walker, and was the only one of Clara's brothers who appears to have emerged psychologically unscarred from his school experience.

When she was ten Clara was sent as a pupil to Notting Hill High and Bayswater High School for Girls in Norland Square, an independent day school founded by the Girls' Public Day School Company in 1873 to serve the daughters of families to the north of Hyde Park. The first headmistress, Harriet Morant-Jones, had begun with her sister as an assistant and just ten pupils. By the time Clara arrived the school was large, flourishing, and achieving outstanding success in the Cambridge Higher Local Examinations due to Miss Morant-Jones's refusal to compromise on academic standards. She was a tall, magisterial figure with a Guernsey accent, habituated to reading aloud the Biblical Parable of the Talents sternly to admonish any girl who did not put her intelligence to good use. Emma, a down-to-earth northerner with 'no side about her', was amused by the headmistress's thinly veiled social snobbery. She would invariably point out the daughters of Judges and Generals to any visiting prospective parents.

Miss Jones's own teaching methods were decidedly old-fashioned. She dictated short paragraphs under headings which had to be underlined and learnt by heart but she had a genius for attracting, remunerating, and retaining enthusiastic young staff fresh from the women's colleges in Oxford and Cambridge. The novelist Winifred Holtby once taught History there, and the distinguished engineer and physicist, Hertha Ayrton, Science. Clara remembered being taught Latin extremely well by Marion Withiel, a Unitarian who was thought to have been passed over for promotion because of her unconventional beliefs. A number of feminist pioneers including Barbara Ayrton Gould, Ernestine Evans Bell, Ada Adelaide Lamb, Gertrude Lowry, Helena Swanwick, and Margaret Haig Thomas, the future Lady Rhondda, all passed through the corridors of Notting Hill.

Margaret, Frank and Clara would all set off on foot together to go to school in the morning. Classes were large: there were forty-four girls in Clara's form. According to her report in the Upper-Third in 1888, Clara's conduct was 'very good on the whole – she talks too much'.[12] The area in which Notting Hill at first made no attempt to emulate the boys' public schools was in games, sport and attitudes to punishment. There were no sports facilities or organised games and Clara's only exercise was a visit to Paddington Baths on a Saturday morning where she first learnt to swim. Unlike their brothers, who were physically beaten, the girls were punished by detention or by missing school 'treats': they muttered darkly that Miss Jones invented 'treats' specifically so that they would miss them. Teaching was from 9.00 to 1.15 with preparation at home in the afternoon when girls were expected to help their mothers. As Carol Dyhouse points out, even the newer high schools for girls were in many ways conservative institutions fostering conventional ideas of feminine behaviour and reinforcing the lessons of family life.[13] Clara sent back three accounts of life at Cambridge University which were printed in the Notting Hill school magazine.

Henry and Emma sent Clara away to St Leonards, a pioneering independent school within the walls of a medieval priory at St Andrews in Fife, in the conviction that St Leonards represented the best academic education for their daughter that was to be found. The school had been established in 1877 by a group loosely associated with the oldest of the Scottish universities who, in defiance of all the ideological and gender constraints of the time, were determined to ensure that a girl should receive a schooling that was as good, if not better, than that received by her brother in one of the leading public schools. Its reputation had spread rapidly in progressive circles by the time Clara arrived as a boarder in 1892. Among the early intakes were Louisa Garrett

Anderson, the daughter of Elizabeth Garrett Anderson, Helen Archdale, the Scottish suffragette and editor of the feminist periodical *Time and Tide,* Margaret Haig Thomas, the founder of that journal, and Agnata Ramsay, the classical scholar. The formidable Louisa Lumsden, one of the three 'Girton Pioneers' who had taken the Classical Tripos in 1873, was the first headmistress. Her towering presence influenced every aspect of school life even after her retirement in 1882 when Frances Dove, another Girton alumna with a strong belief in education for citizenship, took over. Clara joined Miss Dove's house (see Figure 2.5).

Clara's classes were all in the morning. In the afternoon the girls were free to walk alone or in groups along the East Sands or the West Sands; to clamber on the rocks or sink barefoot into the sand dunes. There were magnificent sunsets over the windswept cliffs to the North Sea and they collected crumbs from the dinner table to throw at the shrieking sea gulls circling overhead. Hair-washing was a strictly rationed activity but when permitted they would wash the sand out of their hair in enamel basins. Dreadfully homesick at first, the girls would huddle under the bedclothes and exchange confidences in the glacially cold dormitories, long after they were supposed to be asleep.

Books were Clara's refuge and her escape. She worked her way through the Victorian classics, reading quietly in the dormitory or in the sanatorium: she suffered from minor colds as well as excruciating toothache. She had read Ruskin, Browning, Tennyson, Charlotte Bronte (*Villette*), Dickens (*Nicholas Nickleby* and *The Old Curiosity Shop*) while at St Andrews and was to remain an avid, if somewhat unadventurous, reader of literature throughout her life. Users of the Cambridge University Library who knew Clara in her later years remember her borrowing armfuls of biographies, history, and social studies but with the exception of Joyce's *Ulysses* (which she liked) she showed little interest in experimental, Modernist, or contemporary fiction. Indeed, there was some speculation that her parents may have named her Dorothea after George Eliot's serious, intellectual, protagonist, Dorothea Brooke in *Middlemarch* because Dorothea was not a name in the family (Clara was). *Middlemarch* was always one of Clara's favourite books and she greatly admired Eliot's relentlessly moral vision of life.

There were no motor vehicles on the roads of Cambridge when Clara arrived at Newnham College to read Classics in 1895. The first left-hand drive motor carriage, powered by a Daimler engine ordered from Paris, had travelled from Micheldever in Hampshire to Datchet in July. But it was only in 1896 that the speed limit was raised from four to twelve miles an hour and cars began to appear on the roads. Free wheels for bicycles were invented in 1894[14] and the students took to them in numbers. The large houses in Harvey Road, Selwyn Gardens and Bateman Street built in the 1880s and 1890s for the families of married dons still enjoyed a semi-rural aspect.

The ancient skyline of Cambridge had been altered by two arresting new additions that were, in their very different ways, signs of the changing times. The first was the Church of Our Lady and the English Martyrs, designed by Charles Voysey and situated on the corner of Hills Road and Lensfield Road in the Hyde Park area. Widely admired as one of the most beautiful Roman Catholic Churches in England, the church had been consecrated five years earlier through the munificence of Yolande Marie-Louise Duvernay (stage name Pauline Duvernay), a widowed ballet dancer born in Paris. Her English husband was rumoured to have been the richest commoner in England and to have made his fortune through the invention of moveable eyes on Victorian dolls.

The second was the imposing Victorian sewage works and pumping station with its 173 foot high tall chimney where household rubbish was burned which was hailed as a marvel of Victorian technology on its construction at Riverside in 1894. Steam from the sewage works fuelled the engines that pumped the detritus that had previously been discharged into the river to treatment works in nearby Milton thus helping to ward off the cholera and water-borne diseases that had been the scourge of the town for as long as anyone could remember.

Thanks to a protracted and courageous battle fought by seventeen-year-old Daisy Hopkins in protest against her wrongful incarceration, the power of the university Proctors to arrest and detain 'lewd' women in the infamous 'spinning house' at the Vice-Chancellors pleasure had been successfully challenged and the prison in St Andrew's Street closed down in 1894. Newnham village, Clara's destination, its origins dating back to before the Norman Conquest, was little more than a hamlet on the river Cam with a solitary public house, surrounded by meadows and open fields. Footpaths and bridleways linked Cambridge to the nearby villages of Grantchester, Madingley, and Coton. Many of the present landmarks on the west of the city; St Mark's Church, Eltisley Avenue, and the good new road and bridge over the Fen Causeway had yet to be built.

Newnham College was founded in 1871 by Millicent Garrett Fawcett, Henry Sedgwick, and others to provide 'Lectures for Women' in Cambridge. The first five students lived in a rented house in Regent Street, now the Regent Hotel, under the personal supervision of the first Principal, Anne Jemima Clough, sister of the poet, Arthur Clough, who was related by marriage to Florence Nightingale. The first permanent college buildings in the imposing Queen Anne Style were designed by the architect Basil Champneys in 1875.

The beautiful college gardens without the formality (and ubiquitous geraniums) of the men's colleges gardens, overlooked meadows, and poplar trees and were laid out and planted at about the same time. Women were allowed to walk on the grass unless bulbs were growing in springtime. Clumps of daffodils, superseded by irises as the 'Newnham flower', were to be found everywhere in the college grounds. The year

1895 was a particularly vivid year in student memory. It was the year of the 'Great Freeze' with skeletal trees and red brick college buildings white with snow, and the college ground soaked with heavy autumnal rains and thick with ice. There was the novelty of learning to skate, perhaps on Skaters' Meadow, on frozen college lawns, on either side of Trinity Avenue, or on Parker's Piece. From Newnham they could skate as far as Byron's Pool and Grantchester Mill, and with the wind behind them even from Ely to Cambridge.[15]

Clara was already familiar with the ethos of Newnham College and the feminist history of which she was to become a part. She had visited the college when Margaret was a student and had met two of her sister's closest friends. Blanche Athena (Thena) Clough, was the niece of Anne Jemima, and herself to become Principal, and Philippa Fawcett, daughter of two of the college founders, Millicent and Henry Fawcett, who had stayed with Margaret at Fennes during the Cambridge University vacation. Philippa's brilliance as a mathematician had been recognised by the college which arranged for both Margaret and Philippa to receive coaching from the dour but supportive Ernest Hobson of Christ's, who had been the Senior Wrangler (top mathematician) in 1878. Margaret vividly recalled the jubilation in 1890 when Philippa become the first – and only – woman to secure the highest marks in the Mathematical Tripos, by reputation the most difficult and prestigious of university examinations. She had rushed straight to Senate House, mingling with the huge expectant crowd gathered to hear the results and joining in the tumultuous applause when Philippa's name was read out 'above the Senior Wrangler'. Margaret, a gifted tennis player, had played in the annual Newnham versus Girton tennis match on the day and lost – it hadn't mattered.

Philippa's astonishing achievement was of great symbolic importance. This finally disproved the misconception that women were relational rather than rational beings and incapable of attaining the same intellectual heights as men in mathematical and scientific subjects. The celebrations at Newnham lasted well into the night. Bells rang, gongs sounded, fireworks were set off. Undergraduates from Selwyn College climbed over the railings – and nobody minded. Margaret and her friends festooned the college with streamers and lanterns and carried Philippa aloft as they danced around a huge bonfire until they virtually dropped with happiness, excitement, and fatigue.[16] The two women were to remain the best of friends all their lives until Philippa's death in 1948.

Much had changed at Newnham College since Margaret had left Cambridge in 1891 returning dutifully, and with not a little resentment, to live with her parents at Fennes and undertake the tedious round of ritualised social calls and domestic tasks expected of a Victorian 'home daughter'. Two imposing bronze entrance gates designed by Basil Champneys had been erected in memory of Anne Jemima Clough who had died in 1892.

Nora Sidgwick, married to the college founder, Henry Sidgwick, neice of one Prime Minister, Robert Cecil and sister of a future Prime Minister, Arthur Balfour, had taken on the role of Principal, albeit with some reluctance, fearing that this would be detrimental to her own work for the Society for Psychical Research. In turn, Helen Gladstone, had taken over as Vice-Principal and as Tutor of Sidgwick, Clara's own Hall of residence. Electricity had been installed and the students enjoyed the novelty of turning on and off the new-fangled lights. A hard hockey pitch had been laid out in a secluded part of the grounds away from the prying eyes of passing strangers and the men in the nearby Ridley Hall Theological College.

Newnham College was no longer new but the aura of newness lingered; its past as important as its present; its history recent but conspicuously still in the making, made visible through the naming and renaming of college buildings and rooms. The college founders, the Sidgwicks, the Cloughs, and the Fawcetts were not distant figures to be venerated from afar. On the contrary, an occasional glimpse of them could be caught in the corridors or the dining hall, taking a polite informed interest in students and whatever was going on. The history of women's hard-won achievements and aspirations was everything and everywhere; acquired through the careful accumulation and display of artefacts, furnishings, books, gifts and bequests from grateful parents, benefactors and well-wishers: in 1899 Emma Tabor presented the college with a gleaming Championship Cup for Fives.[17] That Newnham was the 'first institution in either Cambridge or Oxford to be without denominational affiliation'[18] and the absence of a chapel or collective worship confirmed Clara's own deeply held conviction that collegiate intellectual life should always be secular.

In January 1895 Thomas Hardy published his last novel, *Jude the Obscure*. Its anguished stone mason, Jude Fawley, was excluded from study at 'Christminster' (Oxford) and the misery of its sensitive tormented 'New Woman', Sue Bridehead, stemmed from the lack of any outlet for her intellect. Newnham students consciously regarded themselves as pioneers and many had fought exceedingly hard to be where they were; some in the face of family indifference or intense opposition. Clara was probably exceptional in so far as no impediment had ever been placed in the path of her education by Henry or Emma. Jane Harrison, the 'first Englishwoman to make a name in classical scholarship',[19] was asked by an aunt 'what use Greek would be to her when she had a house and family of her own'.[20]

Clara relished the ritual evening after-dinner cocoa parties traipsing from one college room to another clutching her allocation of milk in a large china mug. There were Sunday walks to Grantchester Church, bicycle rides to Hardwick Woods in spring to pick the primroses, summer afternoons lying in a hammock in the college gardens, and nightingales singing as she lay awake at night. Like every woman studying at Cambridge University, Clara came to understand that she was there on sufferance. College life supplied girls with role models who were very different from their mothers and with the company of other women with values which generally legitimated intellectual purposes.[21] But although women were permitted to sit the Tripos examinations from 1881 they were not awarded degrees and their results were recorded in separate class lists. They were required to wear hats and gloves in town and to be closely chaperoned. Even a brother could not be openly acknowledged in the street ('The brother of one of us is not the brother of us all'). The system of chaperonage was exceedingly irksome, particularly because the hard-pressed Principal had to do much of the chaperoning herself, and it was often ingeniously circumvented although not formally abolished until the 1930s.

It was instilled into every student that the edifice of hope, opportunity, and learning assembled by the Sidgwicks and the Fawcetts for her benefit was paradoxically both strong and fragile and that it might topple as a result of one foolish or ill-considered act on her part. Florence Ada Keynes (née Brown) remembers that they all had to be as inconspicuous as possible in behaviour and appearance 'in order not to alarm the doubters'.[22]

The women's colleges in Cambridge attracted curious visitors. Jane Harrison showed John Ruskin the college Library as a student. '"Each book", he said gravely, "that a young girl touches should be bound in white vellum"'.[23] Her idol, George Eliot, complimented her on the 'dolorous' Morris wallpaper in her college room as a 'beautiful background for your face', leaving Jane 'senseless with excitement'.[24] Ruskin, who was prone to self-dramatisation, gave the college copies of his own works bound in serviceable blue buckram.

G. H. Lewes and George Eliot stayed with the Sidgwicks and George Eliot used to visit the Newmarket stables with Nora Sidgwick to feed sugar to the horses.[25] Arthur Balfour came to Sunday lunch as his sister's invited guest[26] and William Gladstone, to visit his daughter, Helen (described by Harrison as the 'most breezy, boisterous creature possible – we called her Boreas')[27] and to plant a tree in the college grounds. A rigid Tory at this time, Harrison 'resolutely refused to join the mob of students in cheering and clapping the Grand Old Man on his arrival'.[28]

Clara conformed to the type of the 'New Woman' in every particular usually associated with the term in popular culture, literary, and non-literary discourse: riding a bicycle, smoking in public, rejecting the conventional expectations of women, demanding emancipation, and benefitting from a Girton education (read Newnham). But the 'New Woman' was already discredited as an outmoded caricature and Clara never used the words in relation to herself. As Talia Schaffer puts it, 'by 1895, the "New Woman" had become a wildly skewed reductive media construct which did not represent the real lives and work of those people it purported to describe.'[29] Moreover, late Victorian feminists 'disliked the caricature intensely as intended to undermine and belittle their work'.[30] Clara made her advanced views known. But she dressed conservatively and did nothing that might shock, antagonise, or confirm the prejudices of the 'doubters' for fear of setting back the causes in which she believed.

Several of Clara's most important friendships date back to her time at Newnham College. One lifelong friend was Susan Arabella Lawrence, then far removed from the militant socialist sent to prison during the Poplar rates protest in 1912 and the Labour MP she was to become. Clara remembered Susan as a 'convinced and even passionate Conservative', short-sighted 'tall, upright and dignified, with a disconcerting habit of looking at her interlocutor through a lorgnette', a piano in her room which she was never known to play, and a Dalmatian dog which followed her on bicycle rides.[31] It was at Newnham College that Clara met her future sister-in-law, Magdalen Harriet Ricardo, granddaughter of the Liberal MP, David Ricardo the younger, and great-granddaughter of the great political economist David Ricardo. Magdalen (known to everybody as Mad) is pictured in the photograph of the victorious Newnham College team alongside Clara (see Figure 2.6).

Clara's other good friends, the Jebbs, Louisa, Eglantyne, and Dorothy, lived in the family home, Springfield, overlooking Queen's Green and the Backs[32] which had once been a harbour for barges bringing goods upstream from Wisbech and King's Lynn in the Middle Ages. Clara was a frequent visitor to Springfield and was particularly close to Louisa who unusually took a diploma in agriculture. On leaving college, Louisa embarked on a hazardous expedition from Constantinople via Tarsus to the river Tigris, sailing to Baghdad and returning to Damascus through the Syrian Desert with a Newnham contemporary, Victoria Buxton. The adventure was described in Louisa's travel book *By Desert Ways to Baghdad* (1909).

Their uncle, Richard Claverhouse Jebb, was elected Regius Professor of Greek at Cambridge when Benjamin Kennedy, the father of Julia and Marion Kennedy, died in 1889. Both Richard Jebb and Benjamin Kennedy before him, were strong supporters of women's education. Some of the first Newnham students sat their examinations in the Kennedy House in Bateman Street with a solicitous Marion, a classical scholar in her own right and Honorary Secretary of Newnham College from 1877–1904, in attendance to provide light lunches: old Dr Kennedy 'sometimes went to sleep and we had to wake him up to light the gas'.[33]

Mary Agnes (Molly) Hamilton, a leader of the Liberal Group in the Political Debating Society, and for two years the Labour MP for Blackburn (1929–1931), remembers that Newnham students were all 'blankly ignorant about sex and its manifestations' but made up for this by talking about love and politics a great deal.[34]

Gladstone and the Liberal Party had been defeated by Salisbury and the Conservatives in the General Election of 1895, but not withstanding the Balfour family connections with the college, the student body in Newnham was predominantly Liberal. The Roll Letter in 1897 noted that the college had been 'most persistently Liberal in Politics during the last few years and in the Political Society, the Liberal Party, whether in power or in opposition ... all powerful'.[35] The Newnham Political Society in which Clara led an 'earnest and united' Liberal Party was a simulacrum of the debating chamber of the House of Commons with Liberal and Conservative 'governments' alternating in power, enabling women students, who were not permitted to join the Cambridge Union until 1963, to acquire confidence in debating skills, to draw up mock cabinets and parliamentary legislation, and to practise the leadership roles that they hoped might one day be open to them. Designating herself President of the Local Government Board, Clara spoke for the Maldon Division of Essex which included Bocking. Louisa Jebb chose Oswestry in Shropshire as her constituency and took the role of Chancellor of the Exchequer. A coalition Ministry of Conservatives and Liberal Unionists was led by Susan Lawrence.[36]

Clara was nominated Captain of the College hockey team in 1897 and led victorious college and university teams in 1897 and 1898. There was some ambiguity about the propriety of cricket in the college, and the college authorities were also anxious lest the sight of young women playing boisterous games provide ammunition for the 'doubters'. But 'Fives', hockey, and lawn-tennis (played in decorous long white piqué skirts or thick green wool dresses because every hall in Newnham designed its own tennis outfit) all had Anne Jemima Clough's personal seal of approval.[37] A photograph of the hockey team shows Clara and her team in the regulation blue serge skirts virtually touching the ground, crisp white blouses and hair swept off the face under the caps, which aped the boys' uniform.

Away from the hockey pitch, Clara was largely indifferent to her physical appearance. Her preferred choice of dress consisted of stout brogues, a simple open-necked blouse, a practical skirt usually in a dark colour for cycling and a tailored jacket; a 'mannish' tie sometimes added for dashing effect when ties were in vogue. The fashion for padded hips, bosoms and voluminous sleeves of the 1890s was largely ignored as were the large showy picture hats favoured later by many Edwardian women. Clara's choice of costume denoted seriousness, respectability, and sexual propriety. With some seasonal adjustments of colours, textures, and fabrics this serviceable 'uniform' established in her student days varied little from photograph-to-photograph and from year-to-year. As an adult she used no cosmetics other than a little cold cream and a touch of lightly applied lipstick on special occasions.

Clara was a strong and confident swimmer. But unchaperoned swimming was strictly forbidden to women students. Gwen Raverat recalled that 'All summer, Sheep's Green and Coe Fen were pink with boys, as naked as God made them; for bathing drawers did not exist then; or, at least, not on Sheep's Green'.[38] Clara was also a proficient long-distant cyclist and would cycle for miles to the surrounding villages and into the Fens, enjoying the birdsong and the sights and sounds of the countryside.

The Tabor sisters, Margaret and Clara, belonged to one of many tendentially progressive intersecting networks of women friends and relations connected to Newnham College,[39] sometimes encompassing more than one generation of the same family. Three of Clara's nieces, Mary Tabor, Lucy Tabor, and Winifred Elisabeth Adams (the daughter of Harris's younger sister, Winifred Rackham) studied at the college, as did Clara's great-niece Anne Hobbs. Barbara White (née Dale), a relative of Clara's by marriage, was a Tutor of one of Newnham's four Halls of residence from 1925 to 1934, appointed Acting Bursar during the Second World War and became the permanent Bursar in 1946.

In *Faith, Duty and the Power of the Mind* Gillian Sutherland shows how Newnham College was 'both symbol and agent of the transformation of educational opportunities for women'[40] using the members of the Clough family to 'make the point that the rise of professional occupations in England is not purely a male affair'[41] and went hand-in-hand with a desire to bring about reform in the university and beyond. She writes that

> In this company the creation of educational opportunities and structures for women took its place with other schemes for enlarging access to education, a concern with class as well as with gender, a concern that Cambridge and Oxford should behave less like corrupt little oligarchies and more like responsible elites.[42]

Clara's decision to read Classics rather than Moral Sciences, History, or Mathematics like her sister was determined very largely by the high quality tuition in the classical subjects in both of her schools – Louisa Lumsden's influence was very long-lived. Clara had been exceptionally lucky. Notting Hill and St Leonards headed the lists of schools sending students to Girton and Newnham who took the Classical Tripos from 1885 to 1899. Notting Hill sent twenty students followed by the North London Collegiate with sixteen students and St Leonards in third place with eight.[43]

In 1882 the Cambridge University statutes had been changed to give permission to Fellows of the college to marry and, as Florence Ada Keynes put it, 'Cambridge became a place where women could be educated and men could be married and the results have not seldom been combined'.[44] In 1887 Agnata Ramsay a student at Girton College, had caused a sensation as the only student of either sex to be ranked in the first division of the First Class in Part I of the Classical Tripos. Agnata married Montagu Butler, the fifty-five-year-old Master of Trinity in 1888.[45] Between them Agnata and Montagu produced a veritable dynasty of classical scholars. Clara was to find herself standing against one of them, Agnata's great grandson, R. A. Butler, in the General Election in Saffron Walden in 1935.

But it was not easy for women. 'The Classics at their most classic – studies not of literature but of words and grammar – were considered by public school masters as the only proper learning for boys; anything outside Latin and Greek were frivolous *hors-d'oeuvres*'.[46] Part one of the Classical Tripos was dominated by translation and composition and, as Mary Beard points out, was 'almost entirely a test of the Latin and Greek Language, designed to test the linguistic skills of men who had been drilled in almost nothing else'.[47] Most women students were severely at a disadvantage and struggled to develop the skills of prose composition in three years. Many found the challenge of Latin and Greek verse virtually insurmountable.[48] Clara was no exception.

If Margaret had witnessed Philippa Fawcett's magnificent triumph, one of the most joyful moments in the history of Newnham College, Clara was present at one of its bleakest. The Grace to admit women to degree titles on May 21, 1897 was resoundingly defeated in a ratio of almost 2.5 to 1 with 662 in favour and 1,713 against, with the women's opponents chartering special trains from King's Cross to bring in non-resident MAs to vote against. An effigy of an advanced young woman in bloomers riding a bicycle ('the Girton Girl') was suspended outside what is now the Cambridge University Press bookshop in the Market Square and set alight. Flour, fire crackers, and rotten eggs were hurled into the crowd and through open windows and the fire brigade summoned to extinguish a raging bonfire.[49]

Marauding undergraduates celebrating their *soi-disant* 'victory' attempted to storm Newnham College – Girton was too far away. Terrified women students taking refuge on the Old Hall roof could hear the clamour of the approaching mob. More damage would certainly have been inflicted had the rioters not found the gates presciently locked against them and been persuaded to turn back. Nora Sidgwick put a brave face on the distasteful episode and the ignonimy of the women's defeat and Clara, rationalised what had happened as an object lesson in the importance of steadfast leadership in the face of adversity ('with what courage and good temper it is possible to fight a hard and losing battle').[50]

In 1896 Helen Gladstone resigned as Vice-Principal having been summoned to the family home in Hawarden to tend to her ailing father. Clara's childhood hero, William Ewart Gladstone, died at Hawarden Castle on May 29, 1898 at the age of eighty-eight on the day before Clara was due to sit Part 1 of the Classical Tripos. Those around her took good care to see that she was not told of Gladstone's death, lest this devastating news affect her performance in the examination.[51] The result was a disappointment although not entirely unexpected. Clara had been placed low in the class lists in the second division of the Third Class. She did not take the optional Part Two which was less narrowly philological than Part I and took the precaution of obtaining testimonials from Katherine Stephen, the Principal, for use should she decide to teach. Her Third does not appear to have dented her confidence in any way.

It was as her college tutor in Classical subjects that Clara first met her future husband. Harris Rackham (see Figure 2.7) was reserved, rather formal in manner, careful and deliberate in his choice of words, and invariably courteous and considerate. He was seven years her senior. Clara's diaries are curiously circumspect in relation to Harris with no mention of how and when they met, other than a cryptic reference to the year 1897 as the 'happiest of my life' and no mention of any engagement. Harris did, however, write to tell his sister, Winifred Rackham, the good news: 'I'm engaged to the girl with blue eyes and blonde hair whom I teach Greek prose'.[52] Clara's hair, variously described as 'brown', 'coppery', and 'blonde' was often parted and drawn back to reveal her strongest feature ('penetrating blue eyes which remained absolutely steady and were quite transfixing').[53]

Harris had won a scholarship to Christ's College, Cambridge in 1887 where he had been a contemporary of Clara's brother, Francis at Emmanuel College. He had graduated with a First in Part One of the Classical Tripos and a First in Part Two. Harris's first temporary teaching position was as an Assistant Master teaching Greek and Latin composition at Winchester College, an ancient religious foundation with its medieval chapel and cloisters founded in the fourth century by Bishop William of Wykeham with the school proverb 'manners maketh man'. Harris returned to Cambridge in 1892 as one of a cohort of trusted scholars from the men's colleges whom Newnham College could always rely on to supervise their students in Latin and Greek. He was meticulous, well-organised, popular with the students and an excellent teacher, and was appointed a Lecturer at Newnham College in 1893 and a Junior Fellow of Christ's College in 1894. This diffident young scholar must have been impressed by Clara's vivacity, good humour, intelligence, irrepressible love of life, and intellectual curiosity. He must also have been aware that his younger brother Bernard, a first-year student reading Classics at Pembroke College, and not Harris himself, was Clara's exact contemporary in age. While the attraction between Clara and Harris was immediate, propriety ensured that a suitable distance between them be maintained, at least until Clara's studies had been completed. Both her own parents and Harris's warmly approved of the relationship from the very beginning.

Harris was born in South Lambeth Road, in London in 1868 to Anne (née Stevenson), from a family of lace-makers in Nottingham and Alfred Thomas Rackham, a legal clerk. Thomas had 'stormed out' of the Church of England in protest at its treatment of the radical theologian, Frederick Denison Maurice, who had played a leading role in the Christian Socialist Movement and the Working Men's College in London and Harris's brother, Maurice, was named after his father's great mentor. When Harris met Clara his family were attending Unitarian meetings. Harris had an older sister Margaret (Meg), and an older brother, the future book illustrator, Arthur, who was to become increasingly important in Clara's life. The age difference between Arthur and Harris was thirteen months and as children the two were virtually inseparable. Younger brothers and sisters arrived in rapid succession: Ethel, Leonard, Winifred, Mabel, Bernard, and Stanley; the last, Maurice, born in 1879. Alfred was promoted to Chief Clerk at the Admiralty in 1875 and in 1881 the family moved to a larger four-storey house in Albert Square, a salubrious mid-Victorian 'garden square' off the Clapham Road and then to Earlsfield Road in Wandsworth.

In 1879 Harris and Arthur were both sent to the City of London School in Cheapside. Harris edited the school magazine and enjoyed playing soccer. Arthur won prizes for algebra and trigonometry. Both loved Chemistry and Physics: 'Harris and Arthur Rackham were among the experimenters at home, constructing *inter alia* an electric battery'.[54]Arthur would smuggle a pen and pencil to bed with him and draw as long as it was daylight and when this was forbidden he secreted the pencil into bed with him and drew on the pillows.[55] A. E. Douglas-Smith, recollected that 'Arthur Rackham delighted us at school, as he has delighted the world since, with his drawings'.[56]When he was caught by his form master drawing lifelike caricatures of the masters, his 'punishment' was being made to draw the same caricatures on the board in front of the whole form. The most famous old boy of the school was Herbert Henry Asquith, the Liberal Prime Minister and an intractable opponent of women's suffrage, who was to cross paths with Clara more than once.

It was a wrench for Arthur and Harris to be parted but in 1883, on medical advice, his parents sent Arthur on an ocean voyage to Australia as a cure for consumption. There was no question of further schooling on Arthur's return to England in 1884 and he was enrolled at the Lambeth School of Art as an evening student until 1890. He took up his first full-time job, as a junior clerk in an insurance company, the Westminster Fire Office, in 1885,

> for the next seven years or so I worked as hard as I could out of business hours (9–5) to equip myself as an artist – not being able to embark on a professional career till I was nearly 25, & then for

> many years getting the barest living from my profession & having to do much distasteful hack work.[57]

Arthur resigned from the Westminster Fire Office in 1892 and took his first tentative steps towards becoming a professional illustrator, with commissions from J. M. Dent, exhibitions in art galleries, and illustrations in *Pall Mall Budget* and *Westminster Gazette.* Harris and Clara were drawn together by their shared interest in questions of urban poverty and unemployment. In 1896 Harris joined a team of social investigators in drawing up case notes for a report on unemployment for the Toynbee Trust. We still have his handwritten notes on the Castle End area of Cambridge between Northampton Street and Castle Hill where the Castle End Mission taught working men to read and write.[58] Here the poor, desperate, and destitute were crammed into overcrowded, dank, fetid, airless courts, and yards – Comet Yard, Worbey's Yard, Gentle's Yard, and Leonard's Yard. The largest of these, Kettle's Yard, later to become the home of Jim Ede and the site of his world-famous collection of modern art, consisted of twenty-six cottages hardly fit for human habitation with six or more people sleeping in one room. Many working-class women were laundresses eking out a living washing college linen at home and drying it on the grassy slopes of Mount Pleasant.[59]

Harris served as the Cambridge University Secretary of Toynbee Hall for ten years from 1894 and was on its governing council from 1895. The pioneering university settlement was founded by Canon Samuel and Henrietta Barnett in 1884 in the working-class parish of St Jude's in Whitechapel notorious for the gruesome 'Jack-the Ripper' murders. The Barnetts encouraged students from Oxbridge to live and work in Toynbee Hall in order to witness the terrible social conditions of the East End for themselves. It was through the Toynbee Hall residential community that Harris first met the socialist economic historian, R. H. Tawney whom he introduced to Clara, and who was subsequently to become a lifelong mentor and friend and to influence her own thinking profoundly.

The radical experiment in communal living was not without its critics who argued that 'Barnett failed to perceive that although the men and women of Whitechapel were poor, they were not without a culture of their own. To him Whitechapel represented a cultural void, into which his own culture had to be poured'.[60] Harris was drawn to Toynbee Hall because it was a practical attempt to apply the social principles of Christianity and the ideals of socialism to modern industrial life. But it also gave him an opportunity to think more deeply about the possibility of non-exploitative relationships between women and men, to question received Victorian ideas about masculinity, and to ask what kind of man he wanted to become inwardly, as part of his engagement with the social and economic problems of a changing world. As Seth Koven puts it, 'If settlements were explicitly experiments in reimagining class relations, they were also implicitly sites to invent a new kind of man' who was 'attuned to the private grief of his neighbours' and was prepared 'to think in new ways about his private and public self'.[61] Although Toynbee Hall only admitted men as full members of its residential community Henrietta Barnett was very prominent in its affairs and had first visited Cambridge in 1887 to talk about settlements. In practice there were many opportunities for Oxford and Cambridge University women to become involved as associates. The Women's University Settlement, at which Margaret Tabor volunteered, was set up in Southwark that year and Helen Gladstone was appointed Warden in 1901.

Henrietta Barnett would sometimes stay with Clara if she was in Cambridge and Clara would stay in the Barnett's home in Hampstead in return. She has left this account of one memorable visit:

> In the house we found a mixed company; there were "convalescents" from the neighbourhood of Toynbee Hall, girls from the Poor Law Schools being trained for service, besides the Barnetts' personal friends. Nor were the old people forgotten: Mrs Barnett saw how wretched the aged women in the Whitechapel Workhouse were in the winter time because of the overcrowding so she had a group of them to live in the Hampstead house in the winter months and they returned to the Workhouse in the summer when the conditions were much better. Everyone seemed very happy but it was not one's idea of a peaceful weekend retreat.[62]

On leaving Newnham Clara returned to Fennes where Henry and Emma had relocated themselves after her grandfather's death. As Ellen Ross put it; 'the endless round of social duties – to accompany their mothers everywhere, to answer piles of letters, to dress and undress several times a day, to entertain sickly relatives' could be exceedingly tedious.[63] Henry and Emma led a busy social life and Clara duly joined in. The Tabors were on calling terms with other county families, and particularly with the Courtaulds, Unitarians descended from seventeenth-century French Huguenots refugees, and known throughout Essex as philanthropists, and patrons of the arts.

Samuel Courtauld had installed a steam engine in his Bocking silk mill and at one time the three Courtauld mills in Bocking, Braintree, and Halstead employed over 3000 workers, in the main, women and girls, manufacturing the ubiquitous black silk crêpe which was the standard mourning attire of choice for the middle classes in Victorian Britain. Clara and her siblings would often walk or drive in the carriage to Gosfield Hall, their sixteenth-century manor house. Marion Ruth Courtauld, whose personal fortune financed much charitable work for girls in the Braintree area, was a very good friend. Edward Tabor and Austin

Courtauld were the same age and remained the best of friends from infancy until old age.

Clara kept guinea pigs and rabbits, set up a branch of the Girls' Friendly Society in the village, and collected the rent from the cottages on the estate. But the Essex countryside was an unwelcome contrast to the lively intellectual ambience of Cambridge which she missed. Neither she nor Harris ever thought twice about cycling the thirty-five mile distance between Cambridge and Bocking. Clara had great physical stamina and was to undertake many demanding cycle tours over the years. In 1894 she travelled to Switzerland, to Germany in 1895, Italy in 1896 and Austria in 1898. In 1899 she cycled across Belgium and in 1900 across the whole of Normandy. Had she lived today she might well have been a competitive long-distance cyclists.

Clara followed the news from Harris's family and her own avidly while living at Fennes maintaining contact through the postal service, frequent and reliable, and a good train service from Braintree to London. Arthur was extremely happy having met his future wife and soul-mate, Edyth Starkie, a vivacious Irish portrait painter, who lived next door to his Hampstead Studio. Bernard had obtained a First- Class degree in the Classical Tripos in 1898. He joined the South Kensington Museum, later the Victoria and Albert Museum, and was quickly put to work to catalogue the museum's vast collection (some 5,000 pieces) of recently acquired pottery and porcelain, a massive project which was to furnish him with his encyclopaedic knowledge of ceramics and glass from all over the world.[64]

Francis's professional career also flourished. On leaving Cambridge he joined the Indian Civil Service in the North-West Provinces and Oudh rising to Magistrate in 1898 and becoming a Sessions Judge in 1901. Margaret had visited Francis in Lucknow, travelling to India in the company of Athena Clough, Anne Jemima's niece, and Philippa Fawcett and parting company with her friends to look after Francis who was ill. The others returned home through India, Ceylon, China, Japan, Canada, and the United States, an expedition that took Athena and Philippa nine months and which circumnavigated the world.[65] Margaret had been appointed Warden of the newly opened University Hall of Residence for women in Liverpool (1900–1905). Edward had found his metier as a civil engineer working on the railways in England, Canada, and the United States until 1899 when he went to Egypt with Messrs. Ransomes and Rapier as a resident engineer on the construction of the steelwork at the Aswan Dam.

Notes

1 Unless otherwise indicated the biographical information on Clara Rackham's early years is taken from her handwritten notebook, 'Recollections of Childhood 1875-1891' (n.d.) with no page numbers, courtesy of Lucy Tabor and Helen Bloxsome, Tabor Family Papers (TFP).

2 Margaret Tabor, 'My Reminiscences', unpublished typescript (c.1949), 10, courtesy of Lucy and Helen Bloxsome (TFP).
3 Ibid., 8.
4 See Marjorie Thompsett, 'The Tabor Diaries 1868-70: Some Aspects of the Mid-Victorian Scene', unpublished MA dissertation, 2012, https://commons.wikimedia.org/wiki/File:HenryTabor Diaries.pdf, accessed October 22, 2018.
5 Tabor, 'My Reminiscences', 19.
6 Ibid.
7 Ibid., 20.
8 Ibid., 21–7.
9 Ruth Barton, 'Sunday Lecture Societies, Naturalistic Scientists, Unitarians and Secularists Unite against Sabbatarian Legislation,' in *Victorian Scientific Naturalism: Community, Identity*, eds Gowan Dawson and Bernard Lightman (Chicago, IL: Chicago University Press, 2014), 189–219.
10 Tabor, 'My Reminiscences', 11, 12.
11 Ibid., 29.
12 Clara Rackham's Notting Hill School reports (TFP).
13 Carol Dyhouse, *Girls Growing Up in Late Victorian and Edwardian England* (London: Routledge, 2014), 59.
14 F. A. Keynes, *By-ways of Cambridge History* (Cambridge: Cambridge University Press, 1947), xix
15 Harris Rackham, letter to *The Cambridge Review*, March 7, 1942, Harris Rackham Archive, Christ's College, Cambridge, Box 129B, courtesy of the Master and Fellows of Christ's College.
16 Alice Gardner, *Short History of Newnham College* (Cambridge: Newnham College, 1921), no page numbers and Tabor, 'My Reminiscences', 57.
17 A game of handball thought to have been first played at Eton and played against the wall of a three sided court.
18 Gillian Sutherland, *Faith, Duty and the Power of the Mind: The Cloughs and Their Circle 1820-1960* (Cambridge: Cambridge University Press, 2006), 4.
19 Hugh Lloyd-Jones, 'Jane Ellen Harrison 1850-1928', in *Cambridge Women: Twelve Portraits*, eds Edward Shils and Carmen Blacker (Cambridge, Cambridge University Press, 1996), 29–72, 29.
20 Ibid., 30.
21 Carol Dyhouse, *Feminism and the Family in England 1880-1939* (Oxford: Blackwell, 1989), 28.
22 Keynes, *By-ways*, p. xii.
23 Jane Ellen Harrison, *Reminiscences of a Student's Life* (London: Hogarth, 1925), 44.
24 Ibid., 45.
25 Helen Fowler, 'Eleanor Mildred Sidgwick 1845-1936', in *Cambridge Women*, 7–28, 12.
26 Ibid., 13.
27 Harrison, *Reminiscences*, 45.
28 Ibid.
29 Talia Schaffer, '"Nothing but Foolscap and Ink": Inventing the New Woman', in *The New Woman in Fiction and in Fact*, eds Angelique Richardson and Chris Willis (London: Palgrave, 2001), 39–52, 49.
30 Gillian Sutherland, *In Search of the New Woman: Middle-Class Women and Work in Britain 1870-1914* (Cambridge: Cambridge University Press, 2015), 6-7.

31 Clara D. Rackham, 'Susan Lawrence', *Fabian Quarterly* (Spring 1948), 20–3, 20.
32 The grounds and gardens of several Cambridge colleges, King's, Clare, Queen's, St John's, Trinity and Trinity Hall back onto this beautiful stretch of the River Cam.
33 Mary Paley Marshall, *What I Remember* (Cambridge: Cambridge University Press, 1934), 16.
34 Mary Agnes Hamilton, *Remembering My Good Friends* (London: Cape, 1944), 46, 47.
35 The Newnham College Roll Letter, 1895 with thanks to the college archivist, Anne Thomson.
36 The records of the Newnham College Political society.
37 For student reflections on the early days of Newnham College, see Ann Phillips, ed., *A Newnham Anthology* (Cambridge: Newnham College, 1979).
38 Gwen Raverat, *Period Piece: A Victorian Childhood* (Cambridge: Faber and Faber, 1952), 108.
39 See Sutherland, *Faith, Duty and the Power of the Mind*, 4.
40 Ibid., 3.
41 Ibid., p.2.
42 Ibid.,.
43 Claire Breay, 'A Gentleman's Education? Women and the Classical Tripos 1869-1914', unpublished dissertation, Newnham College (c.1990.), 41.
44 Keynes, *By-ways*, xv.
45 Mary Beard, Gillian King and Christopher Stray, eds, *The Birds and the Bees: Women in Classics, Cambridge 1871-1948* (Cambridge: Faculty of Classics, 1998), 23.
46 Raverat, *Period Piece*, 67.
47 Mary Beard, *The Invention of Jane Harrison* (Cambridge, MA: Harvard, 2000), 19.
48 Breay, 'A Gentleman's Education?', 35.
49 *The Cambridge Weekly News*, May 28, 1897.
50 Clara Rackham personal papers shown to Rita McWilliams-Tullberg by Mary Tabor, quoted in Rita McWilliams Tullberg, *Women at Cambridge: A Men's University – Though of a Mixed Type* (London: Gollancz, 1975), 141, fn.48.
51 I.H. Quigly, 'Clara Dorothea Rackham (née Tabor) 1875-1966 (Newnham 1895-1898)', Newnham College Roll Letter (January 1967), 48-51, 49.
52 Letter from Harris Rackham to Winifred Adams née Rackham (n.d.), Anne Stevenson Hobbs family reminiscences and anecdotes (ASH).
53 Letter from C. M. Courtney to Joyce Bellamy, dated October 21, 1980 (CDR, U DLB/9/55), Hull History Centre Archive.
54 A. E. Douglas Smith, *The City of London School* (Oxford: Blackwell, 1963), 271.
55 James Hamilton, *Arthur Rackham: A Life with Illustration* (London: Pavilion, 1990), 17. Unless stated otherwise, information about Harris and Arthur Rackham's childhood is taken from James Hamilton's biography.
56 Ibid., 251.
57 Derek Hudson, *Arthur Rackham: His Life and Work* (London: Heinemann, 1960), 30.
58 Harris's notes are in a small, lined black hard-covered notebook (TFP).
59 Enid Porter, 'The Castle End of Cambridge', CHPL 3, 41 (November 1970), 20–22, 21.

60 Standish Meacham, *Toynbee Hall and Social Reform 1880-1914: The Search for Community* (New Haven, CT: Yale University Press, 1987), 60.
61 Seth Koven, *Slumming: Sexual and Social Politics in Victorian London* (Princeton, NJ and Oxford: Princeton University Press, 2004), 240.
62 Clara Rackham, 'Some Distinguished Women I Have Known: Dame Henrietta Barnett', handwritten ms. (n.d.) (TFP).
63 Ellen Ross, ed., *Slum Travelers: Ladies and London Poverty 1860-1920* (Berkeley: University of California Press, 2007), 21.
64 Obituary, 'Mr Bernard Rackham', *The Times*, February 15, 1964.
65 Tabor, 'My Reminiscences', 58.

Figure 2.1 Tabor Family (Henry, Emma, Margaret, Clara, and Francis).
https://upload.wikimedia.org/wikipedia/commons/9/9f/Henry TaborDiaries.pdf.

Figure 2.2 Fennes, the Tabor ancestral home in north Essex.
Courtesy of Helen Bloxsome and Lucy Tabor.

Figure 2.3 A Young Clara Tabor.
Courtesy of Helen Bloxsome and Lucy Tabor.

Figure 2.4 Margaret Emma Tabor.
Courtesy of Lucy Tabor and Helen Bloxsome.

Figure 2.5 Miss Dove's House, St Leonards School, St Andrews, Fife.
Courtesy of Helen Bloxsome and Lucy Tabor.

Figure 2.6 Newnham College Hockey Team.
Courtesy of Lucy Tabor and Helen Bloxsome.

Figure 2.7 Harris Rackham.
Courtesy of Helen Bloxsome and Lucy Tabor.

Figure 2.8 Cambridge Women's Co-operative Guild, Christ's College, Hobson Street.
Courtesy of Helen Bloxsome and Lucy Tabor.

Figure 2.9 (a) Membership card of the Women's Co-operative Guild. (b) Members of the Women's Co-operative Guild, Cambridge about 1905.

Courtesy of Helen Bloxsome and Lucy Tabor.

Figure 2.10 Clara at the Summit of the Gross Glockner, 1907. Courtesy of Helen Bloxsome and Lucy Tabor.

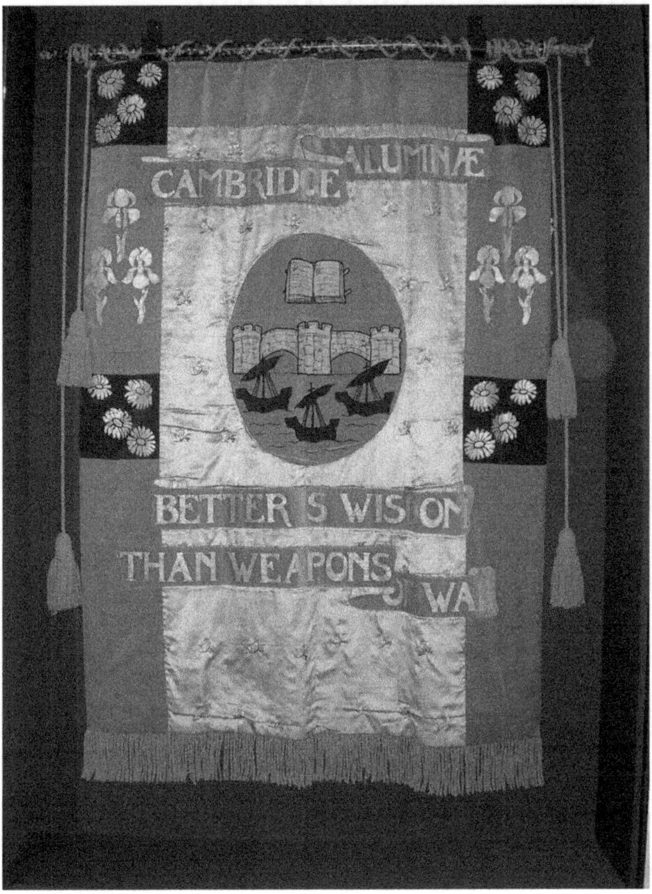

Figure 2.11 Newnham and Girton suffrage banner.
Courtesy of the Principal and Fellows of Newnham College, Cambridge.

2 'Better Is Wisdom than Weapons of War'

Suffragist and Factory Inspector

Figure 2.12 Millicent Garrett Fawcett and Clara Rackham in Hyde Park, the Great Pilgrimage 1913.

Clara and Harris were married in a quiet low key ceremony at the parish church in Bocking on March 16, 1901. The country was preoccupied with Queen Victoria's death on January 22, her lying in state in Osborne House, and her funeral at Windsor, and racked with a sense of loss and uncertainty. They made a stormy sea crossing from Dover to Calais and by train to Basel, Lucerne and Lugano where they stayed in the Hotel Washington, walked round the lake and took the funicular up to San Salvadore. In Milan they saw 'The Last Supper', purchased scent and drank Chartreuse, enjoying the magnificent scenery of mountains and lakes and immersing themselves in antiquities and cultural treasures; the picturesque churches, grand cathedrals, Renaissance art and medieval monuments that Milan, Verona, Padua, Como, and Bellagio had to offer.

DOI: 10.4324/9780429353499-3

Figure 2.13 Clara at the opening of Romsey Labour Club.

In Venice the couple stayed in the Hotel Beau Rivage, mingled with Easter holiday makers, and explored every corner of the city; on foot, taking the steamer, or hiring a gondola (sometimes with Ruskin's *The Stones of Venice* in hand) eying appreciatively everything they saw from the beautiful mosaics at St Mark's Cathedral to the young women making lace at Burano. They would return to Italy and Switzerland again and again.

Like many young feminists of her time, Clara was ambivalent about marriage as an institution. She embarked on her own marriage determined to avoid replicating those patterns of family life which she had experienced as oppressive in her childhood and had taken care to choose a husband who felt much the same way about married women's freedoms and rights as she did.[1] She had an older feminist role model, mentor, and friend in Florence Ada Keynes, who had had three gifted children, Geoffrey, Maynard, and Margaret with the Economist John Neville Keynes, and would go on to combine her own successful marriage with a long and distinguished career as a councillor and magistrate and eventually become the Mayor of Cambridge.

Clara and Harris settled down to a marriage based on the mutual desire to establish an equal union allowing both partners autonomy and the freedom to pursue their separate interests. This was made possible by a succession of devoted long-serving housekeepers, notably a Mrs Jones and a Miss Mills, who became trusted members of the household. In contrast to her sister Margaret, Clara was never to learn how to sew, knit, or cook for herself.

Their first Cambridge home was 4 Grange Terrace in Newnham (now integrated into Grange Road), an area of large Victorian red brick villas with pleasant gardens, popular with academics and their families. Eleanor Sidgwick and her household lived at number one. The Nobel Prize winner, Frederick Gowland Hopkins lived at 71 Grange Road on the site of an old Saxon burial ground with his daughter the future archaeologist Jacquetta (later Hawkes). Marion and Julia Kennedy lived nearby at 7 Selwyn Gardens after their father's death and Mary and James Ward at number 6. To the west of Grange Road the rows of large Victorian villas at the town's edge gave way to flat countryside, golden fields of wheat and huge East Anglian skyscapes with slow-moving clouds.

Harris frequently spent all day at Christ's College with his Thucydides and Greek History and often dined at High Table leaving Clara free to do whatever she wished in his absence. He was very close to the educational reformer and philologist, John Peile, the Master of Christ's, who was also the President of Newnham College Council and Harris was himself made a member of this council in 1905. Peile and his wife, Annette (née Kitchener), had always been great supporters of women's education and he had ensured that his own college was the first Cambridge college to open its lectures to women. The two families became good friends.

Career opportunities, even for well-educated graduates like Clara, were still extremely rare. Married women of Clara's social standing were not expected to work for financial gain and those who chose to do voluntary or charitable work usually prided themselves on their status as unpaid amateurs.[2] But as Margaret Cole, who studied classics at Girton, reflected, 'if you have leisure to think about Roman Society and Greek Society, it is improbable that your thinking will stop there'.[3] Trained to wrestle mentally with the problems of the ancient world, Clara became increasingly taken up with the problems of the new.

Clara did not have to look far to see how other educated women had successfully combined marriage with motherhood and paid or voluntary work. Former Newnham students who married university dons and managed to continue with their careers or with academic research, and to establish their own presence in public life included Margaret Merrifield, married to the classicist, Arthur Verrall, Mary Martin, 'a perfectly delightful Irishwoman, delicate and swift in both wit and humour'[4] – not to be confused with Mary Augusta (Mrs Humphrey) Ward, President of the Women's Anti-Suffrage League – who had married James Ward, the Moral Philosopher, and Mary Paley who married the Political Economist, Alfred Marshall.

Clara's position was anomalous in the context of Cambridge University. She did not regard herself as a 'university wife', although Harris's students were frequently invited to tea, neither did she behave like a 'society woman'. She had no taste for the high life and the grandeur of the old colleges and attended very few social events outside her own college, avoiding society functions and formal university dinners where the all-important conversation took place afterwards in a separate room from which women were excluded, wherever she could do so without giving offence. Instead, Clara and Harris's home became an 'open house' for community groups and supporters of progressive causes. The Cambridge Women's Suffrage Association would sometimes meet there and they would welcome friends like Mrs Foister and Mrs Gray of the Women's Co-operative Guild and a motley assortment of school teachers, charity workers, adult education tutors, Poor Law Guardians, and trade unionists whose company Clara enjoyed.

Harris remained the Cambridge Secretary of Toynbee Hall until 1904, the year in which William Beveridge was appointed Sub-Warden. Clement Attlee, the future Labour Prime Minister, became the Secretary in 1909. The Workers' Educational Association in which Clara was to become very active, was co-founded in Toynbee Hall in 1903 by R. H. Tawney and Albert Mansbridge, who became the full-time General Secretary of the Workers' Educational Association (WEA) in 1905.

In his history of the Co-operative movement in Cambridge, Henry Brown refers to Henrietta Barnett's volume on Canon Barnett in which she noted how Clara had welcomed visiting groups of women from the East End of London seeking contact with higher education, into her own home, and that she 'gave to her Cambridge Co-operative friends similar glimpses of the opportunities for learning while homing'.[5]

Clara was too young to have been a member of the exclusive Ladies' Dining Society which has attracted some recent interest.[6] The society had been established for twenty years by the time of her marriage in 1901, and at the age of twenty-six she was fourteen years younger than Maud Darwin, the youngest member. The closely knit society was a private dining and discussion club founded in 1890 by Kathleen Lyttelton and Louise Creighton and consisted of wives of Cambridge University academics who were strong supporters of women's education; Margaret Verrall, Eleanor (Nora) Sidgwick, Ellen Wordsworth Darwin, Mary Ward, and Mary Paley Marshall. Maud Darwin, Baroness Eliza (Isy) von Hügel and Lady Caroline Jebb were extremely well-connected and enjoyed dining in style. The only outsider was Mary Benson, Eleanor Sidgwick's sister-in-law.

Kathleen was married to Arthur Lyttelton, Master of Selwyn College and Louise Creighton, married to the ecclesiastical historian Mandell Creighton, who was appointed Bishop of Peterborough and then Bishop of London in 1897. When Louise left Cambridge she kept in touch with the others from the Bishops' House in Peterborough and Fulham Palace in London. The members of this influential friendship network continued to drum up support for women's suffrage, charitable works and good causes even after the demise of the Ladies' Dining Society in 1914. Clara remained on very good terms with several members of the group who supported Maud Darwin's advocacy of women police officers to work with women and children who had been subjected to physical and sexual assault and Caroline Jebb's plan for a women's memorial for Queen Victoria to be built in Cambridge. Most notably, they threw their formidable weight behind Eglantyne Jebb's Save the Children Fund which was set up by Jebb and her sister, Dorothy Buxton, in 1919 to transport food and medical supplies to the children in war-ravished Germany and Austria who were starving because of the allied blockades.

Clara, who was becoming increasingly preoccupied with social policy and social reform, was particularly close to Nora Sidgwick who signed her nomination papers for re-election as a Poor Law Guardian in 1912. In May that year Louise Creighton visited Cambridge to talk about the National Council of Women. Clara presided over the meeting to elect the first committee of the Cambridge branch 'keeping the seat warm for' Florence Ada Keynes and 'had the pleasure of moving her into Chair which she occupied with the greatest possible distinction for the next twelve years'.[7]

Florence Keynes had been a Poor Law Guardian since 1907 and as the Hon. Secretary of the Cambridge Charity Organisation Society (the honorific Hon. indicating unpaid) managed to persuade Clara to become the joint Hon. Secretary of the branch. Another prominent figure in the charity world was Helen Bosanquet (née Dando), a contemporary of Margaret's at Newnham College and Secretary of the Shoreditch branch of the Charity Organisation Society. Helen hated doing the branch accounts as much as Margaret loved doing them for her. As Jane Lewis points out, it was largely because both the state and the voluntary sector encouraged women to view work with the families of the poor as an extension of their obligations to their own families that women could aspire to exert real influence over social administration, if not over social policymaking, as social workers and as members of boards of guardians and on school boards.[8]

Clara was initially attracted to the Women's Co-operative Guild (WGC) because it was a democratic voluntary association run by and for women. Almost all the members were married and the vast majority working-class, thus differentiating the Guild from all the other women's organisations that she had known. As Gillian Scott explains, the 'Co-operative Commonwealth was a real ambition for many active members' and a 'historic commitment to sexual equality, a legacy of its Owenite past.'[9] The local Co-operative shops inspired great loyalty in working-class communities because women could see the profits going directly back to their purses in the form of the 'divi' (dividend). Indeed the Guild extolled the principle of co-operation as an alternative to exploitative capitalist modes of production and distribution. But with its stress on mutuality rather than conflict, and accent upon thrift as a means by which the poor could improve their own lives, the Guild must have impressed Clara as reassuringly distant from the militant trade unionism, working-class strikes and labour agitations that marked the turn of the century.

Clara helped to start a branch of the Women's Co-operative Guild in Bocking, founded the Cambridge branch, and was elected its President in 1902. Her first twenty years on the Cambridge committee corresponded almost exactly with the time that Margaret Llewelyn Davies, a Girton graduate and niece of the founder Emily Davies, was in office as General Secretary (1889–1922). Both Clara and Margaret subscribed to a radical idealistic vision of the Guild that aimed to put the needs of married women at the centre of the nation's political debate. Isolated and with no means of collectively remedying their legal and financial disabilities, 'married women in the home had existed apart, voiceless and unseen'.[10] The 'mothers' meeting' (sewing, reading from an improving book and a talk by a 'lady') had once been virtually the only type of meetings open to working-class women. But as one woman who defected from the mothers' meeting to the Guild in disgust put it; 'There is such a different feeling in speaking of trials and troubles to Guilders (where they are real) than to speak to the ladies of the Mothers' Meeting. You know that they have a fellow-feeling being all on an equality.'[11] In Cambridge Clara worked hard to replace the deference and passivity of the 'mothers' meeting' with a lively programme of speakers, discussions, and practical activities which would make an 'educated lady' like herself redundant once working-class women acquired the confidence to raise their voices, organise themselves, and launch their own campaigns. A stalwart of the Cambridge branch, a Mrs A. K. Edwards, described Clara as a 'tower of information' who 'went about her business in a most quiet way',[12] at first conspicuous by her-middle class demeanour and education but then becoming trusted and accepted for who she was. She drew on the list of suitable topics recommended by the central committee as being suitable for weekly discussion and debate. These included 'trade unions for women, protective labor legislation for female workers, women's suffrage, minimum wages for female cooperative employees, national health care for expectant mothers, and the extension of cooperation to the poor.'[13]

Margaret Llewelyn Davies quoted one Guildswoman's feelings:

> "It was a revelation. My spirit felt here is the opportunity I had always been seeking but never put into words. I had longings and aspirations and a vague idea of power within myself which had never had an opportunity of realisation. I felt as I imagine a war-horse must feel when he hears the beat of the drums."[14]

The national membership card, etched in social-realist detail by the artist, Muirhead Bone, later to become Britain's first official war artist, personifies hope, longing and aspiration [see Figure 2.9]. A working-class woman depicted in a coarse apron carrying a market basket stands on a hillside. Her sights are turned upwards, beyond the factory chimneys of the industrial landscape below her, towards a flock of birds on the far horizon signifying the birth of a new dawn. The caption reads: 'A self-governing organisation of women who work through Co-operation for the welfare of the people, seeking freedom for their own progress, and the Equal Fellowship of men and women in the home, the store, the factory and the state'.[15]

The Cambridge Co-operative Society organised excursions to the seaside, visits to 'model' Co-operative factories, warehouses, and Whipsnade Zoo and allowed the Guildswomen to use rooms on the top floor of their flagship Co-operative Department Store on Burleigh Street which opened in 1901 for their weekly meetings which Clara attended without fail. The women relished meeting in the huge, glass-fronted emporium (now Primark) with stylish mannequins in the shop windows which occupied much of the street. With lifts to all three carpeted floors and inducements to the customer to 'save as you spend', the store was billed as the 'finest department store in town' where everything possible has been done to make shopping a real pleasure and the comfort of our customers is the first consideration' and was hailed throughout the district as the last word in modern convenience and design.

It was through the Co-operative movement that Clara first ventured into the world of the social investigators (Lucy Gray, Rose Elizabeth Thomson, Edith Bethune-Baker, Muriel Kenny, Dorothy Jebb) who were invited to contribute to Eglantyne Jebb's edited volume *Cambridge: A Brief Study in Social Questions*. This was published in 1906 by the Cambridge COS under the exacting scrutiny of Mary Paley Marshal and Florence Keynes. Jebb's survey was influenced by the classic study of urban poverty, Charles Booth's *Life and Labour of the People* (1889) based on research by his wife's cousin Beatrice Webb. Like Booth, Jebb appended a 'poverty map' to designate areas of social deprivation and used colour to indicate the average value of rents.

The survey was informed by what Mary Poovey terms the 'feminized epistemology of sympathy'[16] which emphasised the importance of the enquirer listening carefully to her subject and made the work of female social researchers qualitatively different from many empirical surveys conducted by men. Clara stressed the terrible social isolation of her interviewees.

> 'Many of the most respectable women among the poor regard it as a credit to themselves that their lives are bounded by their household cares. How often one hears them say in a tone of pride that they never go anywhere except perhaps to church on Sunday, and that they never speak to anyone.'[17]

Despite the inclusion of the 'poverty map', poverty was not central to Jebb's project as a whole. Neither was statistical analysis: the facts and figures Clara proffers are minimal: there were 4,224 members of the Cambridge Co-operative Society in 1905[18] and the Cambridge branch of the Guild had about 120 members.[19] The topics they discussed included the hardy perennials of 'Temperance or total abstinence?' 'Cash and credit?' and the 'Choice of occupations for girls and boys.'[20]

Clara's own survey of social conditions in Cambridge published in Helen Bosanquet's (edited) social survey, *Social Conditions in Provincial Towns* (1912) was one of a series on provincial towns; Portsmouth, Worcester, Cambridge, Liverpool, Edinburgh (hardly provincial), Oxford and Leeds published in the *Charity Organisation Review* and then in book form. As Mark Freeman puts it, with the local backgrounds, knowledge, and contacts that they brought to their work, Clara, and the others contributors,

> revealed a cultural poverty that transcended the economic condition of the individual or the household, and was experienced collectively as well as individually, and thus they focused on the community as an organic whole rather than a statistical abstraction of the individuals who formed it.[21]

In her advocacy of the importance of connection, neighbourliness, feminine influence and personal contact between the social classes as a way of establishing good, active citizenship, Clara brought the philanthropic tradition of social welfare and the principles of the COS and the university settlement movement to the social survey in order to describe her own community 'in a more relational and synoptic way.'[22]

In its size and appearance the Cambridge of 1912 resembled a glorified Fenland market town with a grime-covered foundry belching out smoke and fumes where Marks and Spencer is located today. The town was dominated by its ancient university. There was no large, well-paid industry and the local economy fluctuated due to the students with seasonal, casual, or part-time work for college 'bedders', servants, and laundry workers. Clara's principal concerns related to 'in work' poverty, slum housing, disease, poor sanitation, the proliferation of public houses, and the high infant mortality (76 per 1,000 births).[23] Wages were low with unskilled labourer earning only about eighteen shillings a week.[24]

> 'There is undoubtedly among some of the artisans a vague feeling of resentment against the University. They have an idea that its influence has been exerted to keep railway works and other large industrial undertakings out of the town, and that this is not by any means compensated for by the trade that the University brings into it.'[25]

Clara hoped the new network of Labour Exchanges introduced by the Liberal government in 1909, which abolished the old custom of men 'tramping' across the country in search of work, might one day be instrumental in decasualising the labour market.[26] In practice, the network implemented by William Beveridge as a Civil Servant at the Board of Trade created no new jobs and therefore did not begin to solve the problem of decasualisation. She distanced herself from those of her contemporaries in the COS who held the poor responsible for their own poverty,[27] envisaging a more proactive, interventionist, and important role for the local authority. Her report praised the introduction of the school nurse, Cambridge's pioneering work in school dentistry,[28] and the 'admirable system of health visiting which ensures that every infant is visited by a skilled and trained worker within a few weeks of its birth'[29] while lamenting the lack of a qualified almoner at Addenbrookes Hospital and of any public baths and wash-houses in the town.[30]

Clara's political activity was interspersed with her enjoyment of family news. Harris and Clara attended the wedding of Harris's brother, Arthur and Edyth Starkie in Hampstead on July 16, 1903, Clara drawing up an annotated list of books as a wedding present.[31] After their marriage, Arthur and Edyth maintained separate art studios. Arthur with his 'prim precise English manner' owed much to the artistic, extroverted Edyth, who was the romantic one in the family and 'his most engaged and stimulating critic' and 'in return he gave her unswerving loyalty and devotion so that the marriage, despite its temperamental ups-and downs, proved a very happy one'.[32] Their only child, a daughter, Barbara, was born when Arthur was forty in 1908.

In 1904 Harris, his sister, Meg, Clara, her suffragist friend, Eliza Sturge, a Quaker, the 'silent Willie', Clara's parents Henry and Emma, all holidayed in Scotland at a Temperance Hotel enjoying the 'magnificent mountains', 'the wildest and grandest in Britain'. Meg Rackham described Emma Tabor as 'really one of the kindest people in the world'. However, 'everyone seemed to regard our party as rather formidable (& perhaps rather learned), from the books on Social Science, Bluebooks & huge volumes of Morley's Life of Gladstone which were generally scattered around us'.[33] Meg noted the other guests breathlessly drinking in their remarks and dead silence in the drawing room with everyone pretending to read, although with only one lamp that was scarcely possible.

There was much to celebrate with family reunions, holidays overseas and news 'home' from the relatives who had emigrated to farm in Canada. The Aswan Dam was finished a year before contract so Edward Tabor was free to go 'gadding around' the world still on full pay. After his return to England in 1903 he joined the staff of the London County Council and undertook major engineering projects including the construction of the Blackwall Tunnel and as resident engineer on the Woolwich Tunnel. Much to Clara's delight, her Newnham friend, Magdalen

Ricardo went out to India and married Francis in Bombay. She told Clara that she knew that he would be a good husband because he was her brother.[34] Before she married, the intrepid Magdalen had trekked in the Himalayas with just one Indian sepoy. Magdalen and Francis had two daughters, Mary and Evelyn. Evelyn was a delicate, nervous child with complex emotional needs who was never able to live independently and was lovingly cared for by Magdalen and Francis at their home, 'Evegate', near Bocking.

Margaret Tabor had also travelled far: to Pretoria at the invitation of Philippa Fawcett who had been deeply moved by the suffering in the concentration camps in the Boer War and given up her Fellowship in Newnham to train teachers in Mathematics and developing farm schools in the Transvaal. In a very brief interval between 1904 and 1907 Trinity College, Dublin decided to award its degrees *ad eundum* to members of the women's colleges in Oxford and Cambridge denied the right to graduate by their own universities. Margaret and Philippa grasped the once-in-a lifetime opportunity and joined over 700 'Steamboat Ladies' who boarded the boat to Ireland to collect their degree certificates in person.[35]

Clara's own expeditions abroad took her further from the beaten track. In April 1908 she scaled the summit of Mount Etna in Sicily by night in a party of five camping in the deep uneven snow and bitter cold. The men were exhausted and overcome by the fumes but Clara, in the peak of health, sat on the edge of the crater enjoying the glorious sunshine and the view.[36] The hotel keeper at Syracuse found it hard to believe that the party included two women. '"They must", he said, "have been ladies of *gran coraggio*"'.[37] In August 1910 Clara made a long-planned visit to United States and to see family in Canada. She and a friend rode for a mile on muleback in the scorching heat along a winding path to the very bottom of the Grand Canyon in Colorado. The sight of the painted desert was 'impossible to describe – vast peaks and ravines, all shapes and all colours, flaming red, purple and blue'.[38] They camped at night in darkness near the Colorado River with only their guide and a fugitive who had killed a man in a fight ('He was a friendly creature, glad of some company'). Their guide and the fugitive left together early next day, to return with the two donkeys for their journey back up the gorge, each carrying a rattlesnake captured among the rocks.

Despite growing misgivings Clara remained loyal to the Liberal Party but the intransigent attitude to women's suffrage and the broken promises of successive Liberal governments from 1906 onward sorely tested her patience. Moreover, the Guild increasingly brought her into contact with socialists such as Clementina Black of the Women's Trade Union League, sister of Constance Garnett, a Newnham graduate, who favoured collective modes of action and a greater regulatory role for the state.

It was Adela Adam (the mother of Barbara Wootton, the first woman life peer), a Lecturer in Classics at Girton College,[39] who was responsible for recruiting Clara into the women's suffrage movement: Clara recalls that

> She came to tell me that she was the Secretary of a small Women's Suffrage Society, the subscription was a shilling a year and would I join? She explained that the society didn't do anything, because there wasn't really anything for it to do.[40]

Little did either foresee the dramatic resurgence of interest in 'the cause' in consequence of the militant activities of Emmeline Pankhurst's Women's Social and Political Union (WSPU) founded in Manchester in 1903 which moved the question of votes for women from the periphery to the centre of the nation's political debates and revitalised the flagging energies of the constitutional suffragists who had worked peaceably for the vote for half a century. Still less could they have envisaged the momentous chain of events that would propel Clara from obscurity to chairing the largest of the constitutional suffrage societies, the National Union of Women's Suffrage Societies (NUWSS).

With the redoubtable Mary Ward, as its Secretary from 1905 the Cambridge Women's Suffrage Association acquired a new lease of life. Committee rooms were acquired at 2 Bene't Street and a shop with merchandise in the law-abiding suffragists' colours of red, white and green. Agnes Ramsey organised the regular market stall at Peas Hill selling handicrafts, preserves, and fresh produce. Newnham College and Girton College amalgamated their suffrage societies to form the Cambridge University Women's Suffrage Society (CUWSS) in 1908. That year Ray Costello (later Strachey) and three other students, took part in a NUWSS caravan tour from Dumfrieshire through the Lake District, Halifax, Huddersfield and Derby to Oxford with a taciturn driver and a horse called Jock.[41] Four hundred students from Girton College and Newnham College marched behind their banner designed by the artist Mary Lowndes and emblazoned with the words taken from Ecclesiastes, 'Better is Wisdom than Weapons of War'[42] [see Figure 2.11]. In 1909 the ninety-seven members of the Cambridge University Women's Suffrage Society in Girton included all the college teaching staff. The feminist and medieval historian, Eileen Power, is regularly listed as the college contact in the NUWSS paper, the *Common Cause*.

The playwright and polemicist Cicely Hamilton once claimed that 'women's suffrage was the first political agitation to organise the arts in its aid'.[43] Mary Ward's own suffrage play 'Man and Woman' was very popular and toured the country as a fund raiser. In October 1910 Hamilton's *Pageant of Great Women* was enacted in the Cambridge Guildhall with Clara as Elizabeth 1st, Agnes Ramsey as Margaret of Anjou, and Edith Bethune-Baker as St Theresa. In a performance of *Britannia's Daughters* at the Co-op in Burleigh Street Clara played herself as a Poor Law Guardian and Rosamond Rootham played the 'Spirit of Freedom'.

Harris presided over numerous meetings as President of the Cambridge University branch of the Men's League for Women's Suffrage. He and Clara were among the many married couples prominent in the women's suffrage movement, among the best known of whom were Frederick and Emmeline Pethick-Lawrence and Henry and Millicent Garrett Fawcett. Although Mrs Fawcett, President of the NUWSS from 1897 to 1919, had left Cambridge after Henry Fawcett's death she was revered in the town and returned to address packed public meetings in the Guildhall. In addition to meetings in the colleges, raffles, 'bring and buy' sales and fund-raising events, intimate 'at homes' took place in suffragist's drawing rooms. Clara was 'at home' with Catherine Marshall in December 1911.

Suffragettes were very much in a minority in Cambridge, a suffragist stronghold. Invitations to speak were, however, issued to virtually all the well-known figures in the movement such as Christabel Pankhurst, Flora Drummond, Lady Frances Balfour, Isabella Ford, Muriel Matters, and Lady Frances Balfour. Jane Brailsford once spoke from the back of a stationary vehicle which was shaken and pushed by rowdy anti-suffragists into the middle of a cricket match on Parker's Piece.

The Women's Co-operative Guild's longstanding support for adult suffrage dated back to a conference vote moved by the Lancashire working-class suffragist, Sarah Reddish, the Guild's first paid organiser.[44] On February 22, 1909 a letter signed by Margaret Llewelyn Davies, Mary Macarthur, and Emily Hobhouse appeared in the *Cambridge Independent Press* announcing the formation of the People's Suffrage Federation as the successor of the Adult Suffrage Society and claiming the support of leading members of the WCG.[45] Adult suffragists including Llewelyn Davies, the new Secretary of the People's Suffrage Federation, wanted the vote for all men and women over 21, an age-related measure that would have extended the electorate to include all disenfranchised working-class men. While Clara disliked in principle the prospect of a limited suffrage for women based on property, she was equally opposed to harnessing the carefully constructed feminist case for votes for women, which had gained much momentum in parliament and the country, to whatever course of action Westminster might eventually adopt in relation to votes for working men. She remained a committed women's suffragist rather than an adult suffragist.

Clara was one of the local Women's Co-operative Guild's best known local publicists and the WCG was among the first of many voluntary organisations in which her organisational skills and powers of analysis were recognised, welcomed, and put to good use. Somewhat surprisingly, she appears to have had no interest in putting herself forward for the national committee or to have had any direct input into national publications. As the number of Co-operative stores grew and the Society expanded its branches and activities, the Guildswomen intensified their campaigns for the right of women to keep their dividends (even when the money had been given to them by their husbands), for a minimum wage, and for equal pay for Co-operative women employees.

Co-operative women were also at the forefront of the campaigns for reform of the marriage and divorce laws and for an end to domestic violence and marital rape. These demands proved to be highly contentious not only because some vocal men in the co-operative movement were extremely hostile to any suggestion of easier divorce and contraception and but also because Guildswomen themselves sometimes subscribed to the conservative social attitudes to the family, contraception and reproductive rights that were prevalent in the working-class communities in which they lived.

In 1912 the annual congress of the Women's Co-operative Guild passed a resolution to make divorce available after two years' separation and to bring it within the reach of the poor. In her evidence to the Royal Commission on Divorce Margaret Llewelyn Davies organised her arguments around the responses which Guild Officials had sent to her summarising in writing each of 131 individual case examples she had received.[46] The Guild reported an 'overwhelming demand amongst married women belonging to the artisan class for drastic reform in the divorce laws'. Moreover, 'No other subject in the life of the Guild has aroused such immediate response and elicited such strength and earnestness of feeling.'[47]

In October 1911 Harris was promoted to Senior Tutor at Christ's College and the couple left Grange Terrace and moved into the Senior Tutor's House at 18 Hobson Street a few minutes from the market square and Great St Mary's Church. Clara enjoyed showing her friends from the Guild around. There is a group photograph of the Burleigh Street branch taken in the grounds of Christ's College in the Tabor family papers. The Guildswomen appear happy, to be enjoying the college surroundings, and dressed in their 'Sunday best' perhaps in readiness for a pleasant excursion which they had planned.

Clara had always admired the housing reformer, Octavia Hill, a founder member of the COS who had given her 'an impression of strength and goodness'[48] and collected rents from her tenants in person. Clara had felt able to relate to women of all classes and backgrounds without condescension since the days when she had collected rents from her father's cottagers. But while she disliked the 'Lady Bountifuls' of her own social class, she was acutely conscious of having grown up in the protected environs of the English country gentry, and that she still knew far too little about the humdrum reality of working people's lives. With some initial hesitation, Clara, put herself forward in 1904 as a Poor Law

Guardian in the Castle Ward where Harris had carried out his investigations for Toynbee Hall. 'There is no harm in the new Guardian acquiring experience as she goes along', Clara was later to write ten years later in an effort to encourage other women to follow her example.[49] After a flurry of excitement caused by the novelty of being asked to vote for a woman the 'popular lady candidate' topped the poll.[50]

As Seth Koven puts it, the 'institutionalization of female friendly visiting as an essential component of early-twentieth century social welfare legislations ... grew out of women's attempts to know and sympathise with their poor sisters'.[51] Thus it was that Clara joined a long line of Poor Law Guardians including Emmeline Pankhurst, Margaret Corbett Ashby, Hannah Mitchell, Henrietta Barnett, Ada Neild Chew, Margaret Nevinson, and Charlotte Despard whose impassioned support for votes for women was inextricably linked to their own feelings of anger and frustration at their powerlessness to do anything about the human misery to which they were exposed. As a columnist in *The Cambridge Independent Press* put it; 'When one thinks of Mrs Keynes and Mrs Rackham doing their best as Poor Law Guardians and visiting the workhouse Infirmary, what better words could there be to describe them than "administering angels"'. However, these particular 'angels' wanted votes for women as well.[52]

The female Poor Law Guardians were required to oversee indoor and outdoor relief for the old, the infirm, the homeless, and destitute. But all the institutions supposedly responsible for them were chronically under-resourced. Clara routinely found herself listening to appalling individual stories of hardship and desperation; little girls infected with venereal diseases, families of eight sleeping in two dank rooms, as working-class women confided in her, and it became patently clear that the Poor Law system was lamentably failing those for whom it was intended.

The Cambridge Workhouse in Ditchburn Place in Mill Road in 1838 was a grim forbidding institution of last resort. In a typical week (October 1909) the guardians dealt with 147 inmates and relieved 185 vagrants. The sum of outdoor relief dispensed (cash, goods, and services distributed outside the workhouse) was £45 and the number of persons who obtained relief was 405.[53] Clara become embroiled in a dispute with the other guardians by siding with the Local Government Board Inspector concerned about ten little girls not being properly looked after by a qualified woman. There was an unsatisfactory report from another inspector, a Mr Roundell, in April 1913. In general, the building appeared clean,[54] albeit old and inadequate. But little or nothing could be done about the detention of children, the cruel separation of (most) husbands and wives – exceptions were made -- and the Cambridge workhouse had a reputation for being more liberal than many – or the inhumane system in which the poor, widows, orphans, unmarried mothers, the homeless, infirm and destitute – were trapped and could spend all day scrubbing floors and picking oakum. At a Church Meeting for Poor Law Reform in Cambridge on September 30, 1910, Clara addressed a very large audiences on the subject of under-funding and over-stretched resources and demanded a better understanding of the structural causes of poverty.

In response to ubiquitous criticisms of the Poor Law, the retiring Balfour government set up the Royal Commission on the Poor Laws and Relief of Distress (1905–1909) which included Octavia Hill, Helen Bosanquet and Beatrice Webb. Jane Lewis describes them as perhaps the 'first of many "token" women'[55] who were being appointed to many official committees. The Commission published its findings in a Majority and a Minority Report in 1911. Led by Helen Bosanquet the majority concluded that the Poor Law should be retained, defending the fear of the workhouse as a deterrent. In contrast, Beatrice Webb, George Lansbury and the minority emphasised the relationship between worklessness and destitution and argued for Labour Exchanges, unemployment insurance, and for transferring responsibility away from private charities and trade unions to the state, albeit at the risk of undermining the notion of individual responsibility.

Following the report Clara wrote to *The Nation* (reprinted in the *Cambridge Independent Press*) reiterating the importance of the Charity Organisation Society. She argued that much of the Minority Report was 'admirable' but questioned whether a scheme could be said to 'put an end to overlapping which takes no account of the work of the provident clubs and friendly societies or of the huge sums dispensed in private charities?'[56] The sums, were in practice, far from 'huge'. Robert Humphreys has shown that the 'value of provincial Charity Organisation Society assistance was often less than the derided Poor Law dole, both as regards unit weekly value and the period over which relief was provided'.[57]

Clara's support for Sidney and Beatrice Webb's campaign against the Poor Law drew her closer to the Labour Party which had thrown its full weight behind the Webbs. In contrast, proponents of 'classic' Gladstoneian *laissez faire* liberalism in successive Liberal governments from 1905 onwards had resisted all demands for reform. The Labour Party also rose in Clara's estimation in 1912 after it resolved not to support any legislation for electoral reform that did not include votes for women. The NUWSS abandoned its political neutrality and, thanks to Catherine Marshall, the Parliamentary Secretary of the NUWSS, set up an Electoral Fighting Fund to help Labour Party candidates.

The NUWSS was by far the largest of the women's organisations working for the vote. At its height it could lay claim to some 450 branches in towns and villages. Organisationally it was divided into sixteen federations. The Eastern Counties with some forty-nine branches although smaller than either London or Scotland was larger than the Manchester Federation. The suffragettes of the Women's Social and Political Union, founded in Manchester by Emmeline Pankhurst in 1903, never had more than a fraction of the NUWSS numbers.

By 1908 Clara was holding open-air meetings and organising motorcades around the villages. Around forty NUWSS branches were in Bedfordshire, Cambridgeshire Essex, Norfolk, and Suffolk. Clara had helped to found a fair number of these branches herself and visited them regularly, She was 'an excellent speaker, being remarkably clear and direct in style' with the 'faculty of putting herself on a level with people of little education'.[58] She was also accepting invitations to travel and speak further afield. At one rowdy open-air meeting at Appleton near Warrington in 1909 chemical fumes were set off:

> 'Many of the men present looked at Mrs Rackham as they might have looked at a witch in the Middle Ages. There was wonder in their eyes, an evident terror of being beguiled out of their sanity, and their laughter was largely nervous. In this county district, a woman speaker was an innovation to be regarded with extreme caution, and it was noticeable that the audience consisted entirely of men.'[59]

Clara redoubled her activities for the 'cause' addressing large public meetings in Swindon and Chiswick Town Hall and at the AGM of the Norwich branch organised by young women from the well-known Colman family (of the extant Colman's English Mustard). She spoke in Kensington, Hull, York, Sutton, Whitby and Filey in 1911. By 1913 she was one of the NUWSS's most sought after public speakers. In that year alone she addressed some forty meetings as far apart as Bristol and Jarrow. These included Cambridge, Canning Town, Ealing, Fulbourn, Great Ormsby, Hampstead, Harpenden, Holt, Hitchin, Hull, Hunstanton, Ipswich, Islington, King's Lynn, Letchworth, Luton, Newmarket, North and East Essex (at Bocking), Newport (Essex), Norwich, Ramsay, Romford, Saffron Walden, Sawbridgeworth, Sheringham, St Albans, Sidcup, Stevenage, St Neots, Sutton, Stratford, Tower Hill, Walworth, Woodbridge, and Yarmouth. It was to the rough and tumble of the suffrage campaigns that Clara subsequently attributed her prowess as a brilliant impromptu speaker. A friend once expressed their envy. 'Ah', she said, 'you didn't learn from a soap box in Trafalgar Square'.[60]

With the encouragement of the veteran Millicent Fawcett, Clara was elected to the Executive Committee of the Eastern Federation in 1909 and to the National Executive Committee in 1910, Vice-Chairman in 1912 and Chairman in 1913. The mood of the country had altered radically after 'Black Friday' in November 1910 when women attending a peaceful demonstration in Parliament Square had been subjected to sexual assaults by the police. In consequence, many women became unwilling to attend the large demonstrations that had been the hallmark of earlier campaigns. Prompted by the failure of the Conciliation Bill the

WSPU embarked on a series of arson attacks and damage to property (although not to persons). Suffragette militancy escalated. A bomb was planted in Lloyd's George's house at Walton Heath, the orchid house at Kew Gardens was destroyed, a jewel case in the Tower of London smashed, and a railway carriage at Harrow set alight, in the course of a few weeks in February 1913.[61]

Cambridge too had its so called suffragette 'outrages'; a homemade bomb in a mustard tin which exploded at the Varsity Rugby Pavilion; a smouldering device in a treacle tin left in the railway station in Great Shelford; a suspicious, though harmless, package in the University Arms Hotel bearing the words 'votes for women'. But by far the most serious incident took place in May 1913 at an unoccupied house in Storey's Way which was burned to the ground by Maria Pratt, a Norwich schoolteacher who was subsequently jailed. Olive Bartels, the WSPU organiser, whose handiwork was detected in the planning of the arson attack, was never charged.[62]

In *What I Remember* (1924) Millicent Fawcett affirmed that the task of the suffragists had been to 'win the hearts and minds of our countrymen to the justice of our cause, and this could never be done by force and violence'.[63] But, as she explained in *Women's Suffrage* (1911), once the NUWSS full council had unequivocally condemned all acts of violence it appeared 'unnecessary to asseverate that they condemn individual acts of violence'.[64] Clara was scrupulously careful to follow Fawcett's example. When questioned about suffragette militancy, she would always point out that suffragettes had had more damage inflicted upon them than they had ever inflicted themselves and protest vociferously against the draconian punishments meted out to the militants, often for minor infringements of public order.

In May 1913 Clara, addressed a meeting in Newmarket Town Hall with Margaret Heitland and Katherine Vulliamy. It was disrupted by a 'concertina, songs, squibs that went off like pistol-shots, and witticisms of a wide range'. Their car wouldn't start because water had been poured into the petrol tank and they had to be rescued by the police.[65] Two weeks later on June 2, Emily Wilding Davison died under the King's horse on the Epsom race track. Relationships between the suffragists and suffragettes, which had been cordial in many towns and villages, were now stretched to breaking point. Suffragists like Clara became exceedingly concerned lest the good will achieved through years of patient lawful activity be lost due to public hostility to suffragette violence.

The Great Pilgrimage of 1913, the most ambitious of all NUWSS projects, was initially the idea of Katherine Harley, the key organiser, sister of General French, a national hero after the Second Boer War, and of Charlotte Despard (née French), President of the Women's Freedom League. The Pilgrimage was meticulously planned, publicised and executed in a matter of weeks with supporters from England and Wales attired in white with the cockle shell – the symbol of the pilgrim – pinned to their hats, retracing the steps of the medieval pilgrims, beginning at Carlisle and Newcastle and finishing at Land's End.

The 'pilgrims' with sashes and placards proclaiming that they were 'non-violent', 'law abiding', and 'non-party' to demonstrate to curious bystanders that they, as constitutional suffragists, wanted the vote, were organised in their Federations. They followed the old 'pilgrim' routes along the Great North Road, Watling Street, the Portsmouth Road, the Brighton Road, and the Pilgrim's Way in Kent, eventually converging in London for an enormous rally in Hyde Park addressed by Millicent Fawcett.[66]

Clara joined the pilgrims along the Eastern route at the village of Burwell. A long procession wound its way through Cambridge on Saturday July 19. The mood was jubilant despite widespread anger prompted by the infamous 'Cat and Mouse Act I' (Prisoners' Temporary Discharge for Ill-Health Act) introduced by the Home Secretary, Reginald McKenna, in March and permitted the government to release and re-arrest suffragette prisoners at will.

Large crowds lined the streets and the procession was largely without incident, other than good humoured banter, until a disaffected working man attempted to down his bag of tools in Magdalen Street in protest (he too did not have a vote). Some marchers stopped at Castle Hill outside Agnes Ramsey's house in Buckingham Road where group photos were taken. The procession made its way to the Maids Causeway and Midsummer Common. After resting overnight at private homes the marchers gathered in the Market Square behind a plethora of colourful banners. The NUWSS banner carried by Hope Mirrlees and Ray Costello said 'No Taxation without Representation'. Women's organisations including the CWSA, the British Women's Temperance Association, the Conservative and Unionist Women, the Women's Co-operative Guild, and the Church League for Women's Suffrage, were out in force. Clara gave a rousing speech from the fountain in the market place. The main Cambridge contingent marched out along the Trumpington Road accompanied by the Sawston band and then via Royston to London along the A10.

Clara herself chose to march to London with the Braintree and Essex section and arrived in Braintree having marched for ten days with the contingent from Hunstanton, with a voice hoarse from much outdoor speech-making. In Braintree she was reunited with her sister, Margaret, several of the Courtaulds, and their good friend, the Rev. Alun Roberts of Bocking. Clara carried one of the poles of the 'Law-abiding Suffragists' banner while Margaret brought up the close driving her motor car. They left Braintree to walk the eight miles to Witham. There they joined forces with pilgrims from Colchester and the east coast and continued via Chelmsford to London.[67] Footsore and weary, they arrived at the outer London suburbs tramping to Trafalgar Square via Piccadilly and thence on July 26 at the massive rally at Speakers' Corner in Hyde Park.

In the well-known photograph of the rally Clara is pictured on the podium wearing a straw hat and cravat seated immediately next to Millicent Fawcett [see Figure 2.12]. 'Never shall I forget the sight of that sea of faces when I was speaking from one of the platforms in Hyde Park; there were fifteen platforms all of them thronged',[68] she recollected in 1966. She was one of a deputation alongside Katherine Harley, Margaret Robertson, Millicent Fawcett, Helena Swanwick, Maude Royden, and Kathleen Courtney. They received at an audience with the Prime Minister. After speaking of her own experiences on the march, Clara asked him directly; 'Do you not think that though not through your fault – something is actually owing to us?'[69]

In December 1913 Susan Lawrence, who had joined the Labour Party, made a welcome return to Cambridge to organise the vast Sweated Labour Exhibition at the Guildhall hosted jointly by the CWSA, the Church League for Women's Suffrage, and the Cambridge University Men's League for Women's Suffrage. Visitors were shown the pittances paid to women making artificial flowers, black braid, brushes, toothbrushes and nursery shoes. Sweated workers came on the platform one-by-one to tell their own stories. One woman spoke movingly of being paid two pence for a gross of matchboxes.[70]

In July 1914, after Archduke Franz Ferdinand of Austria was assassinated by a Serbian nationalist in Sarajevo. Austria–Hungary declared war on Serbia, effectively beginning the First World War. Germany quickly declared war on France and Britain officially declared war on Germany on August 4, 1914 after an ultimatum to Germany to withdraw from occupied Belgium had been ignored. The NUWSS had planned to conduct a campaign in the coastal resorts in 1914 and Clara arrived in Cromer on August 3 to find people 'gathered on the front and gazing out to sea as if they expected the German fleet to appear intent on invasion'.[71] This was not a propitious time to talk of the 'cause' and she promptly turned around and returned to Cambridge.

It was no surprise that Clara topped the poll for the NUWSS executive in February 1915, securing a record number of 473 votes.[72] For in addition to the strategic thinking and the organisational skills shown in the Eastern District, her reputation as a clear-headed thinker able to conduct any meeting impartially and with good humour was second to none.

In her *Commonplace Book* (1970) her friend, the journalist, Mary Stott wrote:

> Mrs Rackham was elected as chairman because she possessed a masterly capacity for guiding a large conference through a maze of resolutions and amendments without expressing personal bias, getting in a muddle herself, or allowing delegates to do so. Presidential and chairmanship qualities do not necessarily go together, and during the many years of her chairmanship, observation of Mrs Rackham's

technique was another phase of our education for citizenship under the auspices of the NUWSS.[73]

It fell to Clara to steer the national organisation through the most turbulent moment in its history in 1915. Substantial sections of the membership, and the majority of the NEC were either pacifists or primarily interested in ending the war by a negotiated peace with Germany. For example, Catherine Marshall was heavily involved with the No Conscription Fellowship. Kathleen Courtney, Margaret Ashton and Mary Sheepshanks, a nearer contemporary of Clara's at Newnham College and editor of the journal, *Jus Suffragii*, were founder members of the Women's International League (later the Women's International League for Peace and Freedom).

Clara herself, maintained a judicious distance from the 'peace faction' on the NEC which included several good friends. She wanted to see a negotiated peace and a public debate on how peace could be brought about through international arbitration. However, many ordinary members were willing to accept the patriotic justification for the war against Germany. In February, Millicent Fawcett declared the 'common cause', the campaign for the vote, was to be suspended for the duration of the war and made clear her own (qualified) support for the war effort. She argued forcefully that until the German armies had been driven out of France and Belgium 'It is akin to treason to talk of peace'.[74] Fawcett called instead for women to give their support to 'devising and carrying out well-thought-out plans of national usefulness'.[75] The kinds of initiative the President had in mind included the Scottish Women's Hospitals for Foreign Services which was founded by the suffragist Elsie Inglis in 1914 or the Endell Street Hospital in Covent Garden, London founded by Flora Murray and Louisa Garrett Anderson, the only hospital staffed entirely by suffragists.

Fawcett, who was idealised by the rank-and file, was able to carry the membership with her against her opponents. As her biographer, Ray Strachey puts it, she 'She stood like a rock in their path, opposing herself with all the weight of her personal popularity and prestige to their use of the machinery and name of the union'.[76] However, when the NUWSS refused permission to send delegates to the International Women's Peace Congress at the Hague in April 1915 the majority of the NEC tendered their resignations: Margaret Ashton, Kathleen Courtney, Isabella Ford, Chrystal Macmillan, Catherine Marshall, Eleanor Rathbone, and Maude Royden, who also resigned as the editor of *The Common Cause*.

Clara was deeply conflicted and struggling to reconcile her own deep-rooted aversion to war in any shape or form with her personal loyalty to Millicent Fawcett, the co-founder of her own college. Although her position as Chairman demanded the strictest impartiality, Clara was immensely saddened by the schism. She wrote in private to Mrs Fawcett to make it clear that 'on questions of war and peace' her sympathies 'to a great extent' were with those who had resigned.[77] The difference between them was that Clara believed that the dissidents should be pursuing the cause of peace outside the NUWSS and not within the organisation. Clara offered to step down as Chairman so that she could participate openly in discussion but Mrs Fawcett was adamant that she should stay and eventually managed to dissuade her.

Clara joined the Union of Democratic Control which blamed 'secret diplomacy' in foreign affairs for the undemocratic way in which Britain had entered the war. The UDC was the most influential of all the anti-war organisations and included many of Clara's friends and associates: Clementina Black, Victoria Buxton, Margaret Bondfield, Mary Agnes Hamilton, Margaret Llewelyn Davies, Susan Lawrence, Eileen Power, Ramsay MacDonald, Mary Sheepshanks, Helena Swanwick, Phyllis Sturge, and R. H. Tawney. On April 14, 1915 Clara chaired a huge national conference in the Westminster Central Hall organised by the UDC consisting of delegates from women's societies convened to reflect their perception that the duty of women was to 'palliate the horrors of war' and to urge the government to 'declare without delay the terms on which the Allies would be willing to make peace'.[78]

In June 1915 a special NUWSS conference was convened. In an electrically charged atmosphere Clara sought permission to vacate the chair to move the crucial motion which was to steer the NUWSS away from the brink of disaster. She proposed that in the absence of any agreement about what to do for the best, the conference should adopt no position whatsoever on matters of war and peace and that individual NUWSS members should be free to pursue whatever course of action they wished. Clara's conciliatory proposal was overwhelmingly accepted by the special conference and the very real danger of the organisation falling apart was averted. As Eileen Price and Joyce Bellamy put it, 'the survival of the NUWSS was due as much to Clara Rackham as to any other single individual'.[79]

Clara did what she could to secure support for the women's war effort, representing the NUWSS at a conference to register women for the Board of Trade in April 1915,[80] lecturing on war and the women's movement in Huddersfield that month and on women's hospitals in Ilkley,[81] appealing to women to 'preserve life in any way, to alleviate the horror of war, and to prevent its repetition'.[82] She spoke about war at a suffrage summer school in Cambridge 'in tones which caused her to be pilloried as a pacifist'.[83] She was also on the Mayor's War Service Committee in Cambridge finding homes for Belgian refugees, and instrumental in setting up a WEA sponsored discussion forum on war and peace.

One well reviewed book made a lasting impression on Clara at this time; Margaret Llewelyn Davies's (edited) *Maternity: Letters from Working Mothers* (1915). The author had written to past Guild officials asking them to reply to her privately describing their experience of maternity, pregnancies, miscarriages and infant deaths. Margaret had found their letters too distressing to read all at once ('How much worse would the experience have been for less well-off women?')[84] and had edited and published 160 letters in September 1915 with an introduction that highlighted the impact of poverty, the lack of maternity care for women and the demand for comprehensive local authority supported maternity services.[85] The maternity campaign spearheaded by the WCG and other women's societies was instrumental in shifting public opinion and led to the Maternity and Child Welfare Act of 1918.

This was a time of personal sadness and anxiety for Clara's family. Margaret had served on Braintree Rural District Council and as a Poor Law Guardian since 1913.[86] A certain Captain Arbrey had 'wanted to know in effect if the lady intended to introduce bombs' despite Margaret's protestations that she was a law-abiding suffragist.[87] She was determined to pursue a life of public service and was co-opted on to the Essex Education Committee in 1916. A little book, *The Saints in Art*, with their attributes and symbols alphabetically arranged that she published for Methuen in 1908 had run to several editions and would be followed with an illustrated guide, *The City Churches* in 1917. Margaret was busy carving out a rewarding life for herself in the countryside. At Fennes, a forgotten little room reached by a step ladder out of the mangle room, and another small room which communicated with the old nursery above the kitchen, had been ingeniously converted with a new large window and a pitched roof into a pleasant little apartment. Margaret furnished this artistically herself with framed watercolours, pretty curtains, and good old oak from the old curiosity shops in the neighbourhood. This became a quiet room of her own with space to read quietly and to build a small library and entertain her old college friends without disturbing the household. Since his return to England in 1903, Edward Tabor had joined the London County Council as a resident engineer and had latterly been promoted to Chief Engineer responsible for the main drainage system in London. In 1915 Edward's wife, Lucy, had died from consumption leaving three children, Lucy, John, and Winifred who were all under ten. The family was living in Blackheath in south-east London. Edward was utterly devastated and Margaret willingly stepped in to oversee the management of his household making regular visits from Fennes to help her brother to bring up the children to whom she became devoted.

It was with some relief that Clara was able to step away from her the NUWSS and to resign from the NEC after she was one of four women appointed to temporary positions as Factory Inspectors by the Home Office, working alongside Jeannette Tawney, alumna of Somerville College, wife of R. H. Tawney and sister of William Beveridge, in 1915. The outbreak of war had drastically depleted the number of undergraduates in Cambridge so Harris returned to Winchester College to teach the Classical Sixth. The time in which Clara worked for the factory inspectorate was the only time during their marriage that she was away from Cambridge for any length of time.

Clara was initially deployed as a factory inspector in Lancashire but was transferred to the Home Office in London where she lived with the family in Blackheath and spent time with the Tawneys. 'Lady Inspectors' like Clara were high-to-medium ranking civil servants appointed to enforce government legislation and to make recommendations for future legislation in their reports. One long-term consequence of the creation of a female inspectorate was to alter public perceptions of what were suitable roles for women and to raise awareness of professions outside the 'caring' professions of teaching and nursing for which women could be accorded status and responsibility.

It was not only middle-class women required to live away from family and friends. In 1914 Labour Exchanges placed 32,988 women in factories away from their home villages or towns and the number rose to 160,003 by 1916.[88] Employment opportunities for women had increased exponentially since 1914. In agriculture, Louisa Jebb was instrumental in setting up the Women's National Land Service Corps persuading farmers to accept women workers on their land. Vast quantities of artillery, shells, machine guns, tanks, and explosives were required in the trenches of the Western Front and thousands of women were recruited into the factories. After the 'Shell scandal' of 1915 when the war effort appeared to be endangered through low morale and a shortage of ammunitions, the Ministry of Munitions was created with Lloyd George as its head and war work in thousands of premises was regulated by the new Ministry.

Existing factories in Manchester expanded and converted their machinery and expertise to wartime production. Women at the Charles Macintosh factory worked on tyres for motor vehicles and other essential rubber products. The huge Metropolitan Vickers engineering works in Trafford Park made the standard machine guns used by the British army. Mather and Platt produced shelling casing, fuses, gear boxes, and motors for submarines at their Park works and at Newton Heath. Herbert Hunt and Sons in Old Trafford had specialised in drills and went over to munitions. Beyer, Peacock switched their Gorton foundry from locomotives to heavy artillery. Thornton-Pickard produced aerial reconnaissance cameras. Basil de Ferranti in Oldham turned over his entire factory from domestic goods to shells and fuses, the British Oil and Cake Mills crushed oil seed for use in war time essentials, soap, and animal feed.

Clara reported directly in writing to Adelaide Anderson, an alumna of Girton College, and a good friend of Margaret Llewelyn Davies, who had given some lectures on economics to the Women's Co-operative Guild before joining the staff of the Royal Commission on Labour. Initially employed as a clerk, Anderson had been appointed as an Inspector in the Home Office in 1892 and made Principal Lady Inspector of Factories from 1897 and in this capacity reported on the work of the women in the inspectorate. Clara is mentioned twice in the reports of the Chief Inspector of Factories and Workshops for the years 1915–1919, once on being employed in Manchester in the annual report of 1915, then again on her departure, in the annual report of 1919.[89] Despite making exhaustive enquiries in Manchester and in the National Archives in London I have not been able to ascertain what happened to Clara's own reports and notes after they had been submitted to Anderson and to establish whether or not they still exist.

In their written reports the lady inspectors were detailed, and precise about specific breaches of law, negligent proprietors, inadequate buildings, faulty machinery, disregard of safety regulations, and incompetent foremen. In private they were scathing about those men in the inspectorate who had been allowed to work complacently to lower standards in their inspection regimes and agreed that greater state regulation was needed. Adelaide Anderson did not spare her punches:

> Why has the manufacture of munitions of war on a terrible scale led at last to systematic introduction of hygienic safeguards that Factory Inspectors have advocated for many years, such as supervision of women by women in factories, provision of means of personal cleanliness, proper meal and rest rooms, and qualified nurses?[90]

Clara was constantly on the look-out for potential accidents caused by faulty machinery, industrial poisoning, especially from white lead used as an ingredient for paint, scalding in laundries, exposure to toxic chemicals in laboratories, inadequate ventilation and explosions. Ironically, women on the massive Turner Brothers assembly line in Rochdale were allowed to produce asbestos mattresses to insulate battleships unchallenged by the inspectorate: asbestos was not recognised as a health hazard until ten years later. A terrible explosion in the Hooley Hill Munitions factory in Ashton under Lyne in June 1917 killed forty-six people and injured hundreds.

Clara was accommodated in a women's hostel in Manchester and in later years would regale disbelieving listeners with stories of having been kept awake by the ghost of an unknown woman walking around in the night. This is the only known instance of Clara, who thought of herself as an intensely rational person, having shown any interest in the supernatural.[91] Clara renewed her acquaintance with Margaret Ashton, the first woman elected to Manchester City Council, a pacifist who had resigned from the NUWSS executive and was a signatory of the Open Christmas Letter to the Women of Germany and Austria published in *Jus Suffragii* in January 1915 and a founder of the Manchester branch of the Women's International League [for Peace and Freedom].[92] Margaret stayed in Cambridge as a guest of the Rackhams on more than on occasion.

As a government inspector Clara was tasked with making visits – frequently unannounced – to the factories and timing the 30-minute lunch breaks punctiliously. She was ideally suited by temperament to the post which required quick thinking, sharp reflexes, close observation and meticulous attention to detail. Night shifts were permitted in factories and workshops engaged in work for the war effort. Like another senior factory inspector, Hilda Martindale, Clara recollected spending entire nights roving factory buildings to check on everything from the state of the lavatories to the use of illegal child labour.[93]

While the trade unions argued for the appointment of working-class women who could speak with the authority of first-hand experience to the inspectorate, Asquith subscribed to a different notion of expertise predicated on the late Victorian association between middle-class women and philanthropy. Moreover, the creation of women inspectors 'fitted in' with the social reforming aspects of the government's 'New Liberal' response to the problems of the industrial age. Clara was typical of the new brand of factory inspector in that she had independent means and was educated to standards to which working-class women could not begin to aspire. Where 'lady inspectors' like Clara had previous contact with working-class women this was as rent collectors, lady almoners, social workers, housing managers, Poor Law Guardians, or through charitable organisations. Factory inspection, however, was substantively different because the direct individual encounter between ladies and the 'poor' imbued with the effects of 'feminine personal influence' was not considered to be part of the work.[94]

In their written reports the 'lady inspectors' were detailed, precise, and frequently damning, about specific breaches of law, negligent proprietors, inadequate buildings, faulty machinery, disregard of safety regulations, and incompetent foremen. In private they were scathing about those men in the inspectorate who had been allowed to work complacently to lower standards in lax inspection regimes and they were agreed that greater state regulation was needed. However, they were constrained by the principle of civil service impartiality and could not be seen to be too closely aligned to activists like Gertrude Tuckwell in the Women's Trade Union League, with whom they shared many objectives, such as raising the occupational health of women workers.[95]

Clara also spent time in Liverpool with Eleanor Rathbone, another member of the NUWSS Executive Committee and volunteered to work in the Liverpool University Settlement. Rathbone had first come to Clara's attention in 1913 in connection with her pamphlet about widows and children receiving Poor Law Relief in Liverpool.[96] The two had much in common and were to become good friends. Clara wrote that

'I worked with her in the suffrage cause, stayed in her home in Liverpool, and often saw her in her House of Commons days. She gave a wonderful impression of earnestness and strength'.[97]

Clara received her only offer of a permanent job; as Director of Studies in Social Sciences at Bedford College which had been founded as the first women's college in the University of London. She had attended lectures at Bedford College studying Roman History with Emily Penrose in 1894 before going to Cambridge. Her sister, Margaret had acted as Principal from January to March 1907 and as Resident Tutor from March to July in 1913. Most students intended to become social workers and the college was at the cutting edge of training in the profession. In 1916 the Charity Organisation Society set up an arrangement whereby the college would provide lectures on social economics and social ethics for the Social Work Certificate course. Clara may well have come to their attention through a series of public lectures on the relief of distress during the war concentrating on the work of voluntary bodies and the State at the LSE in 1915.[98] Clara turned the appointment down because she could not be spared from work of national importance.[99] Had she taken the post her life would have taken a different direction: a professional career in social work and teaching in Higher Education.

Clara was in the Ladies' Gallery in Westminster on June 19, 1917 for the Second Reading of the Women's Suffrage Bill. She considered it a 'wretched little Bill' but wrote that 'we did not worry; the thin edge of the wedge had been well and truly driven in'.[100] In 1917 Harris, who was missing Clara, left Winchester College to be nearer to her in London and was appointed to the German section of the Naval Intelligence Department of the Admiralty. In 1918 he was moved to the Treasury 'A' Division to work on fiscal policy with the allies under the direction of John Maynard Keynes. Both Harris and Clara were present at the historic moment when the Armistice was declared at 11 am on November 11, 1918 but, as luck would have it, neither was aware of the other's presence. Harris heard the momentous announcement from a second-floor room in the Treasury as Lloyd George addressed the people from the window of 10 Downing Street while Clara was in the jubilant crowd outside, having come out of the Home Office where she was working.[101] The couple moved to Doughty Street in Bloomsbury, nearly opposite to Charles Dickens house, renting the first and second floor flats in the building with Edward Tabor. Harris left the Treasury at Easter and returned to Cambridge and in the summer Clara left the Home Office. The Representation of the People Act which granted the vote to most women over the age of 30, to all men over 21, and much to everyone's surprise, the right of women to stand as Members of Parliament, was finally passed in February 1918. By now Clara was a recognised expert on all aspects of industrial relations. Her vision of clean, light, well-ventilated workplaces, of canteens serving nourishing food, statutory rest breaks, paid holidays, equal pay for equal work, the eight-hour day and the forty-hour working week may have seemed radical, if not utopian, to many at the time, but the reforms she advocated were to become widely accepted over the years and lived to see many of them incorporated into the Factory Act in 1937.

Though close contact with working-class women and children was not part of Clara's contractual obligations, interaction with 'rude girls' (and not just with 'nice girls')[102] was impossible to avoid, given the close proximity of many factories and workshops to communities suffering from the extremes of urban deprivation. Clara's wartime exposure to poverty and suffering in London and the industrial heartlands of the north-west left a deep and ineradicable impression on her consciousness and profoundly changed the way that she saw the world. By the time Clara returned to Cambridge her political journey away from the Liberal Party had been completed. Individual membership of the Labour Party was made possible in 1918. Joining would be merely a formality for she had long been a socialist in everything but name.

Notes

1 Carol Dyhouse, *Feminism and Family in England 1880-1939* (Oxford: Basil Blackwell, 1989), 40.
2 See Linda Mahood, *Feminism and Voluntary Action: Eglantyne Jebb and Save the Children, 1876-1928* (Basingstoke: Palgrave Macmillan, 2009), 74.
3 Margaret Cole, *Growing Up into* Revolution (London: Longmans, Green, 1949), 41.
4 K. M. Rathbone, 'A College with Status', in Ann Phillips, ed. *The Newnham Anthology* (Cambridge: Newnham College, 1979), 21.
5 Quoted, Henry Brown, *Co-operation in a University Town* (London: Co-operative Printing Society, 1939), 67.
6 Ann Kennedy Smith, 'The Cambridge Ladies' Dining Society (*act* 1890-1914)', *Oxford Dictionary of National Biography*, https://doi.org10.93/odnb/9780198614128.013.109658, accessed October 20, 2019. My thanks to Carolyn Ferguson for discussions about this society.
7 Records of the Cambridge Women's Suffrage Association 1884–1939, K455/Q1/a/3, Cambridgeshire County Council Archive, Ely.
8 Jane Lewis, *Women and Social Action in Victorian and Edwardian England* (Elgar: Aldershot, 1993).
9 Gillian Scott, Feminism and the Politics of Working Women: The Women's Co-operative Guild, 1880 to the Second World War (London: UCL Press, 1998), 11.
10 Margaret Llewelyn Davies, 'Foreword', in *The Woman with the Basket*, ed. Catherine Webb (Manchester: Co-operative Wholesale Society, 1927), 9–14, 11.
11 Margaret Llewelyn Davies and Virginia Woolf, *Life as We Have Known It by Co-operative Working Women* (London: Hogarth Press, 1931), 40.
12 Letter from A. K. Edwards to Joyce Bellamy, dated October 16, 1980 (CDR, U DLB/55), Hull History Centre Archive.

13 Barbara J. Blaszak, *The Matriarchs of England's Co-operative Movement: A Study in Gender Politics and Female Leadership, 1883-1921* (Westport, CT: Greenwood Press, 2000), 116.
14 Davies, *The Woman with the Basket*, 10.
15 Blaszak, *The Matriarchs*, 117.
16 Mary Poovey, '*Making a Social Body: British Cultural Formation 1830-64* (Chicago, IL: University of Chicago Press, 1995), 43.
17 Clara Rackham, 'Employment and Leisure', in*Cambridge: A Brief Study in Social Questions*, ed. Eglantyne Jebb (Cambridge: Macmillan and Bowes, 1906), 139–42, 139.
18 Clara Rackham, 'Thrift', Ibid., 120-22, 121.
19 'Employment and Leisure', 141.
20 'Thrift', 121.
21 Mark Freeman, 'The Provincial Social Survey in Edwardian Britain', *Historical Research* 75, no 187 (2002), 73–89, 89.
22 Ibid.
23 Clara Rackham, 'Cambridge', in *Social Conditions in Provincial Towns*, ed. Helen Bosanquet (London: Macmillan, 1912), 23–36I, 30.
24 Ibid., 24.
25 Ibid., 33.
26 Ibid., 29–30.
27 See Jane Lewis, *The Voluntary Sector, the State and Social Work in Britain: The Charity Organisation Society/Family Welfare Association Since 1869* (Aldershot: Elgar, 1995), 1.
28 Rackham, 'Cambridge', 32.
29 Ibid., 30.
30 Ibid, 31.
31 Clara Rackham, letter to Arthur Rackham dated July 11, 1908, Anne Stevenson Hobbs (ASH).
32 Derek Hudson, *Arthur Rackham: His Life and* Work (London: Heinemann, 1960), 56.
33 Meg Rackham, letter to Stanley Rackham dated September 25, 1904 (ASH).
34 Information obtained from Anne Stevenson Hobbs, August 8, 2019 who recalled a conversation with a distant member of the Ricardo family.
35 Susan M. Parkes, *A Danger to the Men? A History of Women in Trinity College Dublin 1904-2004* (Dublin: Liliput Press, 2004), 87-90.
36 Clara Rackham, 'Bitter Cold and Scorching Heat', handwritten ms (n.d.) (TFP).
37 Ibid.
38 Ibid.
39 See Liz Gloyn, 'This s Not a Chapter about Jane Harrison: Teaching Classics at Newnham College, 1882–1922', in *Women Classical Scholars: Unsealing the Fountain From the Renaissance to Jacqueline de Romilly*, eds Rosie Wyles and Edith Hall (Oxford: Oxford University Press, 2016), 133-73.
40 Transcript of speeches by Baroness Wootton and C. D. Rackham at Jubilee Dinner of Cambridge, July 9, 1962, 789/Q105, 1-12, 7, Cambridgeshire County Council Archive, Ely.
41 F. E. Rendell and R. Costello, 'The Suffrage Caravan', Newnham College Roll Letter (January, 1908). 22-7.
42 Elizabeth Crawford, *The Women's Suffrage Movement: Reference Guide 1860-1928*, second edition (London: Routledge, 1999), 84.
43 Cicely Hamilton, 'Foreword', in *A Pageant of Great Women* (London: Marian Lawson, 1948), 7.

44 See Scott, *Feminism and the Politics of Working Women*, 104.
45 February 22, 1909, *Cambridge Independent Press*, 3.
46 Ruth Cohen, *Margaret Llewelyn Davies: With Women for a New World* (Cambridge: Merlin, 2020), 154–5.
47 The Women's Co-operative Guild, *Working Women and Divorce: An Account of Evidence Given on Behalf of the Women's Co-operative Guild Before the Royal Commission on Divorce* (London: David Nutt, 1911), 4.
48 Quoted, S. W. Green, 'Freedom Fighters', *The Guardian*, October 25, 1965.
49 Clara Rackham, 'The Need of Women as Poor Law Guardians', *Newnham College Roll Letter* (January 1913), 26–31, 30, 30.
50 *Cambridge Independent Press*, April 1, 1904, 6.
51 Seth Koven, *Slumming: Sexual and Social Politics in Victorian London* (Princeton, NJ and Oxford: Princeton University Press, 2004), 225, 233.
52 *Cambridge Independent Press*, December 24, 1909, 7.
53 Ibid., October 29, 1909, 8.
54 Ibid., April 11, 1909, 7.
55 Lewis, *The Voluntary Sector, the State and Social Work in Britain*, 1.
56 *Cambridge Independent Press*, June 4, 1909, 2.
57 Robert Humphreys, *Sin, Organised Charity and the Poor Law in Victorian England* (Basingstoke: Macmillan, 1995), 10.
58 *Queen*, April 17, 1909.
59 *Common Cause*, October 21, 1909, 361.
60 I. H. Quigly, Clara Dorothea Rackham (née Tabor) 1975-1966 (Newnham, 1895-1898), Newnham Roll (January, 1967), 48-51, 50.
61 Andrew Rosen, *Rise up Women: The Militant Campaign of the Women's Social and Political Union 1903-1914* (London: Routledge and Kegan Paul, 1974), 189.
62 Sue Slack, *Cambridge Women and the Struggle for the Vote* (Stroud: Amberley, 2018), 51.
63 Millicent Garrett Fawcett, *What I Remember* (London: Fisher Unwin, 1924), 192.
64 Millicent Garrett Fawcett, *Women's Suffrage: A Short History of a Great Movement* (London: T.C. and E.C. Jack, 1911), 76.
65 *Common Cause*, May 16, 1913, 5.
66 Jane Robinson, *Hearts and Minds: The Untold Story of the Great Pilgrimage and How Women Won the Vote* (London: Doubleday, 2018), 152.
67 *Chelmsford Chronicle*, July 25, 1913, 5.
68 Clara Rackham, 'Ninety Years' Work for Suffrage and Socialism', *Labour Woman*, March, 1966, 56.
69 *Common Cause*, August 15, 1913, 322.
70 *Cambridge Independent Press*, December 12, 1913, 4.
71 Rackham, 'Ninety Years' Work', 56.
72 David Rubinstein, *A Different World for Women: The Life of Millicent Garrett Fawcett* (Columbus: Ohio University Press, 1991), 274, fn. 16.
73 Mary Stocks, *My Commonplace Book* (London: Peter Davies, 1970), 77.
74 Ray Strachey, *Millicent Garrett Fawcett* (London: John Murray, 1931), 288.
75 Fawcett, *What I Remember*, 219.
76 Strachey, *Millicent Garrett Fawcett*, 291.
77 Letter from Clara Rackham to Millicent Garrett Fawcett dated April 19, 1915, BLP/WIL/5/2, Women's Library at the LSE.
78 Union of Democratic Control leaflet and conference resolutions (CDR U DLB/55), Hull History Centre Archive.

79 Joyce M. Bellamy and Eileen Price, *Rackham, Clara Dorothea (1875-1966) Labour Alderman, Social Reformer and Educationalist*, in Joyce M. Bellamy and John Saville, eds, *Dictionary of Labour Biography* ix (1993), 232–8, 233.
80 *Common Cause*, April 16, 1915, 12.
81 Ibid., April 23, 1915, 15.
82 Ibid, January 8, 1915, 10.
83 Jo Vellacott, *Pacifists, Patriots and the Vote: The Erosion of Democratic Suffragism in Britain During the First World War* (Basingstoke: Palgrave, 2007), 97.
84 Cohen, *Margaret Llewelyn Davies*, 177.
85 Ibid., 183, 185.
86 'Margaret Emma Tabor', *Newnham College Roll*, 1954.
87 *Essex County Chronicle*, May 2, 1913, 5.
88 Mary Drake McFeely, *Lady Inspectors: The Campaign for a Better Workplace 1893-1921* (Oxford: Blackwell, 1988), 141.
89 Annual Report of the Chief Inspector of Factories and Workshops for the years 1915, HMSO, May 1916, [Cd.8276], 5 and 1919, HMSO, May 1920 [Cmd.941], 5.
90 Adelaide Anderson, Annual Report, 1915, 15.
91 See Clara Rackham 'ghost story' (n.d.), a short typewritten account of this incident which may have been intended as a talk for the BBC (TFP).
92 Clara Rackham, letter to Sybil Hutton dated October 31, 1965 (CDR, U DLB/9/55), Hull History Centre Archive.
93 McFeely, *Lady Inspectors*, 133.
94 Ruth Livesey, 'The Politics of Work: Feminism, Professionalisation and Women Inspectors of Factories and Workshops', *Women's History Review* 13, no 2 (December 2006), 232–62, 247.
95 Helen Jones, 'Women Health Workers: The Case of the First Women Factory Inspectors in Britain', *Social History of Medicine* 1, (1988), 65-81, 171.
96 Clara Rackham, 'Some Distinguished Women I Have Known: Eleanor Rathbone', handwritten (n.d.) (TFP).
97 Ibid.
98 *Common Cause*, October 9, 1914, 12.
99 Cathy Hartley, 'Rackham, Clara Dorothea' (1865-1965), [sic] *A Historical Dictionary of British Women* (London: Taylor and Francis, 1983), revised, 2003, 364.
100 Rackham, 'Ninety Years' Work', 56.
101 Bernard Rackham's annotated copy of the Rackham Family Book. Information provided to the author by Anne Stevenson Hobbes.
102 Deborah Thom makes this distinction in *Nice Girls and Rude Girls: Women Workers in World War One* (London: I.B. Taurus, 1998).

3 Cambridge's Clara

Labour Councillor and Magistrate

The Cambridge to which Clara returned had altered beyond recognition; the unhurried calm of the Edwardian years that she vividly remembered shattered forever by the construction of the First Great Eastern Hospital in 1915 (on the site of what is now the Cambridge University Library) where hundreds of war-wounded soldiers in temporary wooden buildings and open air wards had been tended by volunteer nurses – one, a young school teacher, Leah Manning. The Field Hospital was closed in 1919 and its buildings in Burrell's Walk were converted to temporary housing. There had been so many soldiers on the streets that the National Council of Women had set up its own foot patrols and lobbied for the first two women police officers who had been appointed in 1918.

The struggle for full equality was far from over with the partial enfranchisement of women.[1] On the contrary, as Pat Thane has emphasised, women who had spent years fighting for the vote were realistic in their expectations and continued fighting for a multiplicity of reforms, expecting change to be slow, opposition protracted and anticipating an uphill battle to make their voices heard. Indeed, more women, from a wider range of social backgrounds, were actively campaigning for gender equality in the 1920s and 1930s than before the First World War,[2] often working in single issue, occupational, and faith-based groups.

But for all their hard work and visibility during the war, women 'were still located within ideologies of domesticity, not simply as wives but first and foremost as mothers'.[3] In *Housewives and Citizens: Domesticity and the Women's Movement, 1926–1964* Catriona Beaumont argues that popular, home-based women's groupings such as the Women's Institutes, the League of Catholic Women, and the Townswomen's Guilds were working to improve women's lives and towards a broader concept of democratic citizenship[4] and were part of the women's movement although they are not usually considered feminist organisations.

Strongly felt differences between feminists were to become increasingly evident. Eleanor Rathbone and other pro-natalist (or 'new') feminists argued for family endowment and state support for mothers while 'equality first' (or 'old') feminists were working for equal pay and the removal of legal and constitutional barriers to women's advance. In 1919

DOI: 10.4324/9780429353499-4

the NUWSS voted to transform itself into the National Union of Societies for Equal Citizenship (NUSEC). Rathbone took over from Millicent Fawcett as President and encouraged Clara to put herself forward (unsuccessfully) as a NUSEC candidate in the elections for the Cambridge borough council.

The hopes of a better world order for which so many longed were pinned on the newly formed League of Nations which had its first headquarters in London before Geneva. In September 1919, Clara chaired a conference in London bringing all the major women's organisations together and calling for the representation of women at all levels including the Secretariat. The conference resolved to 'appeal to the British Government to put in practice, and in every way support, the appointment of women to serve along with men on the constituent bodies and in the various capacities connected with the League'.[5] Clara also spoke from the NUSEC platform alongside Eleanor Rathbone, Ray Costello and Margaret Corbett Ashby at a demonstration in support of the League of Nations in Hyde Park in June 1922[6] and was elected Vice-Chairman of the Cambridge branch.

Clara was made an Associate of Newnham College in 1918.[7] In 1921 a second vote to allow women full degrees was defeated and an expectant crowd assembled outside Senate House to hear the voting figures. Clara witnessed a clergyman, Percy Hart, exhort the triumphant bystanders to action: 'Now boys, go and tell Newnham and Girton' and rushed to a nearby telephone to warn the Principal, Blanche Athena Clough. By the time the mob arrived in Newnham the college gates were barred. Undeterred, the men used a handcart as a battering ram and inflicted serious damage to the Clough Memorial Gates which were only restored after a university-wide appeal and subscription.[8] The scene was immortalised in a cartoon by Quentin Blake commissioned in 2009 to mark the 800th anniversary of Cambridge University.

Clara was elected as a councillor for West Chesterton in 1922, one of the first three Labour councillors in Cambridge and the first woman in the Labour group.[9] Whereas the number of women MPs between the wars was miniscule, women entered local government in sufficient numbers from the 1920s onwards for a sense of gendered identity and solidarity to develop at a local level, particularly when it came to the protection – we would now use the word 'safeguarding' — of vulnerable women and children. In Cambridge, where Clara, Eva Hartree and Florence Ada Keynes had known each other for years through their work for charities, voluntary and community groups, youth clubs, and after-school play groups including the Cambridge Association for the Care of Girls and the Cambridge Women's Welfare Association gender solidarity very often cut across party political lines.

The annual conference of the newly formed Co-operative Party in 1918 voted in favour of a Co-operative-Labour Party electoral alliance and Clara argued in favour of the financial support needed to make this possible.[10] She resigned as President of the Cambridge branch of the Women's Co-operative Guild when Margaret Llewelyn Davies stood down as the General Secretary in 1921. The ethos of the local Labour Party which had a strong, thoughtful, pacifist element within it, was much to Clara's liking. They had objected to conscription in 1915, to child labour on farms, and to the daily wage of sixpence for the girls who sewed caps for soldiers.[11] Clara was deeply concerned about the punitive aspects of the terms of the Versailles Settlement imposed on Germany and her feelings were widely shared in the Party.

The demographic of the Cambridge Labour Party was socially mixed. It drew considerable working-class support from the railway workers in the Romsey Town area of Cambridge. The Trades Council was strong. Leah Manning was the Secretary of the local association of the National Union of Teachers (NUT) which was very active. During the war the National Council of Women had set up after-school play centres for up to 300 children and converted some old wooden buildings in Vinery Road into an experimental 'open-air' school for children with chronic lung conditions. Leah had been appointed as the first headmistress. The Labour Party had set up a women's section but initially Clara kept a judicious distance from what Hannah Mitchell described as 'a permanent Social Committee, or Official cake-maker to the Labour Party'.[12] Leading members of the local Party included the Christian socialist Agnes Ramsey, a suffragist and Poor Law Guardian, wife of Arthur Ramsey, President of Magdalene College, and mother of the future Archbishop of Canterbury, Michael Ramsey. The physicist Dr Alex Wood, a Fellow of Emmanuel College, was a Scottish Presbyterian who had joined the Fellowship of Reconciliation and was a conscientious objector during the war. Michael and Helen Pease were also pacifists and lived in Girton, which Helen represented on the county council from 1937. Michael a geneticist, had been interred in a German civilian camp, and Helen, daughter of Josiah Clement Wedgwood, MP, a Quaker, had studied at Newnham College and been active in the No Conscription Fellowship.

The MP for Cambridge, Eric Geddes had advocated squeezing the 'German lemon till the pips squeak' at a meeting in the Beaconsfield Hall in the Khaki election of December 1918. Leah Manning was appalled. This 'made our cheeks burn with shame, so despicably un-English was its sentiment towards a defeated foe'.[13] In 1922 Geddes resigned, and, at the suggestion of Clara and Susan Lawrence, the party unanimously adopted Hugh Dalton to fight the by-election. Dalton, the son of Queen Victoria's chaplain, had studied at King's College and invited Leah (née Perret), then a student at Homerton College, to join the Fabian Society. She was always to feel great personal loyalty to Dalton, who had first introduced her to socialist politics.[14]

Clara who was a strong advocate of family planning served on the birth control subcommittee of the Standing Joint Committee of Industrial Women's Organisations (SJCIWO) from 1923. The organisation had been formed when the Women's Co-operative Guild, the Women's Labour League, the Women's Trade Union League, and the Railway Women's Guild, had come together in order to co-ordinate the representation of women workers during the war. Clara had got to know Hugh's wife, Ruth through the pioneering birth control clinic in Fitzroy Street in 1925, one of the first clinics to be set up outside London by supporters of the Society for the Promotion of Birth Control Clinics (SPBCC) including Leah Manning, Helen Pease, Agnes Ramsey, Eva Hartree, Florence Ada Keynes, and Edith Bethune-Baker,[15] all of whom had been active in the women's suffrage movement in Cambridge. The Labour Party Conference of 1926 passed a resolution in favour of family planning moved by Dora Russell 'on behalf of the ancient and honourable Trade Union of Mothers to which I belong'[16] but the issue of contraception was a contentious one for the Labour Party leadership all too aware of the sensibilities of its Catholic voters and supporters.

Ruth Dalton had taught in the Eastern District of the Workers' Educational Association (WEA) since 1915 and when the district ran into financial problems had been drafted in by the national office to take charge of a major fundraising campaign in 1920.[17] What differentiated the WEA was the premium it placed on the teaching of difficult economic and social questions, the right of students to participate in running their own classes, and for branches to choose their tutors and subjects, and its vision of an educational movement controlled by the working class while working in conjunction with the leading intellectuals and universities of the day.

Clara was a founder member of the WEA Eastern District and elected Chairman twice, the first time in June 1920 after the Adult Education Committee established by Lloyd George's Ministry of Reconstruction published its *Report on Adult Education* (1919), much of it written by R.H. Tawney, which was instrumental in producing the massive expansion of lifelong learning between the wars. The fortnight-long residential Newnham College summer schools for working women and girls set up in 1921 under Clara's watch continuing at two-yearly intervals that coincided with the factory holidays until 1951, can be properly understood as part of this wider expansion of adult learning and were enthusiastically championed by Edith Neville, the radical housing reformer and founder of the St Pancras People's Theatre.[18] The schools recruited up to twenty-five students – typically local factory workers, clerks, shop assistants and seamstresses. Some received small grants, to study an evolving syllabus of English, History, and Economics and the Social Sciences. Students were imaginatively taught, sometimes in study circles and informal discussion groups on the college lawns, by sympathetic college tutors, in the main, determined to avoid condescension, and to impart their own intellectual seriousness and joy in books, literature and ideas to their unfamiliar charges to whom they often warmed. Students were encouraged to read poetry aloud and to trace the steps of Marlowe, Milton, Wordsworth and Tennyson with their teacher and to explore a beautiful city crammed with literary associations. In the afternoons they joined in with student activities, picnics, boating, tea parties and punting to Grantchester. Their appreciative testimonials movingly recall their summer school experience as a momentary, joyful, horizon-expanding respite from workaday lives of drudgery; a brief, blissful, never-to-be forgotten break in their routines of unrelenting toil, incessant money worries, recurrent bouts of illness, and responsibility for loved but needy dependants, to concentrate solely on their own desires and educational needs. Not infrequently, women remembered the summer school as a welcome opportunity to enjoy a 'proper holiday' before paid holiday entitlements were introduced in 1937. The summer school was specifically designed to provide students with useful connections and opportunities for those who wished to continue their studies through the WEA and its extensive nationwide educational networks and through Newnham College's links to Hillcroft College which was started in 1920 in Surrey as a residential adult college for working women. Newnham College's commitment to the core WEA principles, and to the values specific to the college, with its long history of recognizing and rewarding the intellectual potential and curiosity of any woman student with an honest desire to learn and to make something more of her life, were retained throughout its history. By 1928 the organizing principles had been firmly established. 'It is now our definite policy to make this summer school a starting place for those who have had little or no other opportunity of continuing their education...' Those whom we admit are chiefly manual workers.'[19]

Whereas the Socratic tradition of Cambridge University, in which Clara herself was grounded, was sceptical about academic knowledge being put to any practical use, Clara was a key figure in helping to shape the alternative democratic tradition of education for a social purpose developing within the WEA. Ethical socialists like Tawney and herself argued that students should be taught to understand, reform, and humanise industrial capitalism so that they could participate fully in the society in which they were citizens. Indeed, Tawney considered his campaign to rescue his students from the tyranny of industrial capitalism to be comparable to the efforts of the nineteenth-century abolitionists of slavery, [20] and while Clara stopped somewhat short of this position, she followed Tawney in her conviction that equality of opportunity should always be pursued.

Clara was to teach over seventy classes for the WEA, mainly literature and history but also 'citizenship', sociological subjects, current affairs and classes for entrants to local government. We still have her lecture notes, visual aids, teaching materials, notes on pedagogy and press cuttings. She was, by all accounts, a conscientious, inspiring teacher. One WEA student remembered that 'Mrs Rackham was once late for a lecture. She plunged directly into her subject and lectured with her usual vigour. It was not until later that it was learnt that she had been knocked off her bicycle on her way and received serious injuries.[21]

Much of Clara's WEA teaching was predicated on an identification of the concerns of the present with prior struggles in history and on seeking inspiration from the past, for example, from the nineteenth-century struggles of working people to secure the franchise and the Diggers and the Levellers in the seventeenth-century. Clara's popular local history classes were focussed on 'town' rather than 'gown' and introduced her students to little-known aspects of Cambridge and its environs; to Stourbridge Common, perhaps the largest fair in Medieval Europe, the Romanesque Leper chapel, the Saxon burial ground, the Castle Mound, and the Roman Road which was older than the ancient university. Clara made no hard and fast distinction between literature and history. Emily Brontë, Dickens, Stevenson, Thackeray, George Eliot, Hardy, and Kingsley were taught so that her students could learn more about the social history of their times. Underlying every aspect of her teaching was the unshakeable conviction in the fundamental decency and rationality of ordinary men and women. Whenever the outbreak of a new war in a distant place or a terrible man-made disaster prompted a quizzical student to question the inexorability of human progress, Clara's pained reaction was initially of silent, discombobulated disbelief. The job of the good WEA tutor was always to make the student believe that hope was possible rather than despair convincing.

Hugh Dalton moved to Panton Street with Ruth and their daughter, Helen. He fought a lively election campaign, largely organised by Leah, assisted by Kingsley Martin, Maurice Dobb, the young Barbara Wootton, and the indomitable Albert Stubbs ('Bandbox Bertie'), a printer on *The Cambridge Daily News*, who would tour surrounding villages on his motorbike in a one man crusade to unionise the agricultural workers. Dalton lost the 1922 by-election to the Conservative candidate but was returned to parliament to represent Peckham in 1924.

Clara made her first attempt to become a Labour MP in Chelmsford in the General Election in November 1922. She stood little chance (all four Labour women candidates had lost in the 1918 General Election) and Chelmsford was hardly auspicious Labour territory. She addressed a large meeting of women in the Chelmsford Corn Exchange with two suffragist friends, Kathleen Courtney and Louise Aylmer, on the platform and held public meetings in Sandon, Broomfield, Boreham, Danbury and Great Beddow.[22] She came third in the poll with 4,887 votes, losing to the incumbent Unionist, E. G. Pretyman.

In the General Election of 1923 Clara had the pleasure of seeing Margaret Bondfield returned in Northampton, Susan Lawrence in East Ham and Dorothy Jewson in Norwich. However, the minority Labour administration led by Ramsay MacDonald was able to achieve very little and a Conservative government led by Stanley Baldwin took office with a massive majority in the General Election of 1924. All three women lost their seats, leaving the young Ellen Wilkinson in Middlesbrough East as the only Labour woman in Westminster. Margaret Bondfield and Susan Lawrence both fought back hard, winning the two by-elections that were called in 1926, in Wallsend and East Ham North respectively. Dorothy Jewson was never elected again despite another three attempts in Norwich and her very short time in parliament is remembered primarily for her convention-defying refusal to wear a hat in the House of Commons.

Clara's long association with the Cambridgeshire College of Arts, Crafts and Technology began when she was appointed a governor in November 1920. Her first duties were hardly onerous. Chairing the Catering Advisory Committee she was required to act as an 'invited guest' and to taste and comment graciously on the meals prepared by the catering students. The 'Tech', situated off the East Road in Petersfield, still owed much to the ideals of John Ruskin who had opened the Cambridge School of Art in Sydney Street in 1858. The School of Art had educated rich and poor students alike since John Ruskin's day (keeping the two judiciously separate for much of the time). Art classes had initially been offered to ladies in the morning (attended *inter alia* by the distinguished Victorian poet Hannah Webster), and to gentlemen in the mornings and in the evening.[23]

After the Balfour Education Act of 1902 transferred Further Education to County Councils, the School of Art was moved to a complex of unprepossessing municipal buildings on Collier Road in 1909. It always held a special place in Clara's affections as virtually the only co-educational place in Cambridge at which working-class adults and young people – often little more than children – went to continue their education after the Fisher Education Act raised the school leaving age to fourteen in 1918. Clara warmed immediately to the college ethos which appealed to her sense of the 'modern'. Unlike the secondary curriculum in schools which changed relatively little between the wars, the FE curriculum was innovative and forward-looking, teaching commercial subjects, preparing students for the building and printing trades, and for careers in science and technology.

There was a dramatic improvement in its fortunes when the ambitious historian, Arthur Bryant, was appointed in 1923. As Sydney Robinson explained, 'Bryant set about transforming a school with less than 300 pupils into a thriving centre of learning, attended by nearly 1,500 boys and girls when he resigned two and a half years later'.[24] The name of the Cambridgeshire College of Arts, Crafts and Technology proclaimed the college's place in the brave new world of science and technology while retaining an emphasis on the arts and crafts that reflected commitment to its Ruskinian heritage. As Ruskin had told a Royal Commission on Drawing in 1857; 'My efforts are directed not to making a carpenter an artist, but to making him happier as a carpenter.'[25] Clara was well used to working with strong-willed characters in local government, albeit not with anyone quite as precocious as the young Arthur Bryant, who was all of twenty-three and managed to endear himself to her by virtue of his enthusiastic teaching for the WEA. Vocational courses at the 'Tech' always contained an element of liberal education for those who had left school early. There were young idealistic teachers for Clara to befriend and not a few were impecunious Cambridge graduates. She liked to visit the workshops and day continuation classes, to talk to adolescent tool makers and plasterers, perhaps chancing approvingly upon the sonnets of Wordsworth or the short stories of Kipling and H. G. Wells in the pockets of their overalls. There were to be six changes of College Principal in Clara's time as a governor. She was to make herself of use to all of them.

In 1922 Cambridgeshire appointed a new, far-sighted Assistant Education Officer, Henry Morris, the son of a Southport plumber who had gone from humble beginnings (of which he felt ashamed) working as an office boy to read Philosophy at King's College Cambridge after being demobbed in the 1914 war. By 1924 Morris had risen to Secretary of Education for Cambridgeshire. His 30 years in this office overlapped with Clara's time as a county councillor from 1929 and chairing the Cambridgeshire County Council Education Committee from 1945 to 1957. Morris was a tenant of Maud Darwin's at the Grange in Silver Street where he surrounded himself with paintings, silverware, ceramics and objects of beauty. The atmosphere of the Grange is memorably evoked in the memoir *Period Piece* (1957) written by her daughter, Gwen Raverat, the wood engraver, for whom Morris had to vacate the building in 1946. Morris was no ordinary local government officer. He looked on himself as a socialist of sorts, and he and Clara, if not exactly friends, got on well and moved in similar social circles, and he occasionally invited her to his dinner parties. He was perhaps the only personal acquaintance who insisted on pronouncing her name with a rounded vowel ('Clara' as in 'Sarah'), and this expressly against her wishes.

In 1924 Morris printed and distributed his Memorandum on the Provision of Educational and Social Facilities for the Countryside, with Special Reference to Cambridgeshire at his own expense.[26] He proposed to reverse the dispiriting process of rural decline through a visionary programme that aimed to transform Cambridgeshire's antiquated system of village schools whereby children between three and fourteen were educated in a school house, often in one room. The under-achievement of children in the countryside was linked to the mechanisation of farms, the loss of traditional crafts and skills on the land, and the migration of young people to nearby towns in search of work. Morris wanted to construct new architect designed village colleges built to the highest specifications which would be open to children and adults alike. Statutory and voluntary agencies would be co-ordinated and new playing fields replace old asphalt schoolyards. Each college would have a large hall, meeting rooms for evening classes, village clubs and societies, shower rooms, a library, a reading room and state-of-the-art laboratories. 'Many of these features are commonplace today. In 1930 they were revolutionary'.[27]

Clara shared Morris's educational vision but not his fastidiousness, having no strong feelings as to whether fresh flowers in schools should be displayed in jam jars or, as Morris insisted, only in vases. Their working relationship was strained by Morris's ambivalence towards the WEA. While favouring a community-based approach to adult education, he wanted non-vocational classes taught in the village colleges and, in contrast to Clara, considered the WEA too narrow in its appeal. Whatever their differences, Clara was to prove herself to be among Morris's most reliable, trusted, astute, politically sophisticated, and well-placed of allies on the village colleges and throughout the tribulations that beset his many schemes for educational reform.

Morris had many admirers in the world of education but far fewer in local government where it mattered. Romsey Councillor, David Hardman was one, as was Helen Pease. Morris's attitude to councillors could be cavalier and dismissive in the extreme veering erratically between the charming, the charismatic, and the curmudgeonly. He did not suffer fools (or philistines) gladly and was curt to the point of rudeness with those county councillors who wanted the village colleges to cost the ratepayer nothing, and if this was impossible wanted Morris to secure the capital costs and any necessary expenditure himself. Morris also had difficulties relating to women. After a contretemps with the Fellows at Girton College he referred to them disparagingly as having 'their wombs stuffed with algebra.'[28]

The building of Sawston Village College was the first time Morris's money-raising abilities were put to the test and he passed with flying colours; a cheque for 45,000 pounds extracted from the Spelman Foundation in the United States,[29] a further 5,400 was found for a consultant architect, the land for the building plot donated by the owner of a Sawston paper mill, laboratory benches cadged from Newnham College: 'It is not exactly pleasant work, this chasing of rich people,'[30] he remarked, but Morris, more than anyone, appreciated the necessity to turn himself into a scrounger *par excellence*. The votes in council were close, rancorous and ill-tempered and Councillors were bitterly divided among themselves, even after the colleges were built. 'Schools are being robed week after week ... They are not receiving what they would receive because the village colleges are taking the money', railed a furious Councillor Nash.[31] It took a full six years of bickering, objections, obstruction, obfuscation, and scrutiny of every detail *ad nauseam* for Sawston Village College to be completed. Clara and Harris were invited guests at the grand opening ceremony by Edward, Prince of Wales in October 1931; the Prince hardly bothering to disguise his displeasure, having been given the impression that he had come to open a college of Cambridge University.[32] Thereafter, Clara was always to take a close diplomatic interest in both Sawston Village College and Sawston Grammar School.

Morris's reluctance to credit the work of others is widely recognised. 'I know Henry Morris admired her greatly', Mary Tabor once told Joyce Bellamy.[33] However, there is no mention of Clara in any his speeches, broadcasts or the papers published as *The Henry Morris Collection* by Harry Rée in 1984, let alone any acknowledgement of the unfailing support from her that he knew that he always received. David Holland, a Tutor at Bassingbourn Village College in the 1950s, who described himself as a 'friend of Henry Morris' wrote to Clara personally ('I know how much he [Morris] owed to you').[34] 'I doubt if Mr Morris would have got through much of his reforms and the village colleges in particular if it had not been for her', volunteered Helen Pease.[35] Writing in *The Fabian Quarterly* in 1945 Clara conspicuously fails to mention Morris by name: 'The main achievement of the Cambridgeshire Education Committee between the wars was the establishment of four village colleges in four villages in the County'.[36] Clara's patient work behind the scenes ensured that Morris got the crucial votes he needed in committee. Without the good working relationships that she built up with concerned teachers and parents, the village colleges, and particularly the two built on her watch as Chairman of the Education Committee, Arthur Mellows Glinton (1949), and Bassingbourn (1954), would certainly have had a rougher passage.

In 1924 Clara was appointed to an eight-person committee set up by the Labour Home Secretary, Arthur Henderson, to report on the medical examination of young persons for employment in factories under the Factory and Workshop Acts. The committee met on ten days, examined twenty-nine witnesses, and published their findings in May, recommending that existing services should be co-ordinated with school medical inspections, and special medical supervision provided for young people working in potentially hazardous conditions.[37] Clara had clearly made an impression on Henderson. She was asked to join the Departmental Committee on Sexual Offences against Young Persons in July. The task of this committee, which was to review the law relating to children subjected to rape, incest, and sexual abuse, was more protracted and difficult. They interviewed seventy-five witnesses and reported in December 1925.

There were two other women: Clara Martineau and Elizabeth Harriott Kelly, both pioneering JPs and, like Clara, known for their liberal views and their experience of working with juveniles. Clara Martineau, a member of the Martineau family prominent in civic life in Birmingham for generations, had represented Edgbaston as a councillor since 1913. Elizabeth Harriott Kelly sat on the bench in Portsmouth and had a long record of charitable work and like Clara had contributed to Helen Bosanquet's 1912 *Social Conditions in Provincial Towns*. The NSPCC Inspector, Robert Parr, a well-known advocate of better child protection, was the final Commissioner. As Louise Jackson points out, the Commissioners had to contend with the widespread public support for the view that the victims of sexual crimes were somehow 'polluted' and that they should be removed from the parental home for reformation and retraining lest their presence in the household contaminate others in their family and community.[38] The committee's far-sighted recommendations included raising the age of consent from sixteen to seventeen and the abolition of the 'reasonable belief' that a girl was sixteen or over as a defence for assaulting a minor. A sexually assaulted child should, wherever possible, remain in the family home. Moreover, the medical inspection of girls should always be carried out by a woman doctor, testimony from girls taken by properly trained women, and separate waiting rooms introduced for young people.[39]

In 1920 Clara was one of the first five women in Cambridge to be appointed a Justice of the Peace alongside Edith Bethune-Baker, Leah Manning, Florence Keynes, and Jane Ellen Harrison. Her sister Margaret was the first woman appointed in Essex, in 1924 and Helen Pease the first in Cambridgeshire in 1925. Anne Logan suggests that Clara's name may have been put forward by Gertrude Tuckwell, President of the National Federation of Women Workers, and the first woman to be appointed a magistrate in London. Initially all the names on a list of seven put forward by the Lord Chancellor, Lord Birkenhead, in 1919, and subsequently all the nominations submitted by the seven women themselves, were made with a view to securing geographical and political balance across England and Wales. Tuckwell appears to have been responsible for the nominations of the Labour Party supporters on the recommended list.[40]

All five of Cambridge's new JPs had been law-abiding suffragists before the war and the picture was much the same across the country. A sizeable proportion of the new women magistrates including Ethel Bentham, Margaret Wynne Nevinson, Elizabeth Garrett Anderson, Louisa Martindale, and Margaret Ashton had supported the non-militant campaigns. Even those like Clara who disagreed with suffragette militancy had been appalled by the conditions of prisons like Holloway and the draconian sentences imposed upon women prisoners for inconsequential infringements of law and order. Many of the new JPs were already identified with what Anne Logan terms the 'feminist-criminal-justice reform network',[41] and were arguing powerfully that 'girls and women were badly served by an all-male legal profession, judiciary, magistracy, police service and penal establishment',[42] and demanding more women police officers, factory inspectors, social workers, local government officers, and lawyers.

Clara sat in the juvenile courts set up under the Children and Young Person's Act of 1908, which abolished prison for children under 14. Straightlaced and severe though she might first appear, those on the wrong side of the law soon learnt that Mrs Rackham was no ogre but no 'soft touch' either. Though infinitely patient and kind when the need arose, she had a reputation for standing for no nonsense. It was clear to Clara that many of the children before her should never have been brought before the courts. As Carolyn Steedman points out, poor children have always looked 'wrong' to the middle-class observer, 'tired, dirty, old before their time, their faces showing only an absence of childhood'.[43] Children from middle-class homes with money, good housing and education, rarely, if ever, found themselves in trouble with the criminal justice system. Those whom Clara saw came disproportionately from the poorer parts of town such as Barnwell and Castle End. They were badly housed, poorly educated, undernourished, and dressed in the shabby clothes and downtrodden shoes that were the hallmarks of their poverty. Many were very young indeed. In 1920 the criminal age of responsibility was seven and was put up to eight in The Children Act of 1935. If these children were guilty of anything it was naughtiness and not criminality.

The magistracy was overwhelmingly male-dominated, steeped in archaic practices, and tendentially resistant to change. Apart from a scattering of working-class men appointed in working-class-neighbourhoods, such as Billy Briggs in Romsey, they were often far removed socially from the communities they served. One problem needing attention urgently was the lack of provision for those too poor to pay their own defence. Clara made representations on behalf of the Standing Joint Committee of Industrial Women's Organisations to the Committee on Legal Aid for the Poor chaired by Viscount Finlay which reported in 1926. The Poor Prisoners' Defence Act of 1930 subsequently laid the foundation of the present day system of free legal aid.[44]

In 1921, Clara joined the Howard League for Penal Reform which had been established after the merger of the Penal Reform League and the Howard League. She was elected to the Executive Committee in 1927 and Vice-Chairman in 1932. The first Secretary was Margery Fry, sister of the art critic Roger Fry, and among the women magistrates appointed in London in 1921. Clara and Margery had met on the executive committee of the NUWSS but it was through their work for the League that they discovered how much they had in common and became lifelong friends. Margery had wanted to study mathematics at Newnham College but her Quaker family objected because 'it bred agnostics'[45] and although it was 'not so fine' or as large as Newnham she had gone to

Somerville Hall instead.[46] Margery's time in Oxford had overlapped with that of Eglantyne Jebb at Lady Margaret Hall. Eleanor Rathbone was also a mutual friend: Margery remembered walking with Eleanor in the Somerville garden: 'We came to the conclusion that Parliament was shut to us, and practically everything was shut to us. There was nothing that it was worthwhile to be ambitious about'.[47]

Both Clara and Margery had been relieved from the duties of a Victorian home daughter, Clara through marriage and Margery by a fortuitous invitation to return to Somerville as a college librarian from 1899–1904. Until the start of the First World War Margery had been the Warden of a new University Hall of residence for women in Birmingham, a job similar to Margaret Tabor's post at Liverpool University. However, an unexpected legacy (estimated in 1917 to be as large as 'the pay of 42,200 certified elementary school teachers'),[48] from Margery's uncle, Joseph Storrs Fry, a bachelor, who made a fortune out of the family confectionery and chocolate business in Bristol, guaranteed Margery's economic independence, enabling her to do pretty much what she wanted for the rest of her life.

In 1919 Margery had moved to London and set up house at 7 Dalmeny Avenue, overlooking Holloway Prison, with her brother, Roger, and his children.[49] Roger's wife, Helen, having been admitted to a mental institution, Margery and her sister Joan cared for Roger's children, Pamela and Julian, during his frequent absences from London. Margery and Clara both took immense pride in the artists in their respective families. Clara's appreciation of Arthur's enchanted world of gnarled trees, elves and goblins was matched by Margery's love of the hand-painted designs from the Omega Workshops that decorated the surface of furniture, lampshades, and textiles in the Fry's London house.

Margery had been persuaded to take on the role of Secretary of the newly formed League by the Quaker, Stephen Hobhouse. Hobhouse, a nephew of Beatrice Webb, had been sent to prison numerous times for his pacifist beliefs during the First World War and edited *English Prisons Today* (1922) with Fenner Brockway. The first meetings took place in the sitting room of the Fry's Victorian house. By 1922 Margery's visits to Holloway had started and she was appointed the first education adviser to the prison.[50] The courts did not provide training for magistrates and Margery was instrumental in setting up the Magistrates Association with Cecil Leeson as the first Secretary for the purpose of providing training and to ensure that magistrates had their own independent voice. Clara joined the Magistrates Association, quickly, found herself on the Executive Committee, and set about introducing a rigorous programme of professional training courses.

Clara was kept busy with requests to give talks on penal reform, for example, to the Association of Assistant Mistresses in 1928 and the National Council of Women in Tonbridge Wells in 1929. One notable improvement in prisoners' conditions with which she was closely associated was the 'regular payment of convicted prisoners for work done, a notable reform given that it was achieved during the years of economic depression,[51] Clara found congenial company on the executive committee. Madeleine Symons, her contemporary at Newnham College, chaired the West London Juvenile Court and had worked as an assistant to Mary Macarthur and Margaret Bondfield. Theodora Calvert (Girton College, née Llewelyn Davies) was the first woman admitted to the Inner Temple and a niece of Margaret Llewelyn Davies. Theodora had married a fellow committee member, Roy Calvert, a Quaker and a pacifist, who, as the author of *Capital Punishment in the Twentieth Century* (1927), and editor of *The Death Penalty Enquiry* (1930), was architect of the League's long running campaign against capital-punishment.

From 1923 to 1934 Clara edited a 'Law at Work' column in *The Woman's Leader*, the official journal of NUSEC, which campaigned for full equality and supported the Six Point Group set up in 1921 by Margaret, Lady Rhondda, founding editor of the feminist magazine, *Time and Tide*.[52] The objectives of the Six Point Group were to end violence against children, protect the widow and the unmarried mother, and to secure equal rights of guardianship, equal pay for teachers, and equal opportunities for men and women in the civil service. Clara thought her column an excellent way of keeping in touch with Eleanor, Margery and her old suffragist friends. However, the relationship between the non-aligned feminists in NUSEC and women in the Labour Party was fraught with suspicion and a motion prohibiting Labour Party members from being members of NUSEC's Women's Citizens'Association was defeated by a slim majority at the annual conference in 1925.[53]

The 'law at work' column was edited by Clara, Margery and a Mrs Crofts, a qualified solicitor whose first name never appeared on the masthead, but in practice Clara, who had no formal legal training, appears to have written and edited much of it herself. Having total editorial freedom, she concentrated on matters for which the League had clearly defined policies, such as the need for women volunteers to advise the boys in Wormwood Scrubs, and to improve conditions in remand homes. The column carried topical book reviews, for example, Isaac Briggs's autobiography *Reformatory Reform*, published by Longman in 1924.[54] Coverage was given to any projected change in the law that affected women, such as the nationality law in July 1921 whereby women forfeited their British citizenship on marriage to foreign nationals.[55] Clara commissioned a moving piece from George Lansbury about the death penalty at the time of the execution of Edith Thompson[56] which had profoundly affected Margery Fry, who, while she was visiting another prisoner, had glimpsed the condemned woman in an adjacent cell.[57] Clara herself wrote a powerful invective against corporal punishment using the kind of European comparators which the Howard League for Penal Reform, which wanted to set a minimum standard for the treatment of prisoners through the League of Nations in Geneva, was using more and more.

> The punishment of flogging is not found necessary in France, Germany, Switzerland, Italy, Norway and Sweden. It has happened that a criminal who had been flogged under English law has ended his days in a foreign hospital, and has by his scarred back made it known to his amazed doctors and nurses that torture is still practised in English prisons.[58]

In January 1924 the Rackhams moved out of the Senior Tutor's house at Christ's and into a property owned by Christ's at 9 Park Terrace in a terrace of elegant white Georgian houses. Their new house was a few hundred yards from Harris's college and had much to commend it. There was a pleasant uninterrupted view across Parker's Piece, a green grassy open space used as a cricket ground and where the rules of Association Football are thought to have started, gifted to the townspeople by Mathew Parker, Archbishop of Canterbury in the sixteenth century, and traditionally used for outdoor rallies, protests, public meetings, and to celebrate royal marriages and coronations. Parker's Piece was transversed by two diagonal paths illuminated at their meeting point by the 'Reality Checkpoint', a large cast iron lamp post which denoted where the colleges ended and the town began. To the east lay Mill Road with its small, and often family-run, neighbourhood shops, pubs, and churches starting at Peter Field and ending at Brookfield. Mill Road ran for about a mile linking Petersfield on one side of the railway bridge and Romsey Town, surrounded on three sides by agricultural land, which Clara was to represent as a councillor on the other side, although she did not know this at the time.

Many of the houses in Petersfield were built on college land. Their residents were often college servants, or otherwise dependent on the university for their livelihoods. The terraces in Romsey were built largely between 1885 and 1895, often with front doors opening on to the pavement and long narrow back gardens and occupied, in the main, by skilled artisans and their families with no connection to the university; initially construction and railway workers.[59] The street names; Madras Road, Suez Road, Hobart Road, and Cyprus Road intimated pride in the British Empire. Few academics in Cambridge University ever ventured much beyond the town centre other than to the railway station built in 1845 away from the town centre to discourage non-essential student travel and prostitutes and petty criminals from London.

Clara and Harris were both exceedingly hospitable. Hardly a week went by without one or other of their family and friends being invited to Sunday lunch. Harris would uncork a bottle of wine or write a note to the porters' lodge ordering a bottle of sherry to be sent over to celebrate a birthday or special occasion. The days of frugal Sunday lunches, the cold lentils of Clara's childhood, were a distant memory from the past. The meals at 9 Park Terrace, prepared by Mrs Jones, Clara's long-serving housekeeper, were good but not extravagant, with a crisp green salad and a freshly made *vinaigrette* dressing. Fresh fruit and vegetables – a pineapple or a coconut for a special treat – were purchased daily from the nearby market. Unexpected visitors were sure of a welcome. There was always a spare bed with a counterpane made up for anyone passing through Cambridge and needing to stay overnight.

Clara and Harris would often spend Christmas at Fennes. A large fir tree would be brought inside and the room decorated with festive holly, mistletoe, home-made paper chains, and tissue paper bells. The family enjoyed old-fashioned board games, charades, puzzles, treasure hunts, and the ritual completion of the General Knowledge Quizzes in the Sunday papers. 'Consequences' would be played in Greek, which made younger members of the family feel inadequate,[60] and, from the children's point of view, Clara and Harris developed the infuriating habit of talking to one another in ancient Greek whenever they did not want them to understand what was being said.

Philippa Fawcett, by now the highest ranking woman on the London County Council, would visit the house, as would Margaret, enjoying some success as a published author of illustrated books for young people and adults. *A Guide to the National Gallery for the Young* (1925), *The Other London Galleries* (1926), and *A Beginner's Guide to the British Museum* (1927) were based on the outings to museums and galleries in London she had enjoyed with her young charges, John, Lucy, and Winifred. As part of the vogue for the lives of 'famous women' Margaret was asked to contribute pen portraits of Caroline Herschel, Sarah Siddons, Maria Edgeworth, and Elizabeth Blackwell to the *Pioneering Women* series published in four sets by the Sheldon Press between 1925 and 1933 and widely available in schools and children's libraries.

In May 1901, shortly after the Rackhams had moved into Grange Terrace, Clara began the practice of inscribing the names of all her house guests in a black leather visitors' book kept on a table in the hallway; a habit which she kept up for over half a century making careful entries in the same black book (which still survives) until 1956. *Inter alia* the names of Samuel and Henrietta Barnett, Jeannette and R. H. Tawney, Philippa Fawcett, William Beveridge, Margaret Bondfield, Hugh and Ruth Dalton, Leah Manning, Marion Philipps, Molly Hamilton, and Edith Picton-Turbervill all appear.

The visitors' book in Grange Terrace, Hobson Street, and at 9 Park Terrace intimates how the Rackham's living quarters acted as a 'salon' where an advanced liberal left-leaning group of intellectuals, writers, social theorists, and policy makers congregated whenever they happened to be in Cambridge. The Rackhams themselves were at the centre of the progressive social, political and educational circles in which they moved. Hospitality was always generous and tea available for whoever dropped in, usually served from a large silver tea pot given to Clara by her mother who inherited it from Anne Allen, Emma's aunt. When Clara was not there her guests would be let in by the housekeeper. Any group that needed a central meeting room at short notice simply had to ask the Rackhams.

Harold Shearman, a WEA activist who became leader of the London County Council, remembered how WEA tutors would drop in and out. 'Before that the Teachers' Labour League met at Park Terrace [Park Parade) and it was at one of those meetings in your house that I first met [George] Pateman'[61] An improvised 'wake' took place when Mary Agnes Hamilton, Leah Manning and Susan Lawrence all decided to converge on Clara and Harris to lament the loss of their parliamentary seats in the General Election of 1931. Given the co-minglings and the incessant stream of visitors at 9 Park Terrace the conversation might cover virtually anything and whatever the topic, after-dinner conversations were usually intense, animated and good humoured often lasting late into the night.

Clara and Harris's early married years were replete with happy memories. In February 1924 they received a moving letter of thanks for their hospitality signed by fifteen old friends:

> We who have so often stayed with you in the old house want to give a little token to remind ourselves and you of the many happy hours we spent there. Never have there been friends so hospitable. Hobson Street was a real centre of enjoyment.[62]

They added that 'Your old friends think of your infinitely kind and steady friendship as one of the most precious things in their lives'.[63] The signatories included Philippa Strachey, Susan Lawrence and Clara's contemporary at Newnham Flora Mayor, author of *The Rector's Daughter*, a moving, quietly understated novel published by Leonard and Virginia Woolf at the Hogarth Press in 1924, greatly admired in its day, although now sadly forgotten.[64]

The Rackham's house-warming present from their grateful house guests was a modern gramophone encased in a mahogany cabinet with a winding-handle which took pride of place in the large high-ceilinged sitting room. Margery Fry, appointed Principal of Somerville in 1926, the year in which Roger was also appointed a Fellow of King's College, Cambridge, was also an occasional visitor to Park Terrace. Margery remembered Harris as a 'rather gauche, buoyant classical don, with a passion for his gramophone, which he is always ready to turn on for you, even when he ought to be translating Aristotle'.[65] The translation in question was probably the Loeb edition of Aristotle's *Nicomachean*

Ethics published in 1926 to academic acclaim. Harris was intensely musical and interested in abstract musical concepts. He was for many years President of the Christ's College Music Society and loved singing in the college choir.

There was always a cat ensconced in the Rackham household, often occupying the window seat. Pussyfoot, a blue Siamese, was very wild and used to run up the curtains. Another favourite cat, Montagu, was mischievously named after the great classicist, Montagu Butler, Master of Trinity College. A large gilt-framed mirror hung over the mantelpiece on which a silver French clock took pride of place. Visitors recollected an assortment of ornaments and souvenirs brought back from abroad: skiing holidays in Switzerland, walking holidays in in Italy and in the Alps. A low occasional table was piled high with newspapers, buff government reports, *Labour Research* and *Fabian Quarterly* alongside the publications from the RSPB with colourful illustrations of unknown birds, for which the children made a beeline.

After years of scrimping as an insurance clerk Arthur was finally attracting serious attention in the art world and from the readers who mattered to him most: the children who would approach him shyly and ask for autographs. Arthur's reputation as a leading illustrator of the 'golden age' of Edwardian book illustrations was now unassailable. His royalties afforded a sufficiently large income to enable him to leave London and to make a new life for Edyth, himself, and their daughter, Barbara in the depths of the Sussex countryside. Harris and Clara's book-lined shelves boasted numerous presentation copies of Arthur's books with customised bookplates, alongside Dickens, Tennyson, Browning, and Rossetti's poems bound in red leather, including the signed and numbered first editions which Arthur generously gifted to his brother and sister-in-law. The walls of the sitting room were hung with Arthur's original prints, paintings, and drawings, each properly stretched, mounted, and framed. There was a striking portrait in oil of Wilhelmina Welland by Edyth Starkie, which they both greatly admired.

By the time that the Rackhams moved into Park Terrace Clara was approaching fifty and had recognised that she and Harris would never have the children for which they had hoped. Mary Tabor recalled that childlessness was a sadness to her aunt although something on which she never allowed herself to dwell.[66] Clara took her responsibilities as aunt very seriously and loved to hear the house humming with the voices of her nephews and nieces. She would always remember their birthdays. Mary's own present was the same every year: a book token. The children saw a playful and boisterous side of their aunt hidden from those who only knew the public Mrs Rackham. 'She was a delightful and original aunt, and great fun' and would entertain her nieces by 'doing mad or incongruous things' such as shrieking out on the upper deck of the bus and referring to the Natural History Museum as the 'dead zoo'.[67] On one occasion Bertha [Bernard Rackham's daughter] and Mary were staying and Bertha 'fell between a rowing boat and the bank'. Clara fished her out and marched them home. 'Bertha was wearing a nice blue Liberty dress which shrank. She got a chill, and was sick in the night'.[68] Clara would take her nieces to King's College Chapel on Easter Sunday and to the beautiful Good Friday service whenever her mother was staying with her in Cambridge.

In June 1925 Harris's sister, Meg, who had been staying with Arthur and Edyth walked out of the house: her body found eight days later on the Sussex Downs. In January 1927 Harris's younger brother, Maurice was killed in an avalanche on a skiing holiday in the Tyrol. We know that Clara was deeply affected by the death of her friend Agnes Ramsey in a road accident when a car driven by her husband skidded and overturned near Huntingdon in August 1927.[69] We can only guess at Clara's feelings about the other terrible crises in the family.

Clara helped to organise the annual congress of the Women's Co-operative Guild in 1925 in the Guildhall in Cambridge. This passed motions calling for the family allowance and free school meals and milk in schools. Free school milk and meals had always been an emotive issue in Cambridge after a little girl called Mary attending Leah Manning's class in the Ragged School in New Street had died of starvation and the tragic death had been widely reported and condemned in the local papers.

In her 'foreword' to Catherine Webb's *history of the women's guild* published in 1927 Margaret Llewelyn Davies argued that the principal contribution of the Women's Co-operative Guild 'to the life of married women has been in changing the whole attitude of the nation towards Maternity' and she applauded the 'emergence of the married working woman from national obscurity into a position of national importance'.[70] Davies struck a note of triumph, if not triumphalism, in her reference to 'the power of the revolutionary weapon – the market basket': 'Women have been transformed from buyers, ignorant of the economic results of their acts, into intelligent Co-operators, conscious that they can undermine Capitalism, and making good their right to share in the control of the Movement'.[71] Henceforth Guildswomen were to become increasingly occupied with the causes of international Co-operation and peace, distributing the white poppy, and were to reach their zenith with 87,246 members and 1,819 branches in 1939.[72]

One project near to Clara's heart was the construction of the Romsey Town Labour Club on the corner of Coleridge Road and Mill Road. Voting in the inter-war period was along class lines and Romsey, which came to be known as 'Little Moscow' or 'Red Romsey' due to the size and reliability of the Labour vote, had developed a strong sense of social cohesion and civic pride with none of the deference to the university that characterised other parts of Cambridge.[73] The railway was by far the largest employer in Romsey and provided jobs for clerks, boiler-makers, fitters, signalmen, and locomotive drivers who lived and worked in the area. The 'knocker up' going from house-to-house in the mornings was part of the daily routine. Trade union membership was at one hundred per cent.[74] The railway workers were a highly organised cohesive, occupational group with the relatively secure jobs, pensions and prospects of promotion that mattered more as unemployment worsened during the 'devil's decade of the 1930s. *In Call Back Yesterday* (1953) Hugh Dalton remembered the railway and construction workers with unqualified respect: Billy Briggs, a railway clerk, Bill Few an engine driver, Jim Overton, Secretary of the Trades Council, Arthur Cross from the building trades.[75] Locomotive Engineers and Firemen (ASLEF) and National Union of Railwaymen (NUR) stalwarts built the club and drafted in friends and workmates bricklayers, stone masons, plumbers, joiners, carpenters (etc.) to work for nothing at evenings and weekends. Clara made a substantial financial investment purchasing a large number of the one pound shares floated to help defray construction costs.[76] She oversaw the building work personally and was one of eight women whose names appear on the Roll of Honour inside the hall.

The Labour Club was designed as a social and recreational centre for labour supporters in Romsey but not for meetings of the central Party and in 1927 they acquired an old knitting factory which was converted into the official Cambridge Labour Hall, later renamed the Alex Wood Hall. The hall in Norfolk Street was opened by George Lansbury and Margaret Bondfield, who had made history as the first woman to chair the TUC General Council, and had supported Susan Lawrence and Leah Manning when they had tried to organise the college 'bedders' and to persuade the women workers in the Chivers jam factory in Histon to join a trade union.[77] Bondfield was a familiar figure in Cambridge and would stay with Leah or with Clara and Harris on her visits. Clara took on the responsibility for organising the Labour Party weekly meetings with invited speakers which took place on Sundays. She also participated in the other educational activities held regularly in the hall such as the discussion groups organised by the Left Book Club founded by the left-wing publisher Victor Gollancz in 1936 to oppose war, inequality, and Fascism.

The Romsey club, put up for sale in 2015 when the Labour Party could no longer afford to run it, was a pleasing unpretentious one-storey red brick structure fronted with two bow windows with a doorway opening on to a billiard room, committee room, reading room, bar and seating area. Above the entrance were intricate carvings of craftsman's tools used in its construction and John Ruskin's maxim; 'There is no wealth but life' in stone. The official opening ceremony took place until its completion in 1928 but the work was sufficiently advanced for Ramsay MacDonald to lay the foundation stone on April 17, 1926. MacDonald arrived in Cambridge to a rapturous welcome from cheering supporters sporting red rosettes. A banner bearing nurse Edith Cavell's words '"Patriotism is not enough". "Only love can save the world"' was hoisted high [see Figure 2.13]. He was greeted by the President, Billy Briggs, who had worked on the railways since fifteen and represented Romsey on the council since 1920. MacDonald, the son of a Scottish agricultural labourer and a maidservant, who had had a meteoric rise to the top from poverty and obscurity was an inspirational figure for ordinary members. Chosen to preside over the outdoor festivities, Clara declaimed that nothing 'could fill them with greater enthusiasm for the cause and give them more determination to work for it, than the presence of Ramsay MacDonald'.[78] The foundation stone was laid less than two weeks before the start of the General Strike.

When the General Strike broke out Clara and Harris offered their basement kitchen to the Cambridge Joint Strike Committee. The strike was called by the Trades Union Congress (TUC) General Council in protest at the attempt by the coal-owners to renege on national agreements on pay and conditions by imposing substantial reductions in wages while demanding longer working hours. Enthusiasm for the strike across the labour movement – strike committees were formed in towns and villages across the country – contrasted with the lukewarm response of the leadership of both the TUC and the Labour Party. The TUC was ostensibly committed to the strike but widely rumoured to want its end as quickly as possible; the ultra-cautious MacDonald was frightened of the party being tarnished with a revolutionary brush by any association with the strikers.

For nine tumultuous days from May 3 until May 12, Albert Stubbs would travel the forty-five mile journey from Cambridge to London on his powerful motorbike, with Leah Manning on the passenger seat, to collect bundles of the TUC strike bulletin which were folded in and distributed from Clara's kitchen with the 'delicious smell of hot coffee and frying sausages'.[79] Some 4,000 workers came out on strike in Cambridge. Support was predictably strongest in Romsey where hundreds attended a rally on the 'Rec' (the Romsey recreation ground) listening to speakers and the Railway Silver Band. Billy Briggs was subsequently victimised as one of the ringleaders.

Cambridge University undergraduates who volunteered to break the strike were given permission to miss lectures and chauffeur-driven to London to unload ships in the Victoria docks. Striking railway workers in Cambridge watched with derision as over-zealous students directed by a Captain Longley, a Conservative borough councillor, crashed a train into the buffers near the Mill Road Bridge. The TUC capitulated and the miners embarked on a nine month long 'lockout' which ended in ignominious defeat. The offer of a class in public speaking for the Strike Committee, made by George Pateman and the WEA, was never needed because the strike had come to an end.

After the disillusionment of the nine days in May Clara and Harris embarked on an ambitious plan to modernise their house. The design of domestic interiors inevitably reveals much about their occupants. The Rackhams disliked ostentation, were at pains to think of themselves as 'modern', to rid themselves of a Victorian 'clutter', and to incorporate the best features of contemporary design into their home. They wanted to move the kitchen to the ground floor so that the housekeeper would no longer be asked to trudge up and down stairs with every cup of tea. Clara supervised the extensive renovations herself. The old basement kitchen was ripped out and a delighted housekeeper duly installed in a kitchen large enough to double as her own sitting room with a view over the walled kitchen garden at the back. A new serving hatch through, which it was possible for Clara and Harris to converse with her was installed between the kitchen and the drawing room. Clara was, of course, a highly experienced, albeit unpaid, working journalist. One of her few sorties into popular journalism is an illustrated feature article written for *Good Housekeeping* entitled 'Banishing the Basement Bogey'. Here she presents herself, somewhat incongruously for any reader recognising her name from other contexts, as the proud designer of a labour-saving home: 'The old basement house, a familiar landmark in all large towns, can be transformed into a labour-saving home with a little ingenuity and careful planning'.[80] Clara explains the rationale for each domestic improvement to satisfy the curiosity of her imagined reader (the house-proud housewife on a limited budget looking for ideas to improve her modest home). Simple woven rugs on stained wooden floor boards replaced musty old carpet. The tiny open coal fires which glowed in their iron grates but left the rooms icy cold were removed. Modern gas heaters were installed in every bedroom doing away with the need to light fires, clean grates, or carry heavy coal scuttles up the stairs. Each bedroom was fitted with its own hand basin and gas ring for the occupants or their guests to heat water for shaving or tea.

Then calamity struck the Rackham household. Harris's horse stumbled and fell into a rabbit hole and its rider was thrown to the ground, suffering severe concussion and memory loss. In a tape-recorded interview with Brian Harrison, Mary Tabor recalled that 'Uncle Harris who had always been a good conversationalist and told very amusing stories suddenly seemed much older and was never the same again'.[81] Clara was exceedingly patient and never gave the slightest intimation that she found Harris's company taxing or exhausting although he took to repeating himself over and over again. The accident put paid to the horse-riding which Harris loved, but undaunted he learnt to drive a car in his sixtieth year before, as he said, it was too late.[82]

In September 1928 Clara was appointed to a Committee set up by the Home Secretary and chaired by Lieutenant Colonel Sir Vivian Henderson to report on changes to the factory inspectorate to allow the Home Office to discharge its duties in relation to the Factory Bill that the government wanted to bring in. The other woman on this committee was Hilda Martindale, the Chief Woman's Factory Inspector.[83] Much against her will, Clara found herself embroiled in a long drawn out and extremely acrimonious policy dispute[84] between, on the one hand, 'equality first' feminists in NUSEC and the Open Door Council such as Monica Whately, demanding the abolition of restrictive laws relating to women's employment and arguing that industrial health and safety should be determined by the nature of the job and not the sex of the worker. On the other, women in the labour movement demanded extra protection for women, especially in the factories, and were deeply suspicious of attempts by 'middle class' feminist organisations to determine the pay and conditions of working-class women. The problems were compounded by the tendency of leading Labour Party figures, including the Chief Labour Party Women's Organiser, Marion Phillips, to frame their arguments in favour of protectionism exclusively in terms of working-class women with no recognition that all women might have common interests that cut across divisions of class. In consequence, many non-aligned feminists were to become increasingly dismissive of the Labour Party which they came to regard as a male-dominated organisation, the *raison d'etre* of which was to further the interests of working-class men. Like other feminists of her generation, Clara did not consider that her identities as a socialist and as a feminist were incompatible but memories of her work to prevent the exploitation of women on the shop floor during her time at the factory inspectorate brought her down firmly on the side of the 'socialist protectionists'. In 1930 she outlined the basic principles that underpinned the case for protection in a well-received talk for the Fabian Women's Group which she had clearly researched in some depth.[85] In the event, the contentious factory legislation never materialised. But the rancorous dispute was to colour the troubled relationship between the Labour Party and feminists for the next decade. While Pamela Graves's claim that 'the Labour Party virtually abandoned its earlier commitment to the equality of the sexes' in its public rhetoric and across a range of publications and policies[86] during the 1930s (the devil's decade') may well be exaggerated, Clara was only too conscious that older feminist like herself, the veterans of the women's suffrage struggles, were becoming depleted in numbers, or given the deepening crisis in relation to Fascism in Europe, opting to devote their reforming energies to international rather than domestic affairs.

In 1929 Clara was elected as a councillor for 'Red Romsey'; which was to vote Labour in every election between 1919 and 1998 with only one exception; a by-election in 1981.[87] On a good day, Clara was able to cycle from Park Terrace to Romsey in ten minutes. She took in the familiar buildings in Mill Road; the workhouse, later the hospital for infectious diseases and the maternity hospital, the cinema (now demolished), the Bath House, the Salvation Army, and the old Victorian cemetery with its marble cherubs and gnarled evergreen trees.

Between 1923 and 1924 Billy Briggs, had presciently argued that all new houses in Romsey should be built with parlours and a minimum of three bedrooms to prevent them becoming the slums of the future and many were built to high municipal standards.[88] The larger houses had bay windows and front gardens with neatly tended privet hedges. Virtually all had back gardens where gooseberries, dahlias, rhubarb, leeks, and runner beans were grown and chickens, rabbits, and racing pigeons were sometimes kept. Clara fought innumerable battles to secure essential improvements. Most houses had outside lavatories with no bathrooms and plumbing, heating, and sanitation were often rudimentary. Many homes did not have running water. Infants were bathed on the kitchen table from a jug of water heated on the stove and took their weekly bath in the kitchen or the living room in a large enamel or copper tub. Matters improved in 1927 when the new public bath house was opened on the corner of Mill Road and Gwydir Street where a bath could be had for four pence.

Clara had the cultural capital and *savoir-faire* that came naturally to a woman of her social class who had enjoyed the privileges of a good education, a happy marriage, financial security, and lacked for nothing all her life. But her strong personal investment in a moral economy wherein privilege must be balanced by a sense of responsibility made her equally at home addressing cabinet ministers or government officials in Whitehall, or talking 'naturally' and without affectation to train drivers and pensioners in Romsey Town. Clara, who never quite lost her 'cut-glass' accent, or pretended to be anything other than the highly educated, middle-class woman that she was, was always spoken of with respect in Romsey. People liked the fact that she queued up with them to shop in the Co-op (her share book number was 3698); that she engaged small children in conversation, and that Mrs Rackham – as she was always called rather formally by local people who had known her for years ('Clara' was much too familiar and 'Dorothea' reserved for family) – troubled to learn and remember everybody's names. They appreciated her ability to listen quietly and her tenacity: her refusal to take 'no' for an answer and her determination to leave no stone unturned to get whatever needed doing in Romsey done. As Clara put it;

> Time spent with individuals listening to grievances, cleaning up misunderstandings and explaining why "they" acted as they did is one of the ways by which Local Government can be made to work. To many of the electors a woman Councillor seems more approachable than a man.[89]

Clara was descended from the English country gentry, in the main, from good, hard-working honest farmers with little interest in status or material acquisitions. Her ethos of social responsibility and public service was largely acquired from the strong reforming tradition of the Woodcocks on her mother's side in Lancashire and the Tabors on her father's side in Essex. The progressive humanitarian tradition to which Clara belonged recognised the worth of all human beings and that working-class women and children were the most vulnerable members of society and therefore the most in need of safeguarding. For much of the nineteenth century this tradition found its 'natural' home in the Liberal Party. However, after innumerable promises on women's suffrage were broken by successive Liberal governments, more and more feminists and social reformers transferred their allegiances from Liberal to Labour. Margaret Llewelyn Davies, Margery Fry, Barbara Wootton, Dorothy Jebb, Madeleine Symons, and other women active in public life, emerged from much the same progressive tradition as Clara and made much the same switch of loyalties from Liberal to Labour early in the twentieth century.

In 'When I am M.P.', published in *The Vote*, the organ of the Women's Freedom League, in June, 1928, Clara describes herself as the prospective Labour candidate for Huntingdonshire and argues for the importance of the specialist rather than the generalist in a changing world where expertise was frequently called for:

> I think the wisest course for an MP who wants to be of use is to acquire as much knowledge as possible on some one subject. The House of Commons will always listen gladly to a Member who is master of a particular subject, and it is at the same time impatient of general statements which do very well for the public platform. I am much interested in criminology and penal reform, and I should try to make a study of that subject.[90]

She added that getting into parliament would give her an opportunity to see the conditions in prisons in India and the Empire.

In 1928 Harris and Clara were guests at a formal evening event at Newnham College held in honour of Dame Millicent Fawcett. The 'Flapper Election' in 1929, the first in which women over twenty-one were allowed to vote, produced a Labour victory although if, or to what extent, the new female electors tipped the result in Labour's direction it is impossible to say.[91] Clara had accepted the Labour nomination for Huntingdonshire in good faith but uncharacteristically, since she hated letting anyone down, withdrew her candidacy. Electioneering away from Cambridge would have meant leaving Harris on his own for long stretches of time and this may well have influenced her decision.

Women may not have been MPs in large numbers but they were called upon time and time again to 'give the women's view' on all legislation once women had the power to vote. By the late 1920s Clara was recognised as an authority on an extraordinarily eclectic range of subjects including factory law, unemployment insurance, adult education, local government, the criminal justice system, and juvenile offenders. Like Margery Fry, she was consulted by civil servants on a wide spectrum of social policies, had the ear of ministers, and was *persona grata* in the Home Office. She had given expert advice to Home Office Departmental Committees on the medical inspection of young persons for factory employment, sexual offences against young persons, and the factory inspectorate.

In view of the astonishing range of experience and qualifications it may well be asked why Clara was never able to fulfil her ambition of winning a parliamentary seat? Brian Harrison sees this as largely a matter of political geography, pointing to the uphill battle that Labour had to establish itself in rural East Anglia where 'Labour lacked the breadth of local appeal that the Liberals had earlier enjoyed'.[92] Others have emphasised the patriarchal values and misogyny within the male-dominated Labour Party. Clara was arguably disadvantaged in having joined the Labour Party somewhat later than Susan Lawrence or Leah Manning, but having done so she was certainly quick off the mark. Although she did not contest the 1919 General Election, only four Labour women did and all were unsuccessful, she was one of only ten women in the whole country to run for Labour in the General Election of 1922. It is worth looking at the question more closely.

Clara was what we would call today exceptionally well 'networked' (the word was not used as an intransitive verb at the time). She had connections to the creative arts through her brother-in-law, Arthur, to adult education through the WEA, to the top universities though Harris and was an Associate of Newnham College. She had long moved in feminist circles through the women's suffrage movement, the NCW and NUSEC. She had numerous contacts in the Labour Party and the Co-operative movement, in local government, and in the criminal justice system, among magistrates and penal reformers. The quality that frequently impressed others, in addition to her kindness – those who knew Emma Tabor said that Clara 'took after' her mother – was the sharpness of her intellect. F. W. Poole, a blind student, remembered, 'the most amazing mind that worked with the precision of a well-programmed computer'.[93] Less charismatic than either Leah Manning or Susan Lawrence, Clara excelled at the accumulation of evidence and facts, however dry, and the framing of rigorous argument. She was unfailingly punctilious and methodical in everything she did with an infinite capacity for taking pains, and made it a point of honour never to miss a meeting on any of the innumerable committees on which she sat.

The number of women elected to parliament as Labour Party MPs between 1918 and 1938 was exceedingly small. They were: Jennie

Adamson, Ethel Bentham, Margaret Bondfield, Ruth Dalton (for 112 days), Mary Agnes Hamilton, Susan Lawrence, Dorothy Jewson, Agnes Hardie, Jennie Lee, Leah Manning, Cynthia Mosley, Lucy Noel-Buxton, Marion Phillips, Edith Summerskill, Edith Picton-Turbervill, and Ellen Wilkinson.[94] It says much about the strength and resilience of the feminist and pre-war suffragist networks and the feminist networks in the Labour Party after the war, that, with the exception of Jennie Adamson, Agnes Hardie, and Edith Summerskill, Clara had occasion to meet or to work with all of them. She was also on very good terms with Eleanor Rathbone, the one fixed star in a changing parliamentary firmament, who had no party affiliation, and ran what amounted to a one woman campaign to persuade the House of Commons of the need for the endowment of motherhood (the family allowance) for some seventeen years. Given the paucity of winnable or safe seats for Labour and the geographical concentration of such seats in the north and the mining areas, selection required persistence, and a penchant for self-promotion (which Clara never had or wanted). Geographical mobility became increasingly difficult for her as she got older and her commitments to people and organisations in Cambridge and its environs became more deeply entrenched. She was unwilling to go far north, for example, to Sunderland, to seek a nomination, as Leah Manning, Ruth Dalton, and Marion Phillips had all been willing to do, in turn. Clara would have been the obvious candidate for Cambridge but this was not considered winnable until the Labour landslide in 1945 took everyone by surprise. The seat was, in any case assiduously nursed by Alex Wood who ran as Labour Party candidate three times. Contesting the Cambridge University seat or one of the two combined university seats for England (all but Oxford, Cambridge and London) was also a possibility, although one was held by Eleanor Rathbone from 1929.

Persistence was essential to becoming an MP. Virtually every female Labour MP between the wars lost her seat and had to steel herself to try again. There were no women elected in the disastrous General Election of 1931 and Ellen Wilkinson was the only woman elected in the General Election of 1935. It was not, however, only well-qualified women who failed to secure the party nomination in a winnable seat. R. H. Tawney, for example, ran for parliament three times in seats where there was no chance of success.

While Clara was extremely well-connected in the Labour Party – Hugh Dalton was her protégé and Dalton's protégé, James Callaghan, an admirer – her friends tended to be from the intellectual echelons of the party; Fabians, the LSE, social theorists and others, and not the influential party agents, organisers, and officials to whom her name was unknown. Of the fifty-seven MPS returned in 1918, forty-nine were sponsored by a trade union, no fewer than twenty-five of whom were nominated by the National Union of Mineworkers (NUM), and four by the National General and Municipal Workers' Union (NGMWU).[95] While Clara was respected for her expertise on factory conditions and unemployment insurance, she had no history of trade union involvement like Margaret Bondfield in the NGMWU, Ellen Wilkinson in the Co-operative Employees' Union, Leah Manning in the NUT, or even Marion Phillips, who endeared herself to the powerful NUM through her prodigious fund-raising during the miners' lock-out. Clara had no prospect of trade union nomination and sponsorship and this put her at a great disadvantage given the symbiotic relationship between the Labour Party and the trade unions.

Clara certainly wanted to get into parliament. However, to argue that she wanted this the expense of everything else in her life, or that her failure was a great source of regret is to do her a disservice. As Anne Logan has argued,

> in researching women's relationship with political life in the aftermath of suffrage, we need to go beyond a preoccupation with the few women who achieved elected office, and interrogate other ways in which feminist women inhabited political, as well as intellectual elites[96]

away from the metropolis.

When envisaging a possible parliamentary career for herself Clara had been left under no illusions about what could or could not be achieved by her friends who had been MPs. The House of Commons worked late into the night and was not a welcoming or hospitable space for women, who in 1930 were consigned to a 'dank, dark dungeon without even a toilet of our own, and a wash-basin with a jug of water and a pail underneath'.[97] Ruth Dalton had not enjoyed her time in the Commons and felt able to accomplish far more on the London County Council. Leah Manning found life in Westminster less rewarding than the teaching in Cambridge she loved and was deeply sorry to leave behind: 'I cannot think now why I gave up something so worthwhile and fulfilling for the frustrating life of politics.'[98]

Misogynistic attitudes in the chamber aside, and these were to be found on both the right and the left of the political spectrum, women MPs felt under intense pressure, albeit often self-imposed, to appear indistinguishable from the men in their Party and to avoid too close an identification with 'women's issues' which they knew would be detrimental to their parliamentary careers. Local councillors, in contrast, felt under no such pressure. As Pat Thane suggest, 'it is questionable whether a backbench MP had more power or influence than... leading [women] pressure group activists'.[99] Leah Manning, responsible with Eleanor Rathbone and the Duchess of Atholl for the magnificent evacuation of child refugees from the Basque country, and Ellen Wilkinson, who led the iconic march of the unemployed from Jarrow to London, won support for their respective causes with their impassioned rhetoric in the regions and not in the metropolis. Neither relied on parliament which initially voted for British neutrality in the Spanish Civil War, or the Labour Party which kept a judicious distance from the hunger marches often regarding them as Communist inspired or controlled. Personal ambition was anathema to Clara because it was antithetical to her ideal of disinterested public service. To leave her beloved Cambridge to become an MP would be to leave everything she loved: husband, home, friends, comrades, and projects, finished and unfinished, past, present, and future. She did not regard herself as a parliamentarian *manqué* and it was quite out of character for her to dwell on what she had *not* managed to achieve in life rather than on what she had. Clara always enjoyed electioneering, door-knocking, and all the razzmatazz of the election campaign. But her sense of responsibility to the Labour Party would have driven her to stand even if she had not. As Eileen Price suggests, Clara's parliamentary candidatures, were undertaken to "show the flag" for Labour in areas where otherwise there might be no candidate at all or an outsider, or a feeble effort put into the election campaign[100] And she knew, at heart, that that she could do far more good by staying put in Cambridge than she could ever hope to achieve by leaving the city.

In November 1929 Clara broadcast her first talk entitled 'How We Elect Our Councillors' on the BBC Home Service at the invitation of Hilda Matheson, the first Director of Talks at the BBC. This was a six-part series 'How we Manage our Affairs', with the letters JP appearing after her name in *The Radio Times*. A broad hint was dropped that there had been talks by other broadcasters on the subject, each duller than the last. Clara self-deprecatingly recollected that 'I gave my talks, and from the amount of correspondence they aroused I had no reason to believe anyone had listened to me and added 'I have not been asked to broadcast again'.[101] Although she did give a few more talks to the BBC she was never invited on to popular radio panel discussions like Margery Fry and Mary Stott who both became household names.

There was some cause for celebration after the Election in 1929 despite the economic gloom and the storm clouds gathering over Europe. Susan Lawrence, Ellen Wilkinson, Jennie Lee, and Margaret Bondfield had all managed to retain their seats, Bondfield promoted to Minister of Labour with responsibility for the unemployed. They were joined in parliament by five new women: Mary Agnes Hamilton in Blackburn, Ethel Bentham (Islington East), Cynthia Mosley (Stoke-on-Trent), Marion Phillips (Sunderland), and Edith Picton-Turbevill (the Wrekin), bringing the number of women on the Labour benches to its highest number before the Second World War.

Notes

1 See Johanna Alberti, *Beyond Suffrage: Feminism in War and Peace, 1914-28* (Basingstoke: Macmillan, 1989) and Cheryl Law, *Suffrage and Power: The Women's Movement 1918-1928* (London: I. B. Taurus, 1997).
2 Pat Thane, 'What Difference Did the Vote Make?', in *Women, Privilege and Power: British Politics 1750 to the Present*, ed. Amanda Vickery (Stanford, CA: University of Stanford Press, 2001), 253–88, 255, 271.
3 Lucy Bland, *Banishing the Beast: English Feminism and Sexual Morality 1885-1914* (Harmondsworth: Penguin, 1995), 308.
4 Catriona Beaumont, *Housewives and Citizens: Domesticity and the Women's Movement, 1926-1964* (Manchester: Manchester University Press, 2013).
5 *Common Cause*, September 12, 1919, 277.
6 *Woman's Leader*, June 19, 1922, 142.
7 A Newnham Associate is an alumna elected by other alumnae in recognition of her notable contribution to the college and its students.
8 Clara Rackham, talk at memorial meeting for Blanch Athene Clough at Newnham College, October 22, 1960, typescript (TFP).
9 *Cambridge Independent Press*, November 7, 1919, 10.
10 W. Henry Brown, *Co-operation in a University Town* (London: Co-operative Printing Society, 1937), 48.
11 Richard Johnson and Ashley Walsh, *Camaraderie: One Hundred Years of Cambridge Labour Party 1912-2012* (Cambridge: Cambridge Labour Party, 2012), 15.
12 Hannah Mitchell, *The Hard Way Up: The Autobiography of Hannah Mitchell, Suffragette and Rebel* (London: Virago Press, 1984), 189.
13 Leah Manning, *A Life For Education: An Autobiography* (London: Gollancz, 1970), 56.
14 Ibid., 37.
15 Claire Debenham, unpublished Ph.D. thesis, 'Grass Roots Feminism: A Study of the Campaigns of the Society for the Provision of Birth Control Clinics, 1924-1938', University of Manchester, 2010.
16 Dora Russell, *The Tamarisk Tree: My Quest for Liberty and Lov*e (London: Elek/Pemberton, 1975), 188.
17 V. Williams and G. J. White, *Adult Education and Social Purpose: A History of the WEA Eastern District 1913-1988* (Cambridge: Graham Cameron Publishing, 1988), 50.
18 'Colleges for Working Women', Newnham College Roll Letter, (January 1921), 43–47, 4.
19 Ibid (January 1928), 1–2.
20 *R. H. Tawney's Commonplace Book* edited and with an introduction by, J. M. Winter and D. M. Joslin, *Economic History Review Supplement*, no 5 (Cambridge: Cambridge University Press, 1972), i–xxiv, ix. See entry September 18, 1912.
21 I. H. Quigly, Clara Dorothea Rackham (née Tabor) 1975–1966 (Newnham, 1895–1898), Newnham College Roll (January 1967), 48–51, 49.
22 *Essex Newsman*, November 1922, 1.
23 Roy Helmore, *CCAT: A Brief History* (Cambridge: Cambridgeshire College of Arts and Technology, 1989).
24 W. Sydney Robinson, *The Last Victorians: A Daring Reassessment of Four Twentieth-Century Eccentrics: Sir William Joynson-Hicks, Dean Inge, Lord Reith, and Sir Arthur Bryant* (London: Robson Press, 2014), 221.

25 Quoted Sarah Atwood, *Ruskin's Education and Ideas* (Aldershot: Ashgate, 2011), 53.
26 Reproduced in Harry Rée, ed., *The Henry Morris Collection* (Cambridge: Cambridge University Press, 1984), 13–33.
27 Harry Rée, *Educator Extraordinary: The Life and Achievement of Henry Morris 1889-1961* (London: Longman, 1973), 43.
28 Quoted Clyde Chitty, review David Rooney, *The Cambridgeshire Village Colleges and Community Education*, *Forum* 56, no 2 (2014), 319–21, 321.
29 Rée, 1984, 5.
30 Ibid, 39.
31 *The Cambridge Daily News*, January 28, 1939, 5.
32 See https://cambsvc.org.uk/category/sawston/, accessed July 5, 2021.
33 Mary Tabor, letter to Joyce Bellamy dated August 17, 1990 (TFP).
34 David Holland, letter to Clara Rackham dated October 25, 1965 (TFP).
35 Helen Pease, letter to Joyce Bellamy, dated October 19, 1980 (CDR U DLB/9/55), Hull History Centre Archive.
36 Clara Rackham, *Fabian Quarterly*, 'The Cambridgeshire Village Colleges', special issue on municipal election, no 47 (October 1945), 12–13, 12.
37 Report of the Departmental Committee on Medical Examination of Young Persons for Factory Employment, May 1924. Cmd.2135.
38 Louise A. Jackson, *Child Sexual Abuse in Victorian England* (London: Routledge, 2000), 65.
39 Report of the Departmental Committee on Sexual Offences against Young Persons, 1925, Cmd.2561. See also *Summary of the Report and Recommendations of the Departmental Committee on Sexual Offences against Young Persons* (London: National Council of Women, 1925).
40 https://first100years.org.uk/gertrude-tuckwell-londons-first-woman-magistrate/, accessed July 10, 2021.
41 Anne Logan, *Feminism and Criminal Justice: A Historical Perspective* (Basingstoke: Palgrave, 2008), 17.
42 Anne Logan, 'In Search of Equal Citizenship: The Campaign for Women Magistrates in England and Wales, 1910–1939', *Women's History Review* 16, no 4 (2007), 501-8, 505.
43 Carolyn Steedman, 'Prisonhouses', *Feminist Review* 20, (1985), 16.
44 Enid Huws Jones, *Margery Fry: The Essential Amateur* (Oxford: Oxford University Press, 1966), 133.
45 Ibid., 30.
46 Ibid., 31.
47 Ibid., 47.
48 Ibid., 91.
49 Fry (Sara) Margery (1874–1958), Thomas L. Hodgkin, *New Dictionary of Labour Biography*, 2004 revised Mark Pottle, 2007, 101–4, 102.
50 Ibid., 101.
51 Mick Ryan, *The Acceptable Pressure Group: Inequality in the Penal Lobby: A Case Study of the Howard League and RAP* (Farnborough: Saxon House, 1978), 32.
52 See Angela V. John, *Turning The Tide: The Life of Lady Rhondda* (Cardigan: Parthian, 2013).
53 Pamela L. Graves, *Labour Women: Women in British Working-Class Politics 1918-1939* (Cambridge: Cambridge University Press, 1994), 120.
54 *Woman's Leader*, December 1924.
55 Ibid., July 17, 1931.
56 Ibid., February 22, 1923, 4.

57 Ibid.
58 Ibid.
59 Allan Brigham, A Community in Transition – Romsey Town, Cambridge 1966-2006, https://www.colc.co.uk/cambridge/tours/articles3.htm, accessed June 20, 2020.
60 Mary Hobbs (n.d.) (ASH).
61 Sir Harold Shearman, letter to Clara Rackham, December 11, 1965 (TFP).
62 E. S. Bennett and fourteen others, letter dated February 23, 1924 found in Clara Rackham's visitors' book (TFP).
63 Ibid.
64 See Sibyl Oldfield, *Spinsters of this Parish: The Life and Times of F.M. Mayor and Mary Sheepshanks* (London: Virago, 1984).
65 Notes about Margery Fry taken by Anne Logan kindly made available to the author.
66 Brian Harrison oral history suffrage interviews, Miss Mary Tabor, interviewed, November 25, 1975, 8SUF/BO62, Women's Library, LSE.
67 Incidents related by Mary Hobbs (n.d.) (ASH).
68 Ibid.
69 *Lincolnshire Standard and Boston Guardian*, August 20, 1927, 11.
70 Margaret Llewelyn Davies, 'Foreword' to Catherine Webb, *The Woman with the Basket* (Manchester: Women's Co-operative Guild, 1927), 9–14, 12, 10.
71 Ibid., 12.
72 Jean Gaffin and David Thoms, *Caring and Sharing: The Centenary of the Co-operative Women's Guild* (Manchester: Holyoake, 1983), 274.
73 Sallie Purkiss, 'Over the Bridge: Another Cambridge between Two Wars: Communal Responses to Political, Economic and Social Changes, 1919-1938', unpublished MA dissertation, University of Essex, 1982.
74 Ibid., 15.
75 Hugh Dalton, *Call Back Yesterday*: *Memoirs 1931-45* (London: Muller, 1953), 130.
76 *Cambridge Daily News*, April 19, 1926, 3.
77 Manning, *A Life for Education*, 64–5.
78 Quoted William Ingram, Mill Road History Project, Building Report, Romsey Town Labour Club, 2015, 13. For an excellent account of the building of the club see https://www.capturingcambridge.org/wp-c ontent/uploads/2014/05/Romsey_Labour_Club 2nd_edn-rev.pdf, accessed June 1, 2020.
79 Manning, *A Life for Education*, 61.
80 Clara Rackham, 'Banishing the Basement Bogey', *Good Housekeeping* 1927, 54, 166, 168 (TFP).
81 Brian Harrison, Mary Tabor interview, 1975, Women's Library.
82 Obituary, Harris Rackham, MA, 1868–1944, *Christ's College Magazine* XLIX, no 159 (Easter 1944), 32.
83 *Woman's Leader*, September 14, 1928, 1.
84 See Law, *Suffrage and Power*, 172.
85 Clara Rackham, 'Protective Legislation in Industry', handwritten notes for a talk to the Fabian Society Women's Group, February 11, 1930 (TFP).
86 Graves, *Labour Women*, 149.
87 Johnson and Walsh, *Camaraderie*, 33.
88 *Cambridge Chronicle*, December 12, 1923 and February 13, 1924.
89 Clara Rackham, 'Old Students and Local Government', Newnham College Roll Letter, 1958, 19–23, 22.

90 Clara Rackham, 'When I am M.P.', *The Vote* XX1X, no 973 (June 15, 1928), 185.

91 Pat Thane, *Divided Kingdom: A History of Britain, 1900 to the Present* (Cambridge: Cambridge University Press, 2018), 103.

92 Brian Harrison, Rackham [née Tabor], Clara Dorothea (1875–1966), Oxford Dictionary of National Biography, 2004, 7223, 723.

93 F. W. Poole, letter to Joyce Bellamy dated October 30, 1980 (CDR U DLB/9/55), Hull History Centre Archive.

94 Appendix 2: Labour Women Members in Parliament, in Lucy Middleton, ed., *Women in the Labour Movement: The British Experience* (London: Croom Helm, 1977).

95 Andrew Thorpe, *A History of the British Labour Party* (London: Palgrave, 2015), 51.

96 Anne Logan, 'Political Life in the Shadows: The Post Suffrage Life of S. Margery Fry (1874-1958)', *Women's History Review* 23, no 3 (2014), 365-80, 366.

97 Manning, *A Life for Education*, 91.

98 Ibid., 75.

99 Pat Thane, 'Women, Liberalism and Citizenship, 1918-30', in *Citizenship and Community: Liberals, Radicals and Collective Identities in the British Isles, 1865-1931'*, ed. Eugenio. F. Biagini (Cambridge: Cambridge University Press, 2009), 66–92, 77.

100 Unpublished paper, Eileen Price, 'Review of Work Done on Study Leave', 1st August to 31st December, 1977, 1-15, 14, courtesy of Marie Thompson.

101 Press cutting dated July 1934, Miscellaneous Press Cuttings Collected by Harris Rackham between 1897 and 1938, Fellows Papers, 129a-b, Christ's College, Cambridge.

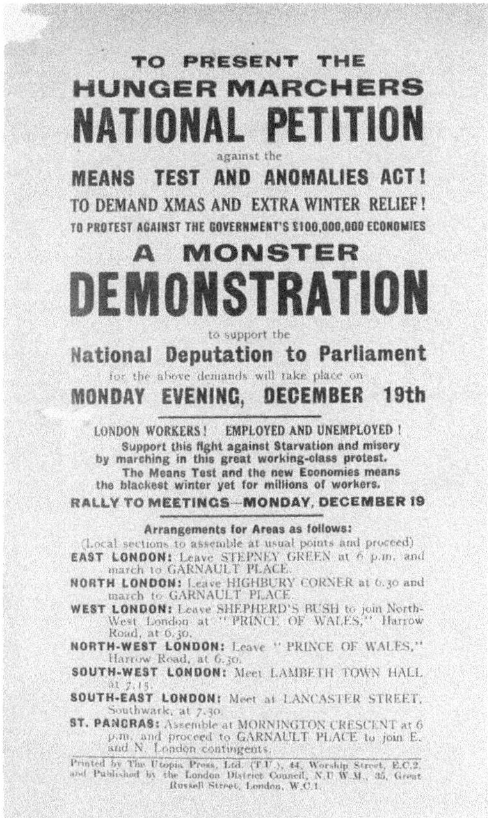

TO PRESENT THE
HUNGER MARCHERS
NATIONAL PETITION
against the
MEANS TEST AND ANOMALIES ACT!
TO DEMAND XMAS AND EXTRA WINTER RELIEF!
TO PROTEST AGAINST THE GOVERNMENT'S £100,000,000 ECONOMIES
A MONSTER
DEMONSTRATION
to support the
National Deputation to Parliament
for the above demands will take place on
MONDAY EVENING, DECEMBER 19th

LONDON WORKERS! EMPLOYED AND UNEMPLOYED!
Support this fight against Starvation and misery by marching in this great working-class protest.
The Means Test and the new Economies means the blackest winter yet for millions of workers.
RALLY TO MEETINGS—MONDAY, DECEMBER 19

Arrangements for Areas as follows:
(Local sections to assemble at usual points and proceed)
EAST LONDON: Leave STEPNEY GREEN at 6 p.m. and march to GARNAULT PLACE.
NORTH LONDON: Leave HIGHBURY CORNER at 6.30 and march to GARNAULT PLACE.
WEST LONDON: Leave SHEPHERD'S BUSH to join North-West London at "PRINCE OF WALES," Harrow Road, at 6.30.
NORTH-WEST LONDON: Leave "PRINCE OF WALES," Harrow Road, at 6.30.
SOUTH-WEST LONDON: Meet LAMBETH TOWN HALL at 7.15.
SOUTH-EAST LONDON: Meet at LANCASTER STREET, Southwark, at 7.30.
ST. PANCRAS: Assemble at MORNINGTON CRESCENT at 6 p.m. and proceed to GARNAULT PLACE to join E. and N. London contingents.

Printed by The Utopia Press, Ltd. (T.U.), 44, Worship Street, E.C.2, and Published by the London District Council, N.U.W.M., 35, Great Russell Street, London, W.C.1.

Figure 4.1 Leaflet advertising a demonstration against the Anomalies Act.

Figure 4.2 Clara and Margery Fry on their European Prison Tour. Courtesy of Helen Bloxsome and Lucy Tabor.

Figure 4.3 Clara wearing a favourite brooch. Courtesy of Helen Bloxsome and Lucy Tabor.

Figure 4.4 At a Children's Tea Party. Courtesy of Helen Bloxsome and Lucy Tabor.

Mr. Robert Davies and Mrs. C. Rackham leading the "No War Over Cuba" protest march.

Figure 4.5 Clara leads the 'Hands off Cuba' Demonstration.

Figure 4.6 Ruth Cohen and Clara on her ninetieth birthday.
Courtesy of Helen Bloxsome and Lucy Tabor.

Figure 4.7 9 Park Terrace as it is today. Courtesy of Carolyn Ferguson.

4 'That Intolerable Woman'

Fighting for the Unemployed

In June 1930 Clara chaired the three-day conference of the Labour Women's Conference in the Kingsway Hall in London, a huge conference with 1,184 participants.[1] The hall was too small, the agenda unwieldy, and the speakers sometimes inaudible. However, Dorothy Jewson reporting the event in *The Woman's Leader* praised Clara as 'an efficient Chairman who did her best to keep us all in order'.[2] The Second Labour Government had been in office for barely twelve months but without a working majority was wholly dependent on the vote of its opponents to get its legislation through parliament and was confronted with a global economic crisis after the crash of the Wall Street stock exchange in 1929.

The women's conference, voted overwhelmingly for the abolition of the marriage bar which compelled women in teaching and local government to give up their jobs on marriage. They endorsed the charter to prevent the exploitation of domestic workers prepared by the Standing Joint Committee of Industrial Women's Organisations (SJCIWO) which Clara had been instrumental in organising and for which she urged support in her opening Chairman's address:

> Last year we welcomed the domestic servants into the ranks of the voters: this year we call upon them to help in framing a charter which may, for the first time, create a general standard of conditions in this, the largest of women's occupations.[3]

The report on equal pay submitted by the SJCIWO and put to conference by Ellen Wilkinson was also passed[4]: 'If Miss Amy Johnson had a job as a motor mechanic she would probably be paid less than a man who had never been up in the air – just because she was a woman'.[5] Jennie Lee,[6] Clara's predecessor as Chairman, spoke in favour of the family allowance, a key issue for many feminists, which she explained was to be funded by direct taxation of the rich. The sums would be 'less than one-third of what we spend nationally on betting, less than one quarter of what we spend on drink, and not much more than one-half of what, with women's help, we spend on smoking'.[7] An emergency motion on unemployment ('a world-wide disaster, bringing its load of misery

DOI: 10.4324/9780429353499-5

to every country; the burden of armaments due to fear and mistrust is worldwide, too')[8] was sent directly from the conference to the Prime Minister.

The Prime Minister, Ramsay MacDonald had no coherent strategy for dealing with the economic downturn and put forward a variety of measures including job creation, taxing higher incomes, funding public works to the tune of one hundred million pounds and creating about 300,000 jobs between 1929 and 1931,[9] but struggled to devise a budget that would include tax rises, cuts in government expenditure, and reductions in the unemployment fund. The rank and file of the Labour Party were in sympathy with the unemployed. Swingeing cuts in unemployment benefits were anathema to them and MacDonald was fearful of a schism within his own party and resignations from his Cabinet.

Clara had already impressed Arthur Henderson and she enjoyed MacDonald's confidence too. Six month later she found herself appointed to the Royal Commission on Unemployment Insurance set up by Margaret Bondfield and chaired by a High Court Judge, Holman Gregory, with the remit of examining the Unemployment Insurance Scheme considered unaffordable, and by 1931 costing the government 120 million per year, only forty million of which was met by contributions'.[10] The other Labour Member appointed alongside Clara was Councillor William Asbury, the forthright Deputy Leader of Sheffield City Council, who was an expert on public health.

Work began in earnest. Raymond Streat, who represented the Lancashire cotton manufacturers, took an instant dislike to Clara, a 'hatchet-faced fanatic if ever there was one', and described their meeting in Manchester thus: 'Mrs Rackham looked daggers at me and got out a notebook – a sure way to stop anyone gabbling light-heartedly'. She 'said the will to work was there: that existing rates of unemployment benefit were too *small* not too large, and thought I had little or no grounds for suggesting the reverse in each case'.[11]

The effects of unemployment in the 1930 were not uniformly experienced but most keenly felt in the 'distressed areas' including Clydeside, the North-East, Lancashire, South Wales, and Yorkshire where the old staple industries of ship building, coal, iron and steel, engineering, and cotton had contracted badly or collapsed. In contrast, new (mostly light) industries manufacturing consumer goods, electrical and electronic devices and processed foods were established in the south, parts of the Midlands, London and the home counties bringing moderate prosperity and improved standards of living and making the 1930s a period of economic growth overall. Clara's own region, East Anglia, was not among the worst affected by the economic recession with some expansion in local industries, for example, at the Chivers jam factory, Pye Electronics, and Marshalls Aerospace in and around Cambridge.

In the 'distressed areas' unemployment compounded the endemic problems of housing, ill health, and poverty vividly described in the fiction, drama, memoirs, and discursive writing of the time such as George Orwell's *The Road to Wigan Pier* (1936), Walter Greenwood's *Love on the Dole* (1933), and Ellen Wilkinson's *The Town that was Murdered* (1939). It was 'this literature more than anything else which helped to shape the popular image of unemployment of unemployment as the principal social evil of the thirties'.[12]

Clara objected strongly to the humiliating household Means Test – detested in working-class communities – imposed by the National Government in 1931 while the Commission was still sitting. The Local Government Act of 1929 abolished the old workhouses and Boards of Guardians, which Clara was glad to see the back of, replacing them with Public Assistance Committees and transferred the responsibilities for poor relief to the local authorities. Relieving Officers were required to inspect the home, furniture, and incomes of the household members of all applicants for assistance in order to calculate (and often recommend reductions in) the 'dole', their visits frequently provoking anger and outrage.[13]

The first report of the Royal Commission, containing both a Majority Report and a Minority Report signed by the two Labour members, was published in 1931. Clara and Asbury disagreed fundamentally with the Majority recommendations and categorically rejected any reduction in the level of unemployment benefits and increase in workers' contributions. They objected in principle to the Majority supported system whereby some of the jobless would receive benefit as of right while others were required to apply to the local authority for relief on grounds of need. Their Minority Report argued for the introduction of a unified unemployment benefit scheme to cover all the unemployed financed by the Exchequer with some contributions from workers and employers administered through a system of Labour Exchanges run by the Ministry of Labour.

Further changes, ostensibly to prevent alleged abuses of the system but with the real purpose of saving millions for the Treasury, were proposed in the 'Anomalies Bill' which was supported in parliament by Marion Phillips, the Chief Woman Officer of the Labour Party, and Margaret Bondfield, Minister of Labour and the first woman ever to hold Cabinet office. The proposed legislation would require a married woman claiming unemployment benefit to satisfy the 'actively seeking work' criterion and to prove that such work existed in her district. As Helen McCarthy puts it, 'What women like Marion Phillips *really* cared about in the 1920s and 1930s was not the rights of working wives and mothers but measures which they had been demanding for decades: general investment in maternal and child welfare services'.[14] They wanted married women who needed to work to be able to do so while at the same time, making it possible for married women who wanted to be full-time homemakers to stay out of the labour market. Clara wrote to *The Times* to object to the discriminatory nature of the legislation in a letter dated December 3, 1931.

Clara was infuriated by the turn of events as were a predictably small number of Labour MPs including Ellen Wilkinson, Susan Lawrence, Jennie Lee, and Charles Trevelyan. 'Why do working women who claim their rights become spongers?' asked one MP, George Buchan.[15] On June 12 the *Common Cause* ran an editorial 'A New Threat to Married Women' urging that a national campaign be launched:

> The figures do not support the suggestion that married women are to any extent misusing the Fund. They are being forced back into industry by financial stringency in the home, at the same time they are the type of employees most readily dismissed when staff reductions have to be made.[16]

Like many men in the Labour Party Asbury was a staunch defender of the 'family wage' which entailed unquestioning acceptance of women's marginal place in the labour force. He made it clear that he stood with the majority of Commissioners on the question of married women[17] and the two Labour Commissioners agreed to live with their differences amicably and to go their separate ways. Clara was left to fight on alone. Women, she pointed out, paid more into the National Insurance Fund than they received. 'Between 1929 and 1931 men contributed more than three times as much as women did to the Fund, but they drew out just under *six times* as much in benefits'.[18] Moreover, it was invidious for the State to apply rules relating to marital status to women and to no other insured persons and to penalise married women who had traditionally worked in the Lancashire cotton mills and the Staffordshire potteries because job opportunities had dried up through no fault of their own. Huge protests, rallies, Demonstrations, and a national petition were organised against reductions in the Means Test and the Anomalies Act by the National Unemployed Workers' Movement (see Figure 4.1) but to no avail and the fiercely contended bill was passed with only thirty MPs voting against. The numbers of married women barred from unemployment benefits was estimated at over 134,000 by the end of 1931.[19]

The Cabinet was split down the middle over reductions in benefit and left office in August 1931, but MacDonald was persuaded to stay on to lead the first National Government and a Cabinet made up of four members of the Labour Party, four Conservatives and two Liberals.[20] It was this Cabinet that implemented the Majority Report including a reduction of unemployment benefits by approximately ten per cent. Clara responded to the news that MacDonald had formed a National Government with shock and disbelief as did the party rank and file. He was expelled from the Labour Party and vilified as a traitor and turncoat for the rest of his life and the Labour Party became the official opposition. All the Labour women MPs, Ellen Wilkinson, Jennie Lee, Edith Picton-Turbevill, Cynthia Mosley, Margaret Bondfield, Susan Lawrence, and even his most devoted admirer, Mary Agnes Hamilton, refused to follow MacDonald and were to forfeit their seats in the next election. So did Lucy Noel-Buxton who had picked up North Norfolk in a 1930 by-election and Leah Manning who won Islington East in a by-election (caused by Ethel Bentham's death that year).

The General Election of 1931 saw the National Government returned with a huge majority in an unmitigated disaster for the Labour Party which was reduced to a rump of fifty-two seats with not one woman MP and only Clement Attlee, Stafford Cripps, and George Lansbury with any Cabinet experience[21] and the pacifist, Lansbury became the new party leader. In Cambridge, a constituency where adherence to high-minded moral principle mattered and pacifist sentiment was strong, Lansbury had always commanded respect. Clara and Helen Pease could still remember Lansbury resigning his seat at Bromley and Bow in 1910 to fight (and lose) another election on the issue of votes for women, and as the defiant leader of the Poplar rates rebellion in which he and Susan Lawrence had gone to jail.

The Peace Pledge Union, which asked its members to sign a pledge renouncing war, founded in 1934 by the charismatic Dick Sheppard, Canon of St Paul's Cathedral, was active in Cambridge. Winifred Adams recollected Clara marching on one of their torchlight processions and that her adult nieces were expected to do so if staying with her, which they duly did.[22] Maurice Dobb was the moving spirit behind the Cambridge Anti-War Council and Bill Few, from the railway workers, chaired a peace rally attended by 10,000 people who listened to the Railway Silver Band on Parker's Piece in May 1935.[23]

Cambridge was not exempt from the miseries of the Depression – nowhere was – but in the gaiety of the May Balls or idyllic afternoons punting on the river it was easy for the young not to notice the shabby men on street corners selling matches and shoe laces. One undergraduate had been fined £3.00 for leaning out of his window at Gonville and Caius College and firing a catapult at a contingent of Hunger Marchers on their way to London to protest against the Means Test.[24] In 1934 John Cornford, a Communist student at King's College, helped to organise the reception for 120 Hunger Marchers from Teesside and Tyneside who passed through Cambridge on their way to London. Their faces left a lifelong impression on many who saw them including the young Margot Heinemann, a student at Newnham College, who had met the marchers at Girton College where they were served roadside meals by the students and medical students attended to painful blisters and sore feet. Clara was present at a large meeting at the Co-operative Hall organised to welcome the marchers addressed by their leader, Wilf Jobling, a softly spoken unemployed miner who died in the Spanish Civil War. The marchers were accommodated overnight in the Corn Exchange.[25] On May 18, 1935 Clara wrote to the *Daily Herald* arguing that children should always be entitled to free school milk on the grounds of poverty alone and never refused milk by claims that they were not *already* suffering from malnutrition.

It was not all work. Clara took her early morning swim in the river Cam every day often accompanied by the housekeeper. This would be followed by a strong cup of coffee, and, unrepentant chain smoker that she was, a cigarette, Egyptian or Turkish rather than Virginian. She sometimes inhaled through a cigarette holder with her eyes, shut, seemingly asleep while listening intently. Whenever she complained about the crowds of *hoi polloi* on the Backs, Harris teased her saying that he was 'more of a Socialist than she was!' adding 'Let them enjoy themselves!'[26] The couple enjoyed their walks along the paths and bridleways around the ploughed fields between Newnham and Coton, and spotted kingfishers and herons on their early evening walks to Haslingfield, Barton, or Madingley. Assorted friends would turn up without warning – those from London often bringing others with them – and after trudging with Clara and Harris through mud, chalk streams and spinneys where siskins, black caps, chiffchaffs, and tree warblers were duly identified, they would all sit up talking animatedly into the early hours of the morning.

Margaret Tabor had joined Essex County Council in 1931 and risen to be Chairman of the Essex Education Committee in 1935. She was never a member of the Labour Party, although thought to vote Labour, as did many of the extended Tabor family in Hertfordshire and north Essex. The raising of the school leaving age to fifteen – the holy grail of educational reformers – and the differentiation of the curriculum between girls and boys (both Margaret and Clara had experience as governors of girls' schools) were absorbing topics of conversation. Clara became a member of the Newnham College governing body in 1933 and Margaret an Associate in 1939.

Margaret, the 'artistic' one in the Tabor family enjoyed sketching, drawing and painting with oils and water colours, transfixed by a medieval saint, a decorative feature in an ancient church, or the contours of a classical sculpture as she filled one penny note book after another with painstaking notes for her short best-selling illustrated guide, *The Pictures in the Fitzwilliam Museum*, published by Heffers Bookshop in 1935. Edward's daughter, Lucy, went to Newnham College to read History in 1925 and was followed in 1926 by her cousin Mary who read Mathematics. There was much jubilation when Mary, having subsequently read for the bar, qualified as a barrister in 1932 and Lucy qualified as a Probation Officer in 1935. Arthur and Edyth's daughter,

Barbara, married Philip Soper, a chartered accountant, in 1935 and the couple moved to Johannesburg.

Clara was becoming increasingly prominent in the higher echelons of the WEA having been co-opted on to the Central (National) Executive Committee in 1934. In 1935 she was joined on the Executive by her friend, Lionel Elvin, Treasurer of the Eastern District, whom she first met when he was a Labour councillor in Cambridge. Elvin, a Fellow of Trinity Hall, who had, *inter alia*, taught the young Raymond Williams, was to become a commanding presence in the adult education movement and to be made Principal of Ruskin College, Oxford in 1944. Clara befriended the left-wing historian John Hampden Jackson, WEA Tutor organiser for rural education in Norfolk and later Director of Extra-Mural studies at Cambridge University. Although he was many years her junior, their attraction was immediate and Hampden's first book *Europe Since the War* published by Victor Gollancz in 1936 has the unmistakable imprint of their discussions about recent history and politics. Another good friendship was with Harold Shearman, Chairman of the Eastern District, appointed National Education Officer with responsibility for drafting national WEA publications in 1935. Clara took over from Shearman as District Chairman and was herself replaced two years later by Arthur Allen, a trade union official from the National Union of Boot and Shoe Operatives, based in Northamptonshire.

Clara frequently stayed with Tawney and Jeannette in their tiny cottage in Elscombe near Stroud in the Cotswolds. Rose Cottage stood alone on a steep hillside with its roof smothered in creeper and a wonderful view across the valley and down to the river Severn from the terrace. The amenities were primitive – drinking water had to be fetched from a distance – but Tawney's company was always stimulating and he would stride happily along on long walks with his sheepdog, Bob, talking about the WEA (he was President between 1928 and 1944) and taking pleasure in pointing out familiar objects in the woods and fields. Clara remembered Tawney as being 'somewhat remote from the practical considerations of life' and Jeannette once telling her about the mice getting into the store cupboard, eating their way through the jam covers and into the jam. His response was: 'Why don't you feed the mice? If you gave them some food for themselves, they would hardly take ours'.[27]

In 1936 the WEA set up a national Educational Advisory Committee with representation from the local districts and co-opted 'experts' with powers to draft policy statements and make recommendations directly to the Board of Education Consultative Committee and to government departments. In addition to Clara and to Elvin, the members included two familiar 'Cambridge names', Barbara Wootton and Shena Simon, a feminist and long-serving member of Manchester City Council who had donated the Wythenshawe Park to the city of Manchester in 1926 for the people of the Wythenshawe Estate.[28] Simon, 'one of the 'steamboat ladies' who had attended Newnham College, was largely responsible for drawing up the government report on secondary schools (the Spens Report) in 1938. The report recommended the introduction of a tripartite system of technical schools and secondary modern schools alongside grammar schools for children with academic ability. Clara, who had become used to defending the grammar schools to a largely unsympathetic and unresponsive Advisory Committee, wrote to Tawney whose *Secondary Education for All: a Policy for Labour* (1922) had been influential in shaping Labour's commitment to free, universal non-denominational secondary education, to express her forebodings: 'I am only a little nervous lest the standard of work in the "Grammar Schools" should seriously decline so that their products can no longer compete with the children of the Governing Classes who are educated in "public schools"'.[29]

In 1933 Clara embarked on a three-week tour of the Soviet Union from July to August 1933 travelling to Leningrad, Moscow, Rostov on Don and Khirkov in the Ukraine. Like many left-wing intellectuals she went to the Soviet Union in an attitude of curiosity; to find out for herself exactly how the Great Soviet Experiment worked. Such trips by socialists, disenchanted with the lack of social advance in their own society, were not uncommon. The novelist, Naomi Mitchison, for example, went on a trip organised by the Fabian Society with a party including Kitty Muggeridge and Christina Foyle in 1932, having discussed with Beatrice Webb what they should look for before they left. H. G. Wells was to go to Moscow in a quixotic attempt to enthuse Joseph Stalin with his own ideas about a socialist world state in 1934.

These tours were carefully orchestrated to allow Western tourists to meet 'ordinary' workers and to see aspects of a Communist society in which the Soviet Union took pride. Clara was shown art galleries, churches, ancient buildings, museums and the usual tourist sights, Red Square, the Kremlin, Lenin's tomb in Moscow and the Hermitage in Leningrad ('the horses look well fed'). She also visited a polyclinic, a children's sanatorium, a crèche, a 'proplylactorum', a collective farm, an elementary school, a workers' flat, a 'park of culture and rest', a tractor factory, an electric factory, a marriage and divorce bureau, and, of particular interest, a prison, where inmates did paid work as well as exercise and study.[30]

Clara would put aside her tiny Cambridge pocket diaries and purchase a small lined exercise book if she needed a more copious record of a special holiday or an important trip abroad, writing her impressions in pencil rather than her usual ink. Her Soviet journal, however, reveals little about her responses to the many contradictions she saw in Soviet society: the dead weight of bureaucracy that was everywhere, the shabby houses in need of paint and plaster alongside imposing *avant-garde* public buildings. There were also wondrous sights as yet unknown in England such as women driving the trams. Her visit did not dampen

Clara's socialist principles but neither did she ever look on the Soviet Union as a socialist utopia.

Clara was essentially a pragmatist. As Helen Pease once put it, she had 'no use for orators' and 'appeared to regard arguments on the "dictatorship of the proletariat" or the "class war"... as futile and mischievous as arguments on the Aryan heresy or Transubstantiation'.[31] She did, however, consider herself to be an ethical socialist, firmly on the left of the Labour Party. Although the Labour Party did not support the 'Popular Front' against Fascism, in which members of the Communist Party were prominently involved, Clara was happy to work with Communists, particularly in relation to the Hunger Marches and humanitarian aid for Spain in the 1930s.

Clara made a final attempt to become an MP in the constituency of Saffron Walden in the 1935 General Election. There were two impressively strong candidates in the constituency each with deep family roots in the Essex countryside. Her opponent, the sitting MP, R. A. Butler – RAB as he was always known – was clever, ambitious, and defending a safe majority of 16,000. His father, Montagu Sherard Dawes Butler was born in Bocking, and his first wife, Sydney Elizabeth, heir to a large personal fortune and the Courtauld world of sophistication, foreign travel, philanthropy, and the arts.

The son of the Governor of the Central Provinces of British Occupied India, RAB was born in India, had been appointed Under Secretary for India in the first National Government in 1932 and was largely responsible for the Government of India Act of 1935 which separated India from Burma. RAB also had family connections with Cambridge. His great uncle was the classicist Henry Montagu Butler, Master of Trinity College. RAB, a classisist himself, had been appointed a Fellow of Corpus Christi in 1925 and knew Harris, with whom there had been some scholarly exchanges. He had left an academic career for a parliamentary one in 1929 and was predicted to go far.

Saffron Walden was a traditional rural constituency, far removed in its demographic from the 'rough' end of Essex and the working-class towns full of East Londoners on the move like Dagenham, Ilford, or Southend-on-Sea. It had its share of rich socialists, and Labour Party benefactors including the idiosyncratic Daisy, Duchess of Warwick, who stood as an Independent Labour Party candidate against Anthony Eden in Warwick and Leamington in the General Election of 1923 and unsuccessfully attempted to give away her ancestral home of Easton Lodge, first to the Labour Party and then to the TUC. The tranquil village of Thaxted was also an unlikely hub of socialist activity: its Christian Socialist vicar, Conrad Noel (known as the 'red vicar') was long remembered for hanging the red flag, and the flag of Sinn Féin alongside the flag of St George in the splendid medieval church.

Clara launched her election campaign at a large enthusiastic meeting in the Co-operative Hall in Halstead addressed by Susan Lawrence who introduced Clara as 'my oldest and best friend',[32] and conducted her campaign on her bicycle touring all the surrounding villages. She apparently addressed eighty-one meetings in a fortnight, sometimes speaking up to six times a day; a remarkable feat, even by Clara's own standards, even if her idea of a 'meeting' was a few people at a bus shelter, clustered on the pavement, in the front room of a private house, or huddled at the back of cottages alongside flapping washing lines and strings of green beans on poles. She stressed not only her thirty years of public service in Cambridge but her local knowledge: she was an Essex woman and a countrywoman – well able to differentiate a Hereford cow from a Jersey or a Norfolk Red – and indeed the only woman to be standing for Labour in Essex. She had also submitted weighty evidence to the Royal Commission on Tithes in 1935.

Labour had set its sights nationally on winning fifty rural seats. The Manifesto in 1935 reflected the party's longstanding desire to redress deep-seated rural grievances. Alongside radical plans to tackle unemployment, and for the public ownership of banks, major industries and utilities, were Manifesto commitments to extend unemployment insurance to agricultural labourers, to abolish 'tied' cottages, to build affordable housing in the countryside, and for the public ownership of land.

RAB was invariably affable, good-humoured and courteous in his dealings with Clara, albeit somewhat amused by her candidacy, and they were to remain on cordial terms throughout his life. Social class mattered to him: Clara was a Tabor and the Tabors were an old Essex family to whom respect was owed. But he was essentially uncompromising in his defence of the austerity measures brought in by the National Government: 'When I am asked by the farm workers whether they will get a rise in wages by just putting a cross against the socialist candidate's name, I tell them that I do not think so'.[33]

Nobody in the tied cottages would admit openly to voting Labour. Clara spent much time talking surreptitiously to farm workers living in insanitary cottages with rotting linoleum, coal dust from the kitchen range, and rising damp on the inside walls. Valentine Ackland's *Country Conditions* had thrown a spotlight on rural poverty and squalid housing in 1934. The lack of unemployment insurance for which the National Union of Agricultural Workers had lobbied was the farm workers' most keenly felt grievance. Who better to represent them than the woman who had fought so hard against the reduction in the dole and who knew the relevant legislation inside out? The Labour-supporting *Daily Herald* which covered the Saffron Walden campaign commended Clara for 'putting up a great fight against the Under Secretary for India':

> She is generally accepted here as the ideal candidate for the constituency, because of her knowledge of local affairs and understanding of problems affecting the agricultural industry. Knowing the difficulties and struggles of the farm workers and their families, she is denouncing the National Government for its wage-cutting policy and exposing the manner in which it has held up the extension of unemployment insurance to agricultural workers. She points out that huge subsidies have been paid to farmers, but nothing has been done for the workers.[34]

Butler retained the seat with a vote of 19,669 seats against Clara's 9,633. Clara was enthusiastically re-adopted as the candidate in Saffron Walden and addressed a crowded meeting in Thaxted Church with Clement Attlee and Conrad Noel in 1937 but further elections were suspended until the end of the Second World War. The General Election of 1935 produced a smaller majority for the second National Government led by Stanley Baldwin. Lansbury resigned after refusing to support the use of force by the League of Nations against Mussolini in Abyssinia and Labour, now led by Clement Attlee, gained over a hundred seats reclaiming much of the ground lost in 1931. For the second time, Ellen Wilkinson, having moved from Middlesbrough to the safe seat of Jarrow, was the only Labour woman in the House.

In July 1936 Civil war broke out in Spain after the nationalist forces of General Francisco Franco overthrew the democratically elected government of Manuel Azana. For Clara, as for countless other socialists, the Spanish Civil War was to become one of the defining struggle of the decade, and indeed of their whole lives. Over 2,500 Britons responded to the Spanish government's appeal to join the International Brigades, over 500 of whom were never to return. Clara was devastated to learn of the death of John Cornford, the son of Francis Cornford and Frances Cornford (née Darwin), and a great-grandson of Charles Darwin, near Córdoba, the day before his twenty-first birthday in December; 1936 as well as numerous nurses, doctors, and others from the Aid Spain movement, including the sculptor and painter, Felicia Browne, the first British and only woman combatant to die in action. Clara had remained close to Leah Manning, Secretary of the Spanish Medical Aid Committee, who made many visits to Spain, and witnessed the destruction of the Basque town of Guernica by the Luftwaffe and Aviazione Legionaria in April 1937, immortalised in the painting by Pablo Picasso. A humanitarian appeal from Eleanor Rathbone had produced a magnificent response and consignments of shoes, clothing, toiletries and blankets were dispatched from Cambridge to the makeshift refugee camps on the French side of the border where disease and sickness was rife.

On May 23, 1937 Leah Manning organised the evacuation of 3,800 children from Bilbao with 95 *maestras* (women teachers), 170 Senoritas as helpers, and fifteen Catholic priests on the steamship HMS Habana which docked in Southampton on May 23, 1937.[35] The Catholic Church in the Basque country being unique in its opposition to Franco and support for the Republic. Twenty-nine of the exhausted and bewildered *niños* on board having been sea sick on a very rough crossing, travelled all day from a transit camp near Southampton and arrived at Cambridge Railway station. They were greeted by 500 cheering well-wishers and were treated to cocoa and iced cake in the Basque national colours at a reception in the Cambridge YMCA. Some went to Cambridge before being accommodated in a vicarage in the village of Pampisford in June, others to Theydon Bois, and the so-called 'Leah Manning House' in the care of the Salvation Army, yet others to Clapton and elsewhere.[36]

In his account of the evacuation *Only Three Weeks* Adrian Bell, suggests that the geographical dispersal of the children on the SS Habana to some 70 different locations was largely done at random and that the particular colony to which any child was sent was very much a matter of chance.[37] However, it is likely that Manning, who had become attached to the children from the orphanage in Bilboa, the Ayuda Social, set up and financed by the Socialist Party for the orphans of militiamen, personally intervened to ensure that the *niños* were sent to Cambridge where she knew that their cultural traditions would be respected.

Clara threw all her organisational skills and energy into the Basque Children's Committee. The Secretary was the historian J. H. Plumb of Christ's College and the Treasurer Francis Cornford, the classicist, who had lost his son in the Civil War. In addition to Clara herself there was Helen Grant, a Quaker and Hispanicist, Eva Hartree, J. A. Ryle, the physician and epidemiologist, F. L. Lucas, the literary scholar, G. E. Moore, the analytical philosopher, and J. B. Trend, Professor of Spanish. A committee stalwart was Jessie Stewart who had studied at Newnham College, and whose most noteworthy achievement before she became a key figure in the lives of the Bilbao orphans was introducing T. S. Eliot to Little Gidding. To support the orphans was to support the cause of democracy in Spain. Trade unionists, town and university groups, and students all wanted to help with fund-raising, organising parties, activities, holidays and outings, many like the Cornfords welcoming them into their own homes. A.S.L.E.F. drivers in Romsey supported two of the Basque children by organising a weekly subscription among their members.

The *niños* been taught to think of themselves 'as the children of heroes' and to honour the politics for which their fathers had given their lives. They did not speak the Basque language, and while they were happy to sing Basque songs, asked to remove a portrait of President Aguirre, leader of the conservative Basque Nationalists from their wall and to replace it with one of the socialist Azana.[38] Jessie Stewart's daughter, Frida (later Knight), who drove an ambulance in Spain, published *Songs of the Basque Children* (c.1938) with an introduction by the Duchess of Atholl and taught the children songs and dances which they performed to enthusiastic audiences in Cambridge and all over the country.

When the Pampisford vicarage could no longer house the niños they were moved to 10 Salisbury Villas, Tenison Road, which was made available to them by Jesus College in January 1938. As Kevin Myers points out, the Cambridge Hostel was an experiment in child-centred education which reflected the Committee's knowledge and understanding of the importance of the children's backgrounds and of their being allowed to discover and explore their own diverse identities. This 'was something that progressive educators in Cambridge clearly understood' and the teaching was conducted on broadly humanistic and secular lines.[39]

Clara would visit the children after their lessons when they were working with paint, clay, and plasticine or taking part in music, improvisation, drama, or dance. They had been deeply affected by the terrible events that they had seen and very few paintings were

> without an aeroplane, a burning house or a battleship belching fire – but after a few weeks village and farm scenes and strange flower pictures appeared more and more frequently and it became rare to see any reminder of the war.[40]

In 1936 Councillor Billy Briggs was appointed the first Labour Mayor of Cambridge and declined to attend the coronation of George V at Westminster Abbey to spare the voters of Cambridge the expense. The twenty-fifth anniversary of the Cambridge Labour Party in March was marked in style. Clement Attlee was the guest of honour at a silver jubilee gala dinner of tomato soup, roast beef or lamb and plum tart or trifle followed by cheese and biscuits at the Dorothy Ballroom attended by 400 people at three shillings per head. Clara addressed the diners after Attlee's speech and moved the toast to all Labour's past parliamentary candidates in Cambridge, including Hugh Dalton who was among the invited guests. In May Clara spoke at the opening of the new public library in Rock Road which served the new and fast growing Rock Estate.

In October 1937 Clara and Margery Fry set out on a fact-finding tour of prison conditions in Hungary and the Balkans (see Figure 4.2). The idea had come from Eleanor Rathbone who returned from a trip to Yugoslavia, Romania and Czechoslovakia with the Duchess of Atholl and reported on the 'strength of Nazi propaganda in all three countries (and of anti-Semitic sentiment in Romania in particular), and paradoxically, a tremendous eagerness for British ties'.[41] Romania was in the grip of a fascist government resembling Hitler's Germany, including similar anti-Jewish laws. Hungary had become stridently nationalistic and reliant on trade with Fascist Italy and Nazi Germany. Bulgaria had a terrible record on human rights.

The Howard League had become increasingly international in its outlook and was working in Geneva to set minimum internationally-agreed standards for the treatment of prisoners. It had its own concerns about violations of civil liberties, solitary confinement, hard labour, political prisoners, and torture in the Balkans, particularly where prisoners were suspected of Communist activity. The two women felt somewhat apprehensive. As Margery admitted, it felt 'curiously interfering' to 'accept their hospitality and help and then proceed to analyse and criticise their penal systems'.[42] The visit, in which Clara and Margery were permitted no access to political prisoners, did little to allay their fears and while they tried to be scrupulously fair in accentuating the positive, confirmed many of their worst suspicions.

In Hungary, Clara thought it 'remarkable to see at the great men's prison at Vac, an up-to-date hospital much superior to any prison hospital in Great Britain'[43] and all the prisoners receiving excellent dental surgery. Also remarkable were the prison industries although the prisoners' earnings were spent on bread in the canteen.[44] There was, on the whole, more light and air than was usual in English prisons, Clara wrote approvingly: 'Windows may be barred, but they are large and low with clear glass and often thrown right open'. Tuberculosis was prevalent. It 'was a sad sight to see long rows of men lying out in caged balconies, gazing it is true at a wonderful view across the Danube, but none of them reading or occupied in any way'.[45] The chief women's prison in the countryside had a large farm run by nuns. The 'atmosphere seemed kindly and punishments few. But it was strangely cold and dead'.[46] Procedures in the juvenile courts and the probation service appeared markedly less formal than in England.

They took an overnight train from Budapest to Romania with Margery paying for a first class sleeper and Clara making do with an ordinary compartment.[47] To avoid any impression of being an official British delegation, they had invited the Swedish psychiatrist and criminologist, Dr Olaf Kingsberg and Maja Kingsberg who joined them in Bucharest. Here they were struck by contrasts of ancient and modern: 'A group of peasants, with high caps, long skirts and tight leggings might have stepped off a Roman bas-relief, oil derricks and huge modern buildings would not surprise one in California'.[48] They were impressed to see women running free clinics, extraordinarily cheap rooms for students and working girls, and a scheme for free legal aid for poor women[49] and were assured by the Inspector General of Prisons that hard labour in the salt-mines had been discontinued.[50] Margery and Clara visited the Correctional Institute for Boys and Girls, remand prisons at Cluj and at Alba Julia, a prison for women serving long sentences at Mislea, and one for men at Aiud. In Bucharest they visited the Prince Nicolei Institution for

Boys, a hospital for girls with venereal disease, the Rescue and Remand Home for Girls and the Patronage Schools for Boys. Years later, in 1954, Anne Hobbs was surprised to receive a rather strange postcard with a photograph of a Boys Reformatory School taken in Bucharest in 1937: 'We were amused by the slightly surprising subject: a tinted photo of short-headed sullen-looking boys eating at a very long table'.[51] The two English women crossed the Danube in a ferry boat at Rustchuk. In Bulgaria they were refused permission to visit the notorious Slieven prison, rumoured to have 600 political prisoners, but shown around three others, Sofia, Vratza, and Plovdiv.

In Plovdiv with its dark wide-arched passages redeemed by sunny courtyards full of glorious chrysanthemums they saw life-sentence prisoners loaded with great chains weighing 60 pounds. 'Plovdiv carried one to the eighteenth century, Vratza to the end of the nineteenth, whilst Sofia wavered between the two', wrote Margery in *The Howard Journal*.[52] There were no children's courts in Bulgaria and no probation service. However, the prisons compared well in the matter of food. 'We saw few of the grey, hollow, shrunken faces so distressing in Roumania. A full kilogramme of bread is allowed per *diem* and meat is given four or five times a week'.[53] The prison system in Bulgaria, Margery's report concluded, 'is one of frank reliance on repression .... and a rather naive belief that fear can be made to act as the sufficient bulwark of society'.[54]

1938 saw the publication of *Factory Law*, Clara's compact and serviceable guide to the working of the Factory Act of 1937. The last general piece of factory legislation had been the Factory and Workshop Act of I90I. Much piecemeal change had come about since then. The new Act consolidated, modernised, or superseded what was on the statute books incorporating into English law the practical measures for which Clara and other 'insiders' in and around the old factory inspectorate had long been arguing. Clara welcomed the opportunity to explain how this would operate on a day-to day basis in simple accessible language directed primarily at the 'common reader'. As far as she was concerned, the arguments relating to the importance of health and safety could not be reiterated too often or to too many different audiences. In *Factory Law*, the history of factory legislation is depicted in Clara's usual amelioristic fashion as a series of incremental changes. Some, like the eradication of child labour from the workplace, of monumental importance, others gradual, almost imperceptible, but all won by and for ordinary working people in the face of entrenched opposition and powerful vested interests. The first chapter, a history of factory legislation from 1802 to 1937, demonstrates her encyclopaedic knowledge of how, when, and why specific industrial practices had changed for the better. This ends with the ironic description of Dickens's hard-nosed mill owners in Coketown in Dickens's *Hard Times* (1854) who consider themselves 'ruined' when inspectors questioned if they were justified in 'chopping people up with their machinery; they were utterly undone when it was hinted that perhaps they need not always make quite so much smoke'.[55]

Clara assigned a leading role to the International Labour Organisation (ILO) in Geneva in raising standards of labour legislation throughout the world. Successive British governments, she wrote critically, had 'not been very helpful on questions in which Great Britain lags behind some other countries'.[56] Moreover, Britain had conspicuously failed to ratify ILO conventions on annual holidays with pay and paid maternity entitlement for women workers. The unfinished business closest to the author's heart, the adoption of the 40-hour working week, was still very far on the legislative horizon.

In the meantime, the new Cambridge Guildhall, designed by the architect Charles Cowles-Voysey, was very near to completion at a cost of 150,000 pounds. It had none of the outward grandeur of John Belcher's designs for the market square that the ratepayers of Cambridge had in their wisdom refused to fund in 1897. But as far as Clara and other 'modernisers' on the borough council were concerned, the building at least had the virtue of being functional. If its façade lacked ornate pillars and columns it did at last provide a council chamber of a decent size and much needed new committee rooms and offices.

Alarming developments were taking place across Europe. The Nazis annexed Austria in March 1938. In September Neville Chamberlain returned from a meeting with Hitler in Munich with a promise of 'peace for our time' and a treaty that licensed the Nazi occupation of the Sudetenland in Czechoslovakia. Dalton suggested the paper that Chamberlain was brandishing at the airport had been 'torn from the pages of *Mein Kampf*'.[57] Clara loathed appeasement and in an impassioned speech to the League of Nations Union in the Mill Road Baptist Church on April 1, 1939 demanded that the League of Nations be strengthened and that it should take decisive action against the aggressors.[58] The pogroms, murders of Jews and attacks on Jewish homes and properties across Germany and Austria intensified after the *Kristallnacht* in November, 1938. In Parliament, Eleanor Rathbone (dubbed the 'Minister for Refugees') – a prophet without honour in her country – made repeated, despairing, and often unheeded appeals for the British to accept their responsibility towards refugees fleeing Fascism.

In May 1939 Clara attended the Labour Party fundraising bazaar in Cambridge opened by Violet Attlee.[59] While her daughters spent their pennies on the sideshows they exchanged snippets of news: the WEA summer party was being planned in the garden of Christ's and Clara had had some success in securing better signage of rural footpaths. Clara also spoke strongly in support of a motion overwhelmingly passed by the constituency Labour Party and the Trades Council roundly condemning the government for the introduction of conscription at the annual May Day rally.[60] With war looming on the horizon, the Education Committee narrowly voted in favour of Clara's proposal to employ married women as teachers. In August 1939 Eva Hartree, Secretary of the Cambridge Spanish Aid Committee, wrote to the *Cambridge Independent Press and Chronicle*, appealing for money to get Basque refugees out of the camps in France and into the countries that would accept them.[61]

War with Germany was declared on September 3, 1939 two days after Germany had invaded Poland. On September 6 Clara and Harris received the devastating news that Arthur had died of cancer at his home in Limpsfield in Surrey. The funeral directors had considered it too dangerous to drive his coffin to London for fear of the cortège being bombed and he was cremated in Croydon. Edyth was to live two years longer. Arthur's wish that their ashes be mingled and scattered at Golders' Green Crematorium, near the scene of their courtship, was respected.[62] No-one thought to raise the question of a public memorial that an artist of Arthur's stature and popularity might have been given in happier times.

The long-awaited opening of Impington Village College was completely overshadowed. Clara and Harris attended the quiet, simple ceremony appropriate to the sombre mood of times, if not to the importance of the college's world-class architectural design which was to influence London's Royal Festival Hall. What Oliver Bennett describes as a striking and understated 'exemplar of humanist modernism'[63] was one of only two buildings in England designed by Walter Gropius, a Jewish refugee from the Nazis and the leader of the German Bauhaus movement, with the English architect Edwin Maxwell Fry. Henry Moore had offered to donate a sculpture 'the family' to the college but the councillors voted against paying for it, despite Moore having said that he would accept a peppercorn fee. Nicholas Pevsner praised Impington Village College as 'one of the best buildings of its date in England, if not the best'.[64]

Notes

1 Dorothy Jewson, 'The Labour Women's Conference', *Woman's Leader*, June 13, 1930, 144. There were 919 delegates representing LP Women's Sections, 106 local parties, seventy-five Trade Unions, thirty socialist societies, and twelve Women's Co-operative Guild.
2 Ibid.
3 Chairman's address, June 13, 1930 (TFP). See Labour History Archive, vol. 3, Domestic Workers, LP/Dom/30, 44–65, 1930, People's History Museum, University of Central Lancashire.
4 See Laura Beers, *Red Ellen: The Life of Ellen Wilkinson, Socialist, Feminist, Internationalist* (Cambridge: Harvard University Press, 2016).
5 *Woman's Leader*, June 13, 1930, 144.
6 See Patricia Hollis, *Jennie Lee: A Life* (Oxford: Oxford University Press, 1997).
7 *Woman's Leader*, 144.

8 Joyce Bellamy and Eileen Price, 'Rackham, Clara Dorothea (1975–1966)', in *Dictionary of Labour Biography*, vol. ix, eds Joyce Bellamy and John Saville (Macmillan: Basingstoke, 1993), 232–8, 235.
9 Pat Thane, *Divided Kingdom: A History of Britain, 1900 to the Present* (Cambridge: Cambridge University Press, 2018), 112.
10 John Stevenson, *British Society 1914-45* (Penguin: Harmondsworth, 1990), 298.
11 Marguerite Dupree (ed.), *Lancashire and Whitehall: The Diary of Sir Raymond Street 1931-1939*, vol. 1 (Manchester: Manchester University Press, 1977), 45.
12 John Stevenson and Chris Cook, *Britain in the Depression: Society and Politics 1929-39* (London: Longman, 1994), 88.
13 Stephanie Ward, *Unemployment and the State in Britain: The Means Test and Protest in 1930s South Wales and North-East England* (Manchester: Manchester University Press, 2013), 100.
14 Helen McCarthy, *Double Lives: A History of Working Motherhood* (London: Bloomsbury, 2020), 155.
15 Keith Laybourn, '"Waking Up to the Fact That There Are Any Unemployed": Women, Unemployment and the Domestic Solution in Britain, 1918–1939', *History* 88, no. 4 (292) (October 2003), 606–23, 621.
16 *Common Cause*, June 12, 1931, 147.
17 *Sheffield Telegraph*, July 5, 1931.
18 Royal Commission on Unemployment Insurance, 1931–1932, Final Report, xiii, cmd.4185, 242–3. See also Susan Pedersen, *Family Dependence, and the Origins of the Welfare State, Britain and France 1914-1945* (Cambridge: Cambridge University Press, 1993), 304.
19 Stevenson, *British Society 1914-45*, 276.
20 Piers Brendon, *The Dark Valley: A Panorama of the 1930s* (London: Pimlico, 2001), 161.
21 Stevenson and Cook, *Britain in the Depression*, 119.
22 Winifred Adams, letter to Joyce Bellamy dated October 21, 1980 (CDR U DLB/9/55), Hull History Centre Archive.
23 *Cambridge Independent Press and Chronicle*, May 10, 1935, 8.
24 *Linconshire Echo*, October 28, 1932, 1.
25 *Hartlepool and Northern Daily Mail*, February 19, 1934, 1.
26 Winifred Adams (née Rackham) (n.d.), Anne Stevenson Hobbs (ASH).
27 Clara Rackham, 'Tawney at Home', typescript (n.d.) (TFP).
28 Chih-Hao Lee, 'The Workers' Educational Association and the Pursuit of Oxford Idealism, 1909-1949', unpublished Ph.D thesis, University or Cambridge, 2018, 229, 300, 301.
29 Clara Rackham, letter to R. H. Tawney dated January 7, 1939, quoted Lawrence Goldman, *The Life of R. H. Tawney: Socialism and History* (London: Bloomsbury, 2013), 212.
30 Clara Rackham, notebook, 'Russia 1933' (TFP).
31 Helen Pease, letter to Joyce Bellamy dated December 4, 1980 (CDR U DLB/9/55), Hull, History Centre Archive.
32 *Essex Newsman*, December 1, 1934, 1.
33 *Chelmsford Chronicle*, November 15, 1935, 12.
34 *Daily Herald*, October 30, 1935, 12.
35 Ron Bill and Stan Newens, *Leah Manning* (Harlow: Leah Manning Trust, 1991), 44.
36 Leah Manning, *A Life for Education: An Autobiography* (London: Victor Gollancz, 1970), 132.

37 Adrian Bell, *Only for Three Months: The Basque Children in Exile* (Norwich: Mousehold Press, 1996), 82.
38 Kevin Myers, 'National Identity, Citizenship and Education for Displacement: Spanish Refugee Children in Cambridge, 1937', *History of Education* 28, no 3 (1999), 313–25, 317.
39 Ibid., 325.
40 Jessie Stewart, *Recuerdos – The Basque Hostel at Cambridge* (Cambridge: magazine distributed by the *Cambridge Daily News*, 1939), 9.
41 Susan Pedersen, *Eleanor Rathbone and the Politics of Conscience* (New Haven, CT and London: Yale University Press, 2004), 284.
42 Margery Fry, 'General Survey', *Howard Journal* 5, no 1 (January 1938), 8.
43 Clara Rackham, 'Hungary', *Howard Journal* 5, no 1 (January 1938), 17–20, 17.
44 Ibid.
45 Ibid, 17.
46 Ibid, 18.
47 Anne Logan, *The Politics of Penal Reform: Margery Fry and the Howard League* (London: Routledge, 2018), 147.
48 S. Margery Fry, 'Roumania', *Howard Journal* 5, no 1 (January 1938), 20–7, 20.
49 Ibid.
50 Ibid., 44.
51 Anne Stevenson Hobbs, postcard from Clara Rackham, dated September 6, 1954 (ASH).
52 Fry, 'Roumania', 28.
53 Ibid., 30.
54 Ibid., 28.
55 Clara Rackham, *Factory Law* (London: Nelson, 1938), 20.
56 Ibid, 152.
57 Frank McDonough, *Neville Chamberlain, Appeasement and the British Road to War* (Manchester: Manchester University Press, 1998), 106.
58 *Cambridge Daily News*, April 1, 1939, 8.
59 *Cambridge Independent Press and Chronicle*, May 19, 1939, 5.
60 Ibid., May 12, 1939, 9.
61 Ibid., August 18, 1939, 9.
62 James Hamilton, *Arthur Rackham: A Life with Illustrations* (London: Pavilion, 2010), 165.
63 Oliver Bennett, 'Bauhaus and Moral Purpose: The Very Model of Modern Community Schools', *The Guardian*, November 17, 2015.
64 Nikolaus Pevsner, *The Buildings of England: Cambridgeshire* (Harmondsworth: Penguin, 1954), 332.

5 War

The term the 'People's War' coined by *Tribune* on May 31, 1940 was co-opted by the Ministry of Information to denote the war against Hitler and Fascism waged by and for the common people. The war arguably not only fostered a sense of national unity and purpose but also made a vastly extended state apparatus capable of gigantic feats of planning and mobilisation in the national interest acceptable across every strata of society.[1] It was a term that Clara and other socialists, working for a planned, democratic post-war society took to their hearts and quickly incorporated into their own rhetoric and strategic thinking.

As Cambridge prepared for war, ladders, buckets, sandbags, and syphons were assembled for fire-fighting rotas. Iron fencing posts and railings were removed; the cast iron bollards retained for their functional purpose of protecting pedestrians and keeping cows on the grass.[2] Children took the injunction to keep their gas masks with them at all times literally and took them into the learners' pool at Sheep's Green. Uniforms were everywhere; Red Cross Officers in stripes, the Women's Voluntary Service in plum and dark green, Royal Air Force officers in blue, the Women's Land Army in green. Academics left to join the armed forces or the civil service, some like J. H. Plumb quietly disappearing for top secret code-breaking duties in Bletchley Park. Two thousand students and staff from the University of London were relocated to Cambridge including old friends of Clara and Harris: Eglantyne Jebb's sister, Geraldine Jebb, Principal of Bedford College sent her students to Newnham College, some lodging with Maud Darwin. If Clara had ever felt happy and surrounded by kindred spirits in any institution it was the London School of Economics. By the time William Beveridge resigned as Director in 1937 the LSE had grown into a huge teaching centre with a global reputation. It was said that he had 'ruled over an empire on which the concrete never set'.[3]

Many LSE permanent staff and students were housed in Cambridge at Peterhouse College. One LSE student, Joy Dalling met her future husband, the socialist cultural critic, Raymond Williams, at a dance at the Dorothy Ballroom organised by the Cambridge University Socialist Club at which he was taking the admission tickets.[4] Male students and staff

DOI: 10.4324/9780429353499-6

from the School of Oriental and African Studies (SOAS) were sent to Christ's. Homerton College welcomed teacher-training students from badly bombed Portsmouth and Hull and allowed the Women's Land Army to train in their college grounds. Male students and academic staff from Queen Mary were evacuated to King's College and women to Girton, their presence swelling the ranks of the progressive left-leaning intelligentsia among whom Clara and Harris felt entirely at home.

Clara signed up for Air Raid Precaution duties believing it right to take her full share of the risks of war. 'ARP patrol' features regularly in her diary so we can conjecture that she set out for foot patrol with her regulation helmet, lapel badge, and armband, to greet neighbours, enforce the black-out, check the shelters, and report any shrapnel or overnight damage. Donkey Common was requisitioned as a holding camp for the Auxiliary Territorial Service (ATS), the women's branch of the army and temporary 'H shaped' huts with wooden bunk beds erected. Clara enjoyed talking to the khaki-clad recruits awaiting instructions to train as welders, drivers, and mechanics, and sorted out whatever practical problems for them that she could. Work had to be found for willing hands. When a vast consignment of antiquated First World War rifles arrived from the United States coated in machine oil, the Guildhall was commandeered for 250 women volunteers to clean and repair a batch of 8000 guns in a fortnight.[5]

Clara accepted LSE students as lodgers getting used to the hum of new voices on her staircase and the disconcerting sound of strange latchkeys in her own front door. Having resisted rearmament for as long as was decently possible – an admixture of hope, naivety, and a visceral detestation for war never really left her – Clara served as the Trades Council representative on the local tribunal that decided the fate of conscientious objectors. Only three per cent of COs went to jail, compared with thirty per cent in the First World War.[6] The very few who refused conscription, work on the land, or medical service outright included the pacifist Jack Overhill, a curmudgeonly pro-Soviet shoe repairer and autodictat, who would take his wonderfully vivid wartime diary with its fascinating account of working-class experience in Cambridge with him into the air raid shelter, leaving his money in the house.[7]

In February 1939 a memorial service was held at the Corn Exchange in memory of 5 Cambridge men who died in the International Brigade. In March the first train in the *Kindertransport* arrived bringing 2,000 children aged from 5 to 17 to East Anglia and over a hundred to Cambridge. On December 18, 1939 the *Cambridge Daily News* reported that refugees had increased from 350 to about 1250 since the war broke out and that, excepting London, Cambridge had accepted more refugees than any English town. Many joined refugee units of the British Army or worked in agriculture or domestic service. Others were 'men of learning'. When an elementary Red Cross first-aid class was started, a young instructor was surprised to find his class largely composed of famous scientists.[8] Greta Burkill, a Newnham alumna was behind much of the activity to bring refugees to safety in England. The fate of those fleeing the unimaginable horrors of Nazi-occupied Europe was never far from Clara's mind. She and Eva Hartree redoubled their efforts to see that all refugee children were welcomed. Housing refugees was voluntary as there was no government funding. Temporary homes with families or foster parents had to be found for them as well as places in schools. And not for the first time, Clara began knocking on the doors of her neighbours, and importuning her friends. Cambridge had two voluntary committees. The Secretary of the Cambridge Refugee Children's Committee responsible for unaccompanied children was Sibyl Hutton, a one-time suffragist and, like Eva and Clara, a longstanding member of the National Council of Women. Sibyl was married to Robert Hutton, the first Professor of Metallurgy, and the Huttons and the Rackhams became friends. Like the Burkills, the Huttons took refugee children into their own family home, in Latham Road.

The Cambridge Refugee Children's Committee 'comprised primarily of women, was concerned with the welfare of unaccompanied refugee children'; the Cambridge Refugee Committee, 'primarily men, raised the funds, controlled the money and were responsible for the needs of refugee families'.[9] By April 1940, the '55' club, a social centre with a canteen, reading room, music room, lecture room, and table tennis, was opened in a house rented at a notional cost from Jesus College at 55 Hills Road, and both committees moved their offices to the top floor of the building.[10]

Clara and Harris quickly reconciled themselves to an unfamiliar world of air-raid precautions, black-out regulations, and the privations of food queues and rationing which they acknowledged as not merely tolerable but eminently fair and reasonable. Besides, there was no need for anyone to fear the wolf at the door. A 'British Restaurant' guaranteeing one good, nutritious, coupon-free meal a day was installed in the aristocratic Pitt Club in Jesus Lane and in the Romsey Labour Club, had Clara been tempted by either. She was not.

At the outbreak of war, the Cambridge University Botanic Garden Syndicate appealed for help in the gardens. Harris, who had enjoyed outdoor work at Fennes and on his brother-in-law's farm in Canada, volunteered immediately and could be spotted hard at work with his hoe every afternoon.[11] Clara and Harris would tread their way home gingerly, leaning on one another's arm for support in the pitch darkness, past the ATS huts and the deeply dug air raid shelter trenches on Parker's Piece, in good time to draw the black-out curtains. During the winter afternoons and evenings they sat together in quiet companionship making do with a light, cold supper off a tray. The new egalitarianism of the war was well suited to their own ethical code; that nobody should benefit unfairly from the war, that privileged people like themselves should throw their lot in with everyone else. They followed foreign affairs closely: Clara, was a strong supporter of Nehru and the Indian independence movement. They would tune in to the BBC Home Service on the wireless at 6.00 pm to listen avidly for news of the war. The bulletins frequently ended with 'A number of our own aircraft are missing'. They would peruse their books and papers, often in silence, until it was time for bed.

In February 1941, the Cambridge Labour Party passed motions objecting to the suppression of the Communist *Daily Worker*, to infringements of civil liberties and free speech at home by the government, and to the arrest and detention of opponents of British policy in India.[12] Clara was kept busy with her committees and her council responsibilities. She organised the speakers for the popular Sunday meetings and discussions which flourished in the Labour Hall throughout the war and the activities that the Labour Party referred to as 'winning the peace' which were intended to ensure the sacrifices of ordinary people would be rewarded by vast improvements in post-war health, education, and living standards. On September 11, 1942 she gave a talk to the Fabian Society Women's Group in London suggesting how pressure might be exerted on local authorities to ensure that the advances that women had made by stepping into jobs in local government previously occupied by men could be continued after the war was over.[13]

What people expected from Clara were clearly-written, cogent reports, plans, and proposals (often without her name if they were for the local Party or for an organisation she supported) with structured arguments, findings, and recommendations. The reason that Clara was deputed to write so often was quite simply because nobody else could be found with her subject expertise and writing skills. For Clara, the act of writing was sedentary, requiring a desk or table top with ink-well and blotting paper to hand. She possessed a rickety old typewriter but more often than not her documents were handwritten and required silence and intense concentration. Moreover, reports could be exceedingly time-consuming. The Minority Report on Unemployment, for example, ran to 500 pages. She would fill her good fountain pen with black ink; it was either that or a sharpened pencil, covering sheet after sheet of paper in the neat, confident handwriting that had changed little since she was a girl. There was a small mahogany cabinet with shallow drawers alongside her desk. Anne Stevenson Wright, who inherited the cabinet, described it as 'an interesting artefact from the history of the Labour Party: remnants of labels still adhere to the drawers ('PENAL REFORM', 'UNEMPLOYMENT', 'LABOUR PARTY' etc.) and a much treasured – and very useful – piece of furniture'.[14]

On Tuesdays and Sunday afternoons there was the ever-popular 'Brains Trust' on the wireless and from 1942 a chance of hearing Margery Fry, Bertrand Russell, Jennie Lee, Barbara Wootton or Ellen Wilkinson join the regular panellists of Julian Huxley and Air Commander A. B. Campbell and C. M. Joad to answer 'brain teasers' sent in by the audience on a postcard. Joad was well-known in Fabian circles as a philanderer expelled from the Fabian Society for misbehaviour at a summer school.[15] Both Barbara and Margery were appointed governors of the BBC. In 1940 Winston Churchill replaced the discredited Neville Chamberlain as Prime Minister in the wartime coalition, the Labour Party having categorically refused to enter any government that Chamberlain led. Attlee, Morrison and Dalton, who had never wavered in their hatred of appeasement, were brought into government. Dalton's brief as Minister of Economic Warfare, housed in the Houghton Street buildings which the LSE had vacated in their move to Cambridge, was to apply his mind to the practical challenges of austerity. What should be prohibited in time of war? He decided that the proscribed items of clothing should include pleats, pockets, and long socks.

Margery had moved temporarily into a hotel in Cambridge persuaded by Susan Isaacs, an educational psychologist, to become joint Honorary Secretary to the research committee of the Cambridge Evacuation Survey set up to monitor the welfare and personal development of children evacuated to Cambridge. Cambridge had expected 24,000 evacuees but had received 6,700. By November 11, 1939 only 3,650 remained.[16] The others, missing family and friends, feeling lost, bereft and bewildered by their first encounters with cows and sheep and the unfamiliar domestic regimes of the countryside, were taken home by their parents, very largely because the expected bombing never materialised during the 'phoney war'. There were 'rather too many lions for the Xtians, i.e. psychologists, students, workers for the children',[17] Margery remarked in irony, and feeling decidedly under-occupied she set sail for France to investigate what could be done to help European artists and intellectuals fleeing the barbarians at the gate.

Mary Tabor made regular visits to her aunt and uncle in Cambridge. She left her job as Estates Manager for Norwich Corporation, to take charge of rehousing in Camberwell Borough Council in 1940 and then for the London Borough of Holborn in 1945.[18] Demand for rented accommodation for bombed-out Londoners far outstripped supply. She often recalled her baptism of fire: a singularly depressing time of 'going through agonies as to who these two rooms with a sink on the stairs was going to be let to and saying if only I could have a terrace of nice little houses with garden'.[19]

Another welcome visitor to Cambridge was R. H. Tawney, who took a room at 8 King's Parade and travelled by train from London and Gloucester to give lectures in Cambridge as Professor of Economic History at the evacuated LSE, two or three days a week.[20] Tawney, in uncharacteristically sombre and lugubrious form, dropped in to see Clara and Harris in Park Terrace more often than he had envisaged; he and

Jeannette having been bombed out of their London home in Mecklenburgh Square in October 1940 in the same bombing raids that gutted the house of the Tawney's illustrious neighbours, Leonard and Virginia Woolf.[21] Susan Lawrence's house in Millbank, once the home of Sidney and Beatrice Webb, also suffered severe bomb damage, forcing her out of London, but a task which gave her much pleasure was the selection of 365 extracts from poetry and prose for the diary produced by the Labour Party in 1940.

Clara took to attending meetings of the Cambridge Women's Co-operative Guild again. They had been valiantly advocating peace through international co-operation and selling the 'white poppy' since 1933, but pacifism had limited appeal once war broke out and her old branch was now much depleted. The Guild's chief campaigning issues included the establishment of nurseries, the prevention of juvenile delinquency, and the demand that the government compensate women living at home injured in bombing raids. In 1943 the Guild celebrated its Diamond Jubilee in the Royal Albert Hall and Clara's friends conferred her with a beautiful illuminated scroll and the 'freedom of the branch' to commemorate her forty-one years of membership. They also gave her a small silver brooch to mark the Cambridge branch's fiftieth anniversary in 1950 when Mrs Edwards was the President and Clara their guest of honour.[22] Clara promised to wear this at meetings and to pay a shilling into the funds if she forgot.

The intense public demand for information underpinned a massive expansion of adult education involving *inter alia* Labour Party branches, local education authorities, adult education institutes, the WEA, the Women's Co-operative Guild, and the Army Education Corps. The WEA flourished, its activities expanded and its influence and reputation grew exponentially. Mary Stott was appointed editor of the WEA journal, *The Highway*. William Temple, the first President of the WEA, whom Clara had known since they had played together as children, was appointed Archbishop of Canterbury in 1942. The Eastern District had lost Harold Shearman to the ranks in Mesopotamia and Lionel Elvin to the American Division of the Ministry of Information. In the absence of men of fighting age, the Eastern District recruited nineteen young women graduates ('the Sabine Women') as full-time tutor-organisers who between them 'held together the framework of the District's organisation in the counties throughout the war'.[23]

Clara no longer chaired the Eastern District but remained influential on its Executive Committee. In the first months of the war the district developed educational provision for evacuees from the industrial areas, refugees from Czechoslovakia and civil defence workers.[24] After the allied invasion of France the district proposed to start classes for German Prisoners of War 'to the consternation of the Foreign Office which claimed that WEA classes might infringe the prisoners' rights under the

Geneva Convention'.[25] Clara worked closely with Hampden Jackson and the new District Secretary Frank Jacques to develop classes in rural Norfolk and to use the war as a unique opportunity to develop working-class education. Years of organising and teaching summer schools for factory girls in Newnham College, of cycling in all weathers from one rural WEA class to another, had produced an intimate understanding of the needs and living conditions of the ordinary working-class students whose support was essential to upholding WEA democracy at a branch level during the war.

Other luminaries of the Eastern District; the principled, thoughtful Quaker, George Pateman, whom Clara had initially met at a NUWSS meeting in Letchworth, Harold Shearman, the mercurial Lionel Elvin, and Jackson himself were all committed socialists, and, like Clara, authorities on the problems of the rural areas. An occupational survey of WEA students conducted in 1938–1939 indicated that thirty-four per cent were manual workers, of whom twelve per cent were agricultural employees, the rest having office and clerical jobs together with a smattering of teachers and housewives.[26] The WEA in Norfolk under Jackson had a stronger history of engaging with agricultural workers than the village colleges in Cambridgeshire, a fact that was not lost on Henry Morris, and which Clara, did not allow him to forget.

WEA classes in the war were heavily reliant on the voluntary input of left-leaning women like Clara, tasked with directing the attention of factory workers from fuzes and widgets to ancient Rome or Elizabethan England and with educating the middle classes about working-class life. The most famous WEA lecture, Virginia Woolf's 'The Leaning Tower', was given to the WEA in Brighton in May 1940. Like Clara, many WEA tutors imparted their own reforming enthusiasm into courses on government, citizenship, and current affairs which inevitably returned to questions of defeating Fascism in Europe, or promoting social reform at home, thus helping to contribute to the well-chronicled shift to the left in the war years. Clara's own very popular university extension course 'How we are governed', held at Linton Village College from 1939–1940, reflected the insatiable demand for education in citizenship throughout the country.

The essential work order of March 1941 directed 'mobile women', i.e. women under the age of forty without dependants, into the war effort; engineering, shipbuilding, the buses, the railways, milk delivery, electrical works, hospitals, the Women's Royal Navy Service (WRENS), the Women's Auxiliary Airforce (WAAF), and the land army. If Clara was disappointed not to be asked back into the factory inspectorate, she gave no sign of it. But she must have marvelled at the skilled precision engineering work done by women in the factories which astonished even Churchill, warmed inwardly at the successful outcome of the first ever strike for equal pay by men and women, at the Glasgow Rolls Royce

Hillhead Factory in August 1942 and the gleaming new aircraft factories, with 'Music While You Work' broadcast by the BBC depicted in Lauder and Gilliat's morale-boosting melodrama *Millions Like Us* (1943).

In May 1941 Clara received a confidential letter from Churchill's Private Secretary, Anthony Bevir, informing her of the Prime Minister's intention to recommend her for an OBE in the King's forthcoming Birthday Honours List.[27] Clara refused the OBE due to a combination of modesty, dislike of the antiquated Honours system and anti-imperial sentiments. This was something that she never spoke of and indeed very few people, including close family, ever knew that the OBE had been declined.

Cambridge was initially lulled into a false sense of security because it was widely believed that the Luftwaffe would avoid the town to prevent Heidelberg being targeted by the RAF and that Hitler would not bomb Oxford because he planned to make it his headquarters if Germany won the war. While Cambridge was never bombed intensively like Portsmouth, Swansea, Coventry, or Hull, enemy planes would drop surplus bombs indiscriminately over isolated farms, agricultural land, and fenland villages in 'tip and run raids' on their return journeys. Marshall's Airport and the Mill Road railway station were used for troop movement and some terrible casualties were concentrated in the small tightly knit communities in Victorian and Edwardian terraces off Mill Road and the East Road.

Clara was deeply affected by the bombing on the night of June 18 to 19, 1940 which flattened numbers one to six Vicarage Terrace and badly damaged numbers seven to ten. It was a devastating attack which shook the community to its foundations. Of the nine people killed and three injured five were children. One, a baby, died in her cradle. The communal grief and horror was compounded on January 30, 1941 when another fatal bomb exploded on the Mill Road Bridge reducing two small railway workers' cottages to rubble, claiming the lives of two people and injuring ten others.

Air raid wardens and firewatchers were sometimes caught up in the carnage. Clara's friend, Peticia Courselles Robertson, who had organised shelter marshals for the whole borough, was on duty during the bombing raids of February 24, 1941 and died instantly. Peticia was married to Donald Robertson, Regius Professor of Greek at Trinity College, a friend of Harris's and of Francis Cornford. Like Clara, Peticia was a feminist, a suffragist and a member of the Labour Party. She had also been a pacifist and a supporter of the Women's International League for Peace and Freedom. Harris and Clara both attended her memorial service in the Chapel of Trinity College, Cambridge. In a separate incident in Romsey Town on August 29, a direct hit on Great Eastern Street demolished two houses leaving yawning craters in the street, claiming two deaths and seven injuries. In the main, college and university buildings escaped relatively unscathed although the Union Society building was badly damaged in 1942. In Cambridge it was the poorer parts of the town that accounted for most of the thirty people killed, and up to seventy injured, and where many of the fifty houses that were totally destroyed were located.

The Romsey Labour Club became a favourite haunt of the First Army after the ignominious retreat from Dunkirk in 1940 and before the allied invasion of Morocco and Algeria in 1942. The main hall was requisitioned as a community feeding centre and the old kitchen as a store for ARP wardens, but the rest of the club kept for recuperation and recreational purposes. Mill Road came into its own at weekends. Beer, thought to be crucial for civilian and military morale, was never rationed. Free club membership was offered to anyone in uniform, and soldiers awaiting orders to depart for North Africa, propped up the bar and took to the dance floor for their last tango or foxtrot at the morale-raising dances on Friday and Saturday nights.

The inspiration of the Cambridge Anglo-Soviet Friendship Society was Joseph Needham, a biochemist in Gowland Hopkins's world-famed laboratory. Needham approached Clara personally, inviting her to join a provisional committee under the Presidency of the Master of Trinity, including *inter alia* Albert Stubbs, Billy Briggs, Jessie Stewart, J. B. Trend, Max Newman, mathematician and code-breaker, Marxist economist, Maurice Dobb, Geraldine Jebb, and Vladimir Minorsky of SOAS, a Russian Orientalist.[28]

Clara's time was taken up organising film shows, exhibitions, lectures, and exchanges of leading scientists and scholars from what was always referred to as 'our great ally, the Soviet Union'. The society's most impressive achievement was to raise funds for two mobile X-ray units for the Russian front. Cambridge was the first English town (Edinburgh led the way) to hold an Anglo-Soviet Friendship week in September 1941. The greetings book contained 1,000 messages from the people of Cambridge to the Soviet Union. A flag day was to follow. Knitting parties were organised and collections of very English 'comforts' (cigarettes, razor blades and chocolate) for Christmas parcels for the Red Army.

After the Axis invasion of the Soviet Union in 1941, The Soviet Union became exceedingly popular. Factory workers enthusiastically turned out tanks for 'Uncle Joe' and as news of massive Soviet casualties came in, a campaign was launched to open a 'second front' in Europe. While much of the nation was in the grip of frenzied pro-Soviet feeling, the Ministry of Information (MOI) was attempting the impossible, trying to demonstrate its support for Soviet allies and to promote public understanding of Russian cultural achievements without encouraging support for the Communist Party at home.

Clara was one of three signatories of a controversial telegram sent to the Prime Minister. The others were Needham and the Reverend Martin Charlesworth, President of St John's College, a distinguished classicist recruiting code-breakers for Bletchley Park. Their missive stated that 'in common with the mass of our countrymen, we shall gladly support any action that relieves the pressure on our great ally, whatever sacrifice that imposes on ourselves'.[29] A lively exchange ensued in the *Cambridge Review* with an editorial pointing out that the three august signatories calling for sacrifice from others were unlikely to be asked to make any themselves. The irony of a pre-war pacifist or neo-pacifist like Clara demanding a more efficient and rigorous pursuance of war did not escape attention. It was suggested, moreover, that their actions had been instigated by the Communist Party, which all three strenuously denied.[30]

Clara helped to organise a crowded anniversary meeting and exhibition of daily life in the Soviet life sponsored by the MOI in Cambridge in June 1942'.[31] Needham left Cambridge for China in August and was instrumental in founding the United Nations Educational, Scientific and Cultural Organisation (he was said to have put the 'S' in UNESCO). In 1946 Clara opened Needham's *History is on Our Side* and was touched to see that he had dedicated the volume to her.[32]

The bombing of Pearl Harbour in 1941 vindicated those like Clara who had been outraged by the Japanese invasion of China 1937, the capture of Shanghai, Beijing and the massacre of women and children at Nanjing. Clara began to attend meetings of the Cambridge branch of the China Campaign Committees (CCC) run by Dorothy Woodman, Secretary of the Union of Democratic Control, and the long-term partner of Kingsley Martin. The committee was led nationally by Margery Fry and the left-wing publisher, Victor Gollancz and its principal objectives were providing humanitarian aid for China, the promotion of ancient Chinese civilisation and literature, and the culture of the modern Chinese Republic. They also organised a consumer boycott of labels of Japanese origin, cheap manufactured goods, tinned salmon, and crabmeat and most importantly of Japanese silk which was widely used in the manufacture of stockings. The boycott was aimed primarily at women – rayon and lisle stockings were promoted instead of silk – and was supported by the Cambridge branch of the Women's Co-operative Guild and Co-operative employees.

In 1942 the long-awaited Beveridge Report commissioned by the war time government was published, with its proposal for a new National Health Service free at the point of delivery, and a comprehensive system of social insurance 'from cradle to grave'. The report became a runaway success: well-thumbed copies circulated among the troops overseas and millions were sold at home: indeed, the queues to purchase an abridged version published by HMSO rivalled those of the other famous wartime queues; outside Billingsgate fish market or the cinema to see *Gone with the Wind* in Leicester Square. Within two weeks, a Gallup Poll discovered that nineteen out of twenty people had heard of the Beveridge Report and nine out of ten thought it should be implemented.[33] Writing to congratulate her brother, Jeannette Tawney confided that 'so many people are asking me to speak on your report but I say that I am not up to its technical details'.[34]

It was precisely the technical details in which Clara was interested. As she did the relevant calculations it became clear that Beveridge's projected reforms did not go far enough. Writing alongside the young Barbara Castle in an essay collection edited by William Robson of the LSE for the Fabian Society in 1943, Clara argued that the unemployment insurance 'scheme cannot be described as insurance in the commonly accepted use of the term as there is not and never has been any attempt to make the contributions cover the benefits'.[35] Moreover, the only way to finance this properly would be for the State's contribution to be greatly increased. But whatever her reservations, the Beveridge recommendations were the most comprehensive and far reaching that she had witnessed. And it looked as if the vision of a welfare state long dreamed of by progressive social theorists like herself was at last within reach.

In the meantime, RAB Butler (promoted from junior rank in the Foreign Office to President of the Board of Education despite his support for appeasement), had succeeded in persuading the Prime Minister of the need for educational reform. Churchill may well have accepted Butler's proposals in order to deflect attention away from the more radical Beveridge Report. The Butler Education Act which received its second reading in January 1944 and Royal Assent in August, sought to provide free education for children from the ages of five to fifteen and to create a tripartite selective system of grammar, secondary modern and technical schools administered by the local education authorities. School places were to be allocated according to the child's performance in the eleven-plus examination.

Butler, was, as ever, scrupulously fair and consulted dozens of educationalists, interested groups and individuals including the WEA, Tawney, Clement Attlee, the future Labour Prime Minister, Hugh Gaitskell, Attlee's Chancellor, and many of his other political opponents. Not for nothing did the term 'Butskellism' (a reference to Butler and to Gaitskell, a leader of the Labour Party) signify consensual government after the war. The Butler Education Act was implemented during the educational reconstruction from 1945. Only in the 1950s did the growing mistrust from educationalists and parents disillusioned by uninspiring 'secondary mods', 'sink schools', underfunded technical schools, and above all a glass ceiling on children's aspirations imposed at the age of eleven, gain momentum. The Act did, however, satisfy diehard defenders of the grammar school like Clara, whose specific objections were not to selection but to its lack of plans to raise the school leaving age to sixteen and not fifteen and the fact that direct grant schools were still to be permitted to charge fees. These two key features of the educational reorganisation undermined, she felt, the egalitarianism that was implicit in other aspects of the Welfare State such as the National Health Service.

1944 ushered in not only educational reform but for Clara also personal tragedy. Harris Rackham died quietly on March 20, 1944 in the week in which the allies captured the beautiful sixth-century abbey founded by St Benedict at Monte Cassino in the mountains of Lazio. Sortie after sortie of American-led bombers had reduced the splendid monastery to a black, sorry, charred, reproachful ruin. Many of the abbey's priceless art treasures and tens of thousands of medieval books and Latin manuscripts had been transferred to the Vatican by German Officers for safekeeping just a year earlier. It was an exceptionally lovely spring with yellow crocuses and white snowdrops blooming in profusion and blue scillas and blue and white wood anemones on the Cambridge Backs. Harris had been ill but still working on his translation of Pliny until a few days before his death. 'I am glad I was able to nurse my husband to the last and his end was very peaceful',[36] Clara confided to Helen Pease. Harris did not to live to celebrate the allied victory in Europe, the capitulation of Rome before the D-Day landings in Normandy, or to see Cambridge erupt with joy on VE day on May 8, a year later with jubilant crowds, singing, making VE signs, thronging the market place and dancing on Parker's Piece. Tables and chairs were set out for a street party in Gwydir Street which Clara attended dressed in black. She was still feeling grief-stricken and in no mood for festivities.

Harris Rackham was a sensitive, cultured man whose devotion to classical scholarship was only matched by his love of his wife, his home-life, and his extended family. The marriage was 'modern' in the sense that it was predicated on a commitment to an equal partnership. It was companionate in that it was cemented by their shared love of outdoor activity, sport, adventure and foreign travel. There was no place for deference in the Rackham household and any residual trace of their initial teacher-student relationship had disappeared with the old century. Clara was 'never any good at ski-ing' – Harris was – but she remembered 'some good fun with it at Villars and in the Engandine – Celerina'.[37] The couple had braved the skies together in an aeroplane on an unforgettable holiday in Corsica, wandered without a care around the fairy-tale pavements, stared at the standing stones of Palaggiu and the citadel at Ajaccio, and at the azure sea below. Holidays like this had been exhilarating and rejuvenating keeping them both remarkably fit and youthful for their respective ages.

The marital relationship might well have been different had either Harris or Clara resented the time the other spent on classical scholarship, and in the labour and women's movement respectively, but this was never the case. Hugh Dalton who knew them both well, once dismissed

Harris as 'rather an academic eunuch',[38] not a 'real man' by Dalton's standards, the implication being that Harris was effeminate or allowed himself to be totally dominated and 'henpecked' by his wife. But few, if any, of their acquaintances would have concurred. Rather, those who knew them best accepted Harris for what he was; a quiet, serious, diffident, limelight-averse intellectual, happy to be left alone with his gramophone records and Latin and Greek translations, but at the same time unfailingly supportive of Clara, deeply proud of her achievement, and totally committed to the causes in which she was often the more prominent but in which they both believed. Clara, in turn, was happy with a husband who had always loved her unconditionally, albeit too reserved and proper an English gentleman to feel much need to put his feelings into words. Reflecting on over forty years of married life together she must have looked back appreciatively on the many occasions when she had known, without needing to ask, that she could rely on Harris's presence and support; his tireless work as the President of the Cambridge Men's League for Women's Suffrage, and during the heated battles over the Anomalies Act which had reduced her to near despair. The unsigned obituary in *The Times* praised Harris's for his innovative translations of Cicero and Aristotle in the Loeb series published by Heinemann, designed to make the text accessible to the widest non-specialist readership printing the Greek or Latin on one side of the page and an English translation on the other. But *The Times* obituary brushed over Harris's political commitment, noting simply that 'in politics, he sympathized strongly with the Labour Party'.[39] In fact, Harris's socialist convictions differentiated him from the majority of those of his own social class. He was the first Chairman of the Cambridge University Labour Party when it was set up in 1923,[40] two years before Clara chaired the borough party in 1925. Until 1945 Cambridge University constituted a separate parliamentary constituency.

Friends were solicitous and not a little concerned about Clara's wellbeing. She appeared understandably subdued and sometimes a little distrait but they noticed that she was more inclined to be kind to herself: she joined an amateur play reading group, and enjoyed the films that came to Cambridge, particularly Anthony Asquith's war time drama *The Way to the Stars* and David Lean's adaptation of *Blithe Spirit* with Rex Harrison and Margaret Rutherford in 1945 but no distraction could compensate for the enormity of her loss. Clara's antidote to sadness had always been activity rather than introspection. As she never tired of explaining, she felt it necessary to devote so much of her life to solving other people's problems because she considered herself exceedingly fortunate to have had so few of her own.

Clara loved her home and the objects in it, but was attached to objects for their associations rather than their monetary value. With Harris gone, Arthur's rare presentation copies of his illustrated books lay unopened and gathering dust. Decisive action was necessary. Clara consigned the unique collection of, for the most part, signed and numbered limited editions, Lewis Carroll's *Alice in Wonderland* (1907), Oliver Goldsmith's *The Vicar of Wakefield* (1929), Christina Rossetti's *Goblin Market* (1933), and other gems, some with Arthur's three colour illustrations pasted in by hand, to packing cases and donated them to the Cambridge Central Library in 1944. The books were duly catalogued and kept intact and safe in the library's labyrinthine vaults far out of reach of the most determined of book thieves until the present day. Prescient librarians also purchased and added several volumes to what Arthur Rackham's biographer James Hamilton praised as 'probably the most important single collection in public hands in Great Britain'[41] after the acquisition of Flora Annie Steel's *English Fairy Tales* in 2011.

The pacifist history, the hallmark of the constituency party's activity in the 1930s, now struck many Labour Party activists as a liability, and non-violence as a woefully inadequate response to the horrors of Fascism in Europe and beyond. The pacifist Alex Wood remained a leading figure in the Cambridge Party having narrowly survived a tense meeting to discuss his differences with the Party in December 1936 – a letter from Clara who was unavoidably absent having been read out in his support.[42] But his influence was waning and he resigned as Labour's parliamentary candidate in 1943 to be replaced by Arthur Lesley Symonds, a local man who had attended the Perse School and Jesus College before leaving Cambridge in the 1930s to teach history in a boys' school in Cornwall.

Wood and Symonds were polar opposites. The latter had a distinguished war record with the eighth army in the desert and in the Italian campaigns, mentioned in dispatches and rising to the rank of Major. Symonds returned to Cambridge from Italy as a 'war hero' to fight the Election in military uniform while the war on the Eastern front still raged. He was, by all accounts, a brilliant speaker, described himself as a 'patriot' on his election address appealing to the ordinary voter in the familiar rhetoric of the 'People's War': 'the whole people must win the war, the whole country must win the peace' on his election address.

The General Election of 1945 resulted in a landslide for Labour with a net gain of 239 seats and 47.7 per cent of the total vote. In Cambridge, Symonds was elected as the Cambridge's first Labour MP, at the age of thirty-four the youngest in parliament, with a majority of 682. Years of campaigning for Labour in the villages on his unmistakeable motor bike had paid off for Albert Stubbs who was returned as the MP for Cambridgeshire by a wafer thin majority of forty-four votes. The WEA stalwart, Arthur Allen, of the National Union of Boot and Shoe Operatives, was elected to represent Bosworth. Two other old friends of Clara's, former Romsey councillor, David Hardman, and Leah Manning were returned as MPs in Darlington and Epping respectively, Leah having prudently ascertained that Winston Churchill would not be her opponent in the new Essex constituency before putting herself forward. Hugh Dalton was back in the Cabinet as Chancellor of the Exchequer but not for long: he was forced to resign when leaked information was published in the evening papers before the budget speech in 1947.

Clara had very high hopes and expectations of the Attlee government. All around her she could see ordinary men and women reading the Labour-supporting the *Daily Mirror*, some radicalised and transformed by their struggle against Fascism abroad, many excited by the Labour Party's promise to create a fair and democratic society with jobs and opportunities for everyone at home. As Paul Addison put it; taking the war years as a whole, 'the Right was politically quiescent while the Left kept up a barrage of activity and propaganda'.[43] Now it seemed as if all the hard work put in to ensure that good adult education during the war would produce an educated democracy and good governance afterwards had paid off. More than one hundred of the Labour MPs who sang the 'Red Flag' in the House of Commons in August 1945 'were connected to the WEA in some fashion, whether as students or as tutors'.[44]

Notes

1 See James Hinton, *Nine Wartime Lives: Mass-Observation and the Making of the Modern Self* (Oxford: Oxford University Press, 2010) for a study of how Mass-observation volunteers explored the paradoxes of wartime identity and how their diaries often reveal a very different sense of selfhood from that of the cheerful cockney stoic immortalised in the nostalgic 'myth of the blitz'.
2 Allan Brigham, *A Brush With the Past: Cambridge Local* History (Cambridge: Cambridge Place Publishing, 2020), 20.
3 Quoted, Ann Oakley, *Barbara Wootton, Social Science and Public Policy in the Twentieth Century* (London: Bloomsbury, 2011), 189.
4 Raymond Williams, 'My Cambridge', in *Raymond Williams, What I Came to Say* (London: Hutchinson), 1989), 314, 7.
5 Angus Calder, *The People's War: Britain, 1939-1945* (London: Jonathan Cape, 1969), 125.
6 James Hinton, *Protests and Visions: Peace Politics in 20th Century Britain* (London: Hutchinson Radius, 1989), 130.
7 Peter Searby, ed., *Cambridge at War: The Diary of Jack Overhill 1939-1945* (Cambridge: Cambridgeshire Records Society, 2010), xvii–xlviii, xxxix.
8 *Cambridge Daily News*, December 18, 1939, 6.
9 Preface to Gertrude Dubrovsky, *Six from Leipzig* (London: Valentine Mitchell, 2003).
10 Ibid., 46.
11 Obituary, 'Harris Rackham' (n.d.) Christ's College, Cambridge.
12 CLP Minute Book, June 4, 1936–November 1936–May 5, 1941 (K634/ob1/7/), Cambridgeshire Archive, Ely.

13 Clara Rackham, 'Women in Local Government', handwritten notes, September 11, 1942 (TFP).
14 Anne Stevenson Wright, own recollections (n.d.) (ASH).
15 Oakley, *Barbara Wootton*, 97.
16 Calder, *The People's War*, 45.
17 Enid Huws Jones, *Margery Fry: The Essential Amateur* (Oxford: Oxford University Press, 1966), 196.
18 Mary Ruth Tabor, MBE, Newnham College Roll Letter, 2003.
19 https://www.stevenage.gov.uk/stevenage-museum/blog/mary-tabor-housing-officer, accessed March 16, 2021.
20 Lawrence Goldman, *The Life of R. H. Tawney* (London: Bloomsbury, 2013), 251.
21 Ibid., 251–2.
22 A. K. Edwards, letter to Joyce Bellamy, October 16, 1980 (CDR U DLB/9/55), Hull History Centre Archive.
23 V. Williams and G. J. White, *Adult Education and Social Purpose: A History of the WEA Eastern District 1913-1988* (Cambridge: Graham-Cameron, 1988), 130.
24 Harold Sherman, 'The First Months: The WEA Carries on', *Adult Education* xii, (1939), xiii.
25 John Field, 'Survival, Growth and Retreat: The WEA in Wartime, 1939-45', in *A Ministry of Enthusiasm: Centenary Essays on the Workers' Educational Association*, ed. Stephen K. Roberts, (London: Pluto Press, 2003), 131-52, 136.
26 Vivian Williams, 'The Eastern District of the Workers' Educational Association: Growth and Development, 1913-40', unpublished Ph.D. thesis, University of London, 1979, 587, 601.
27 Anthony Bevir, letter to Clara Rackham dated May 21, 1941 (TFP).
28 'Anglo-Soviet Friendship' (NCUACS 54.3.95/k.120), 118–22, Cambridge University Library Dept of Manuscripts and Archives.
29 Ibid.
30 *Cambridge Review* LV111, no 1533 (October 25, 1941), 1.
31 Ibid., k.119.
32 Joseph Needham, *History is on Our Side: A Contribution to Political Religion and Scientific Faith* (London: Allen and Unwin, 1946).
33 Calder, *The People's War*, 528.
34 Quoted Goldman, *Life of R. H. Tawney*, 267.
35 Clara Rackham, 'Unemployment Insurance', in *Social Security*, ed. William Robson (London: Allen and Unwin, 1943), 125–37, 137.
36 Clara Rackham, letter to Helen Pease dated March 26, 1944, (C.525, Pease, H. B., letters to Helen Bowen Pease, chiefly from C. D. Rackham, 1944–1964), Cambridgeshire Collection, Cambridge Central Library.
37 Clara Rackham, letter to Anne Hobbs, dated January 21, 1965 (ASH).
38 The Political Diary of Hugh Dalton 1918-1940, 1945-1960, December 6–8, 1919, unpublished ms, quoted Joyce M. Bellamy and Eileen Price in 'Rackham, Clara Dorothea (1875–1966) Labour Alderman, Social Reformer and Educationalist', Joyce M. Bellamy, and John Saville eds. *Dictionary of Labour Biography*, vol. ix (1993), 232–8, 233.
39 Obituary, Harris Rackham, *The Times*, March 21, 1944, 6.
40 Lionel Elvin, 'Socialism in the University', in *Silver Jubilee, 1912-1937: Twenty Five Years in the History of the Cambridge Labour Party*, ed. David Hardman (Cambridge: Cambridge Labour Party, 1937), 26–7, 26.

41 James Hamilton, *Arthur Rackham A Life with Illustration* (London: Pavilion, 1990), 191.
42 December 1936, CLP Minute Book, June 4, 1936–November 1936–May 5, 1941, (K634/ob1/7/), Cambridgeshire County Archive, Ely.
43 Paul Addison, *The Road to 1945: British Politics and the Second World War* (London: Jonathan Cape, 1975), 128.
44 Goldman, *Life of R, H. Tawney*, 271.

6 After the Deluge

The Labour landslide changed everything. Clara put herself forward as a councillor for Romsey for the last time in 1945, having co-authored the far-sighted manifesto *Labour's Plan for Cambridge*, and was returned unopposed. But ordinary people returning to Cambridge after the war, reacting with disappointment to drabness, rationing and austerity, were finding it psychologically impossible to understand how a victorious nation was literally verging on bankruptcy and beholden to the United States to the tune of millions under the Marshall Plan. The pressing need confronting the cash-strapped local authority was for new housing; for as many 'prefabs', flats, and houses to be built as fast as possible. The council housing list of 2,500 people was expanding at 500 per annum,[1] and some families on the waiting list were still living in accommodation that had been condemned as unfit for human habitation.

In the 'spirit of forty five', and the brave new world initiated by the Attlee government, the Labour Party in Cambridge had formulated ambitious proposals to build an abattoir, a central concert hall, a municipal sports ground, and a new public library as well as the covered swimming pool for which 2,000 people petitioned in 1950 and for which the requisite land, money, and planning permission had somehow to be found. The more intractable the intellectual and practical challenge before her, the happier Clara, who could still reckon on the energy and stamina of someone half her age, appeared to be. Her health, apart from her hearing which was deteriorating rapidly, was remarkably good. But she was quite open about the problems that her deafness was causing her; lip-reading as best she could while struggling hard to hear what was being said in meetings.

In 1947 Clara reviewed Seebohm Rowntree's survey on the housing and care needs of the elderly. Her review for the Nuffield Foundation was an opportunity to take stock of the available housing options if and when she became too frail to live on her own. Mary Tabor remembered that her aunt 'felt most proud of her part in changing attitudes to the poor, e.g. the improved conditions for the old in residential homes as compared to the Workhouse'.[2] Rowntree's investigators had uncovered no cases of the kind of acute poverty found in rural Cambridgeshire

DOI: 10.4324/9780429353499-7

before the war. Clara attributed this to the Pensions Act passed by the wartime coalition in 1940 and to the supplementary pension. Moreover, the report identified a demand for new purpose built self-contained bungalows and flats and small residential homes with prive rooms where residents could live in communities and come and go as they please. She noted that 'Where such Homes or Hostels exist to-day, their waiting list is very long'.[3]

The time had come to dispose of Arthur's paintings and drawings so that they could be enjoyed by the public *ad perpetuum*. Clara loaned several to the Cambridgeshire County Council Pictures in Schools Scheme instigated by Nan Youngman, the county Art Advisor, appointed by William Morris, who had been active in left wing and anti-Fascist causes in the 1930s. Youngman had moved to Cambridge in 1946 with her partner, the sculptor and educationalist Betty Rea, and the two women set up home together at Papermills in Newmarket Road. Betty was a founding member of the Communist Party Artists' group, the Artists' Refugee Committee, and Chair of the Arts Peace Campaign. She and Nan were committed to art as a medium for change, to communal childcare and many progressive causes and attracted other creative left-leaning artists and activists around them. Papermills was to become the hub of exciting artistic and community-based initiatives in and around Cambridge after the war.

Uncharacteristically, since Clara was meticulous about such things, no record appears to have been kept of the whereabouts of Arthur's pictures. They disappeared from schools, art galleries, colleges, cash-strapped local authorities, and public buildings and found their way to sale rooms and private homes as did other paintings which had been loaned out.[4] In 2012 an exquisite pen and ink watercolour by Arthur Rackham, 'The Incoming Tide' was rescued from a rubbish skip at an educational establishment in Cambridge by two passers-by who put it up for sale at Phillips auction house. The sale was stopped when a vigilant Anne Stevenson Wright spotted the listing in the Sotheby's catalogue and successfully disputed ownership. The painting is now back with the family and destined for public display in the Fitzwilliam Museum.[5]

Clara resigned as a JP in 1950 having reached the age limit of seventy-five. She relates some of her early experiences in 'Thirty Years on the Bench': 'I was to see you once a fortnight and stop thieving for a year, one boy had said when asked if he understood what Probation meant.[6] Clara was elevated to Alderman by the borough and by the county in 1950. She joined the Humanist Association and took to waiting outside the council chamber until the prayers held before meetings had finished. Clara turned down the Mayorality of Cambridge which organised acts of religious worship before council meetings but agreed to chair Cambridgeshire County Council which did not.

In a letter to Joyce Bellamy, Helen Pease described Clara as a 'militant atheist' but this description was queried by Mary Tabor and the words 'militant atheist' were subsequently never used in the *Dictionary of Labour Biography*.[7] What is not in dispute is that Clara had come to feel increasingly resentful about the churches' opposition to the two things in which she had always believed passionately, women's rights and free non-denominational education and was finding ways, subtle and not so subtle, or venting her displeasure. Church schools appear to have been a key issue of contention. Nobody could ever remember her attending the opening of a new church school by the Bishop and she was sometimes suspected of conducting a war of attrition with the diocese while at the same managing to remain on good terms with individual Anglican clergymen.[8]

Visits to Cambridge by younger members of her family were a never-ending source of pleasure. Her great-niece, Anne Hobbs recalled visiting Clara with her mother when she was six in 1948 and that 'we stayed (all of us?) when I was 12, in 1954. I vaguely remember a housekeeper, but not her name'.[9] Her other great-nieces, Helen Bloxsome and Lucy Tabor, recollected the picture books at Park Terrace and being told bedtime stories. Helen once arrived with a cold and was solicitously tucked up in bed. Sarah Rackham has memories of singing songs with Clara and being taught the words of the anthem, 'Jerusalem' by William Blake.[10]

Clara resumed her friendship with Ruth Cohen who had returned to the Faculty of Economics. Economists in Cambridge and across the world, were mourning John Maynard Keynes, who died without warning shortly after the Bretton Woods Conference of 1945 leaving his mother, Florence, Ada Keynes and much of the Cambridge intelligentsia in a state of shock. On New Year's Day in 1946 Clara's old friend Eleanor Rathbone also died unexpectedly, having lived to see parliament vote for the Family Allowance in her wheelchair, and to launch her final courageous humanitarian mission; to send food to the starving people of Germany.

Among Clara's newer friends was Lucy Munby, married to Lionel Munby, the Communist Historian at the Board of Extra-Mural Studies. Lucy recollected an impromptu visit to Park Terrace with her daughter, Zoë, and feeling thoroughly disconcerted by Clara's advice that she should attach the toddler to reins which were fashionable at the time: 'Clara Rackham knew nothing about children and I was much too polite to tell her that harnesses were intended for horses and dogs and certainly not for my little girl'.[11]

Clara kept herself busy opening fetes and flower shows, addressing teachers and Parent's Associations, and attending the school-prize givings for which she was in constant demand as a speaker, for example, at King's Lynn School, Bottisham Village College, Burwell School, Orton Hall School Peterborough, Ely High School, Impington Village College, and Sawston Village College.[12] Getting the train into London took an effort and when she did so it was often for business meetings, for example, with the Howard League, the Fabian Society and 'Old' Fabians led by William Robson who were 'developing radical solutions for the problem of poverty' and carrying on the 'traditions laid down by the Webbs and other leading Fabians of the last generation'.[13] Robson's edited volume *Social Security* published in 1943 contained chapters by Herbert Marshall, Joan Simeon Clarke, and a young Barbara Castle. In her own contribution on unemployment insurance Clara applauded the vindication of her battles against sexual discrimination in the 1930s: It is a

> welcome fact that the Anomalies Regulations which applied special and onerous conditions to married women who claimed unemployment benefit have been swept away, and married women who remain in insurance will not in future have to satisfy any conditions which do not apply to men.[14]

Lawless Youth: A Challenge to Europe prepared by the International Committee of the Howard League for Penal Reform was published in 1947. The book, researched by an international committee consisting of Clara herself and Margery Fry, M. Gruhut, Hermann Mannheim and Wanda Grabinska, sets out a policy for the Juvenile Courts across Europe. Clara draws comparisons with Holland, Norway, Poland and Switzerland, appraising the aftercare of boys and girls leaving approved schools and children's homes to live in hostels, 'boarding out', in lodgings or foster-parents, and reviews the ancillary services provided for them by voluntary bodies and local authorities.[15]

In October 1947 Clara received the news of the death of Susan Lawrence. Her obituary for the *Fabian Quarterly* (1948) was warm, affectionate, rich in detail, and deeply appreciative of the integrity and the inimitable idiosyncrasy of one of her oldest friends.

> She had an incurable habit of losing her possessions, especially when travelling. Once asked what wish she would chose to have granted, she suggested the return of all that she had lost and pictured the fountain pens, umbrellas and handbags rushing back to their owner. "But", she added, "I should have to engage the Albert Hall."[16]

Clara was inordinately proud of her nieces, Mary and Lucy Tabor who were regular visitors to Park Terrace. Lucy vividly remembered a prison visit where she overheard a terse altercation between Clara and the governor who seemed to have different ideas about the 'dole'.[17] She shared Clara's interest in the criminal justice system, worked in the Probation service throughout the war and as an Inspector in the Children's Department of the Home Office until 1953 and was appointed a magistrate in 1962. Mary and Clara were very similar in temperament, innately kind and formidably efficient, with a forensic turn of mind and a genius for getting things done. Both were experts on local authority housing programmes. Mary had been appointed Housing Manager for the Stevenage New Town Development Corporation in 1951. Stevenage was the first of the architect-designed new towns known as 'pram city' due to large number of pregnant women or mothers with small children; the 'baby boomers' of today.

As Mark Clapson puts it, the New Towns Act of 1946 was one of the few *grands projets* of the British state, designed to reflect the Labour Party's manifesto commitment to decentralised planned communities with good housing and co-ordinated public services but enjoying bipartisan support.[18] Mary was responsible for meeting all new tenants, interviewing them, and handing over door keys and the Bible (the tenants' handbook). Problem-solving was par for the course; gardens with no top soil, roads that led nowhere, taps with no running water, muddy fields with cows grazing on the site where a factory was promised. What confronted so many deracinated Londoners, however, was chronic loneliness. Mary recalled that 'People used to talk about missing the bright lights of London... but what they were missing was their families'.[19] It was Mary who organised meetings with the Gas and Electricity Board as well as 'welcome parties' for the homesick and the Good Friends' Club for the old.

After four years as a widow Clara was still missing Harris deeply. The house was too big for her to manage although she did take in the occasional student from Christ's or friend of Margery's. In 1948 she invited her sister to move in with her. Margaret was profoundly affected by the death of her life-long friend, Philippa Fawcett in June, a week after her eightieth birthday and shortly after the statutes were altered to permit women to receive Cambridge University degrees. Philippa had retired from the London County Council in 1934 and she and Margaret had celebrated the fiftieth anniversary of their friendship by taking a leisurely motoring tour of Cornwall with Margaret driving Philippa to Fowey and home through the Somerset and Oxfordshire countryside. Philippa's letters to Margaret arranging the tour ended ominously with the initials 'H.P'. (Hitler permitting). This was in the year of the Munich crisis.[20]

Margaret had slowed down physically with stiff fingers and aching joints but could still be amusing, and on occasion light-hearted. She took up braille and corresponded with the visually impaired. She had ostensibly turned her back on Essex County Council which had made her an Alderman in 1937 to facilitate her move to Cambridge. In addition to being a Governor of Homerton Teachers' Training College, she had played a key role in the opening of St Osyth's Teachers' Training College in Clacton and was delighted when one of their halls was named after her.

With the notable exceptions of grammar schools and nuclear disarmament, Clara was broadly in line with official Labour policy after the war. Labour narrowly won the General Election of 1950 with a majority of five but Lesley Symonds and Albert Stubbs lost their seats. Clara supported Aneurin Bevan, John Freeman and Harold Wilson who resigned when the Attlee government proposed to introduce prescription charges and charges for NHS spectacles. She was unhappy with the proposal to transfer funds from the National Insurance Fund to pay for rearmament in 1951, the year in which a re-emboldened Conservative Party led by Winston Churchill, won the General Election.

'The election results are wonderful', wrote Dalton, 'we were out at just the right moment and our casualties are wonderfully light'.[21] But few shared Dalton's optimism and the ministerial careers of Attlee, Cripps, Dalton as well as Bevan and Gaitskell were over. Clara supported Bevan's unsuccessful challenge to the incumbent Herbert Morrison In the elections for the Deputy Leader of the Labour Party in 1953. The Labour group on the borough council in that year numbered ten including Clara as one of two Aldermen. Jack Warren described her as 'probably the most effective member of our group'.[22]

Margaret's health had deteriorated: 'My sister's memory has almost quite gone and she takes little interest in her surroundings', Clara informed Helen Pease sadly in December 1953.[23] Margaret was eighty-six, the cause of death was coronary thrombosis, and Clara was at her bedside. The death certificate recorded her as a 'spinster of no occupation' according to the custom of the time. The governors of St Osyth's sent condolences: 'Miss Tabor will be sorely missed for her sweet personality'.[24] Helen wrote the obituary for the Newnham Roll. She noted appreciatively that 'it is to people like Margaret Tabor that we owe the magnificent tradition of public service which inspires the "Old Newnhamite" in every part of the world'.[25] That same year Ruth Cohen was appointed Principal of Newnham College, much to Clara's satisfaction: Ruth was a not only an old friend but also a strong supporter of the Cambridge Labour Party.

Clara stayed in Park Terrace for three more years struggling to cope as best she could: 'CDR seems rather tired and sad. It is going to be a wrench to give up Park Terrace and yet I think she's wise to do it', wrote Margery Fry. 'But she must find a nice landlady ... She's a Spartan. I'm afraid of her "making do" with something below the mark'.[26] It was a difficult decision but Clara grasped the nettle. She moved into Langdon House, opened by Princes Margaret in 1957, a pleasant residential home with landscaped gardens in Chesterton run by the Cambridge Housing Society which Clara helped to found in 1927 and had supported ever since. Clara was happy in her new home but decided altruistically that she must vacate her room for an old person who needed it more. She had mixed feelings about Meadowcroft, to which she transferred. The committee installed a TV set in the dining room, and a well-wisher presented the home with a lift, but Clara was relieved to move back again to Langdon House when another room eventually became available.

Like it or not, Clara had become an *éminence grise*: whenever she spoke, in the constituency Labour Party or outside it, others listened. Clara never fully embraced Labour's post-war support for comprehensive education and believed that small selective grammar schools were of more benefit to working-class children. She expressed her position forcefully in internal party debates, on the WEA Educational Advisory Committee, and to the world at large. Clara emphasised the popularity of the grammar school with working-class and also middle-class (and potentially Labour-voting) parents. Writing in *The Political Quarterly* in 1952, she argued: 'It is not the grammar school which makes our English education undemocratic but the fact that we have two systems, the free maintained schools on the one hand and the fee paying schools on the other'.[27] While there was complete agreement among the Labour Party rank-and-file about the need for teacher recruitment and raising the school leaving age, the call for 'multilateral schools', as comprehensive schools were first called, was always internally divisive. Even the formidable Ellen Wilkinson, Minister of Education in the Attlee government, and herself a grammar school product, had concentrated on teacher recruitment and raising the school leaving age, implemented shortly before her tragic death in 1947.

Clara could not, or would not, be shifted. What others saw as inexcusable stubbornness and recalcitrance made perfect sense in relation to Cambridge which was dominated by private schools. Clara strongly believed fees should play no part in state-subsidised education, a viewpoint then considered radical – the direct grant was only phased in 1975. 'It is desirable that direct grant schools should come into the national system by making their places free and filled by the same method of selection as are those in the maintained schools'.[28]

Clara's influence was clearly discernible in the decision of the Cambridge CLP to mandate its delegate, Councillor Phyllis Clarke (later Lord Mayor of Hull), to oppose Labour's policy on comprehensives put forward in the document *Challenge to Britain* at the party conference of 1953. The evidence of 'experts' on intelligence testing such as the psychologist Sir Cyril Burt used by supporters of selective education was only fully discredited from the 1960s onwards. Those in favour of comprehensive schools including Phyllis Clarke, who chaired the Cambridge Labour Party from 1952 to 1955 were in a minority, albeit a very vocal and disaffected one, and would in private cite Clara's presence behind the scenes as one reason for the very late conversion of the constituency party to the comprehensive ideal.

In November 1956 the Soviet Union marched troops into Hungary, brutally suppressing a popular uprising against the repressive Stalinist government of Mátyás Rosenfeld and the domestic policies imposed by the Union of Soviet Socialist Republics. Hungarian refugees fleeing the Russian tanks began to arrive in Cambridge and Clara once again began to collect money and to solicit offers of accommodation. Dr Alice Roughton, an idealistic medical practitioner, peace activist, and conservationist *avant la lettre*, wrote to *The Cambridge Daily News* appealing for clothes and blanket for the Hungarian Refugee Fund.[29] She and Clara 'often spoke on the same political platforms and were near contemporaries'.[30] Alice's ramshackle Victorian house at 9 Adams Road in Newnham had long served as a sanctuary for any wandering artist, writer, intellectual, displaced person, or 'free spirit' in need of shelter and nourishment. She welcomed Hungarian refugees to live with her, much as she had welcomed the German Jews in 1939.

In the very same month as Hungary, the Suez crisis was precipitated by British, French, and Israeli military action against Egypt after Colonel Nasser's nationalisation and closure of the Suez Canal. Like much of the country, Cambridge was divided into two bitterly opposing camps over the Suez debacle which was to end in national humiliation, the ignominious withdrawal of British forces, and to bring down Anthony Eden's ill-fated premiership in 1957. For many avid listeners to the BBC Home Service or those able to follow the news on their tiny Bakelite television sets, Suez seemed the nearest that the United Kingdom would ever come to a civil war.

Walking at the head of the anti-Suez protest march organised by the Labour Party on November 3 and addressing the demonstration on Parker's Piece on November 4, Clara must have been transported back to the rowdy demonstrations of her 'votes for women' days as the intrepid protesters were pelted with smoke bombs, eggs, and toilet rolls and dowsed with water. Pro- Suez undergraduates noisily disrupted the Labour Party's 'No War over Suez' meeting in the Cambridge Union building where two Labour MPs, Anthony Wedgwood Benn (Bristol) and Kenneth Younger (Grimsby) struggled to make their voices heard above the din.[31]

The old Cambridge that Clara knew was changing. A Roman sarcophagus with its inner lead coffin (the Arbury coffin) containing the remains of a woman, a shrew, and mouse was dug up during the excavations for a large new housing estate. Sylvia Plath, then a visiting postgraduate student at Newnham College, happened to see the unnerving skeleton when it was displayed in the Museum of Archaeology and Anthropology and it inspired Plath's 1957 poem, 'All the Dead Dears'. Sewers and roads were laid on the Arbury Road Estate on a site of around 100 acres for those on the council waiting list thankful to be rehoused with proper bathrooms and running hot water. There was some attempt to establish a new 'village style' community with shops, a primary school, two churches, and a public house in Arbury but a chronic lack of amenities in the north of the city where the neighbouring King's Hedges area was also being developed for housing. The residents' battle for better amenities to alleviate the 'deserts of asphalt' was to be long and protracted. Clara was a founding member of the voluntary committee which set up a experimental adventure playground on the Newmarket Road in 1957, accessible to several of the nearby housing estates so that the children did not have to play on muddy building sites or in the street, and was responsible for compiling the report for the Cambridge Adventure Playgrounds Committee based on the diary of the play leader.[32]

Clara was becoming increasingly conscious that her hearing had worsened to a point where it could no longer be ignored. She retired from all public duties citing deafness as the cause. As early as 1902 Clara had organised and spoken at a large protest meeting organised by Liberal women against proposals in the Balfour Education Act of 1902 to end the right of women to stand for direct election to school boards.[33] In June 1903 she was attending management meetings of the Eden Street Girls Higher Grade School. Fifty-five years later, as Conservative Mayor, Cyril Ridgeon, pointed out, Clara had not only served on most council committees but was still on the Catering, Commons, General Purposes, Selection and Public Health committees and had been on the Education Committee since 1929. On January 27, 1957 the news of Clara's resignation was reported in the local papers. The many readers who struggled to take in the news with their tea and digestive biscuits reacted with shock, dismay, and disbelief.[34]

It was hardly a surprise: Clara was eighty-one. But the public response was overwhelming; the sense of regret, loss and sadness palpable as dozens of letters poured in. Many of the correspondents, like the canteen staff and the meals supervisor at the Girls' High School ('I shall always remember your kindness when I first started') wrote privately to Clara expressing their thanks. The letters that meant the most to her came from teachers. F. M. Mansfield of the Cambridge Teachers' Association lamented the loss of the 'teachers' champion' and a 'tireless advocate of child protection ... the staunchest friend they have ever had'. 'You must know that you are held in universal affection by friends and opponents' wrote Hamilton Kerr, the Conservative MP for Cambridge. The Reverend Mervyn Stockwood said simply: 'You have been a wonderful inspiration and example'. One moving tribute came from County Councillor P. F. Dennards, who remembered growing up in grinding poverty in the area near the Castle Street Mission which Clara had represented as a Poor Law Guardian and Harris had surveyed for Toynbee Hall.

> May I also thank you as a very humble and poor boy from Castle End Boys' School for the great work you did in your early days to bring about such a great change in the life of children... We never see children with shaven heads owing to vermin these days. I am sure

no one will ever know how much this is due to you and your friends who worked so hard.

Over a hundred teachers gathered in Gresham Place to say their farewells. Miss D. A. Humphries for the city teachers, and Mrs Kay for the county, presented Clara with a luminous clock, a bouquet, and dinner at the University Arms Hotel. Clara took home twelve gifts ranging from a black nylon stole and the promise of a made-to-measure tweed skirt from students at the Coleridge Evening Centre where she had been on the management committee since 1930. At a party organised by the Staff Association at the 'Tech' the Principal, Deryck Mumford, presented Clara with a leather wallet and a cheque.

Clara refused to have a bust of herself, a severe and distinctly unflattering one which she disliked intensely, put on public display in the Shire Hall during her life time but stipulated that the council could do could do whatever it thought appropriate after her death.[35] G. E. Edwards, the Chief Education Officer, was tasked with tackling Clara on the subject of the bust: He reported that 'She ordered me immediately to abandon this monstrous proposal' and that he had had 'to prevent her from struggling to carry the bust away in her bicycle basket!'[36] Clara also declined to allow her name to be put on a seat in a school garden or a school in the city to be called by her name.[37]

Many tributes to Clara were elegiac, some seeing her loss as marking the end of an era of disinterested public service although she stressed that she fully intended to continue working for the Labour Party and the WEA.[38] Clara was to become a familiar and much-loved figure in the streets of Cambridge in her later years, making light of her deafness, riding everywhere at speed on her bicycle, wilfully ignoring traffic lights, and stopping abruptly without notice to chat to friends young and old. One policeman referred to her as a 'tough old bird' after a particularly nasty fall from her bike.[39]She still liked hopping on and off double-decker buses much as she had done as a child and usually refused offers of lifts to meetings because a bicycle was much less trouble than a car. Whenever anyone she spoke to 'expressed a wish – to find a new job or just a desire for a book or a holiday... It was always "How can I help you to get it" and she would suggest a solution days afterwards without forgetting'.[40]

Clara enjoyed visiting those whom she described as 'the aged', although they were often some years younger than herself. She read aloud to the blind including one old lady in an almshouse who requested Arnold Bennett's novels although Clara considered them dated. A law student whom she had helped with his studies wrote apologetically 'I am afraid we only got a third' – Clara being greatly amused by his use of 'we'. Frederick Poole a student at Fitzwilliam College named one of his two daughters, Alison Dorothea in her honour.[41]

Clara broadcast five short talks for the 'Indian Summer' series of the BBC Home Service between August 1957 and April 1961. Janet Walters from the Talks Department recorded them in the BBC studio in the ADC premises in Park Street apologising that a comment about Gladstone and Colman's mustard 'could not be used because of the advertising implications'.[42] The inclusive fee was 7 guineas per talk. Clara still favoured the Co-op with her custom, but was sometimes dressed by Elizabeth Rackham's mother. She remarked after a smarter-than-usual outfit had been specially made for her: 'I can't wear this. My old ladies won't know me' and gave the costume to Lucy Tabor.[43]

The 1950s had not been an auspicious time for feminism. Winifred Adams remembered Clara lamenting that she 'had given up the best years of her life to open doors for women who didn't really want them to be opened'.[44] 1957 saw the release of Elvis Presley's 'Jailhouse Rock' in the United States, the launch of Sputnik into space by the Union of Soviet Socialist Republics and the Wolfenden report recommending the legalization of homosexuality between consenting adults, which was duly ignored by the Conservative government. The United Kingdom tested its first Hydrogen bomb at Malden Island in the Pacific. Petrol rationing ended after Suez. Helped by a strong economic boom and a general feeling of material well-being – one in five householders had a washing machine and one in twenty a refrigerator – the Prime Minister, Harold Macmillan, made his famous declaration that 'most of our people have never had it so good' at a rally of the Tory faithful in nearby Bedford before the Conservative Party again swept to victory in the General Election of 1957.

Events had forced Clara to modify the pacifist world view formed in her suffragist days. However, her feminist internationalism and her belief that peace could be secured through co-operation and international arbitration remained as strong as ever. Horrified by the devastation caused by the atomic bomb in Hiroshima, by Britain joining the Soviet Union and the United States in testing nuclear weapons, Clara was among the first members of the Campaign for Nuclear Disarmament when it was formed by Canon John Collins of St Paul's Cathedral in 1957. Both the Rackham and Tabor sides of the family were tendentially progressive in their politics. As Sarah Rackham put it, the 'peace movement was in the family DNA'.[45] The extended family turned out in force in April 1960 for the third Aldermaston March, from the Atomic Research station at Aldermaston in Berkshire to London, organised by CND.

Anne, Ernest, and Christopher Hobbs trudged along from the first day of the fifty-mile protest.[46] It was a tiring but unforgettable experience with the mood of the marchers veering from sombre to jubilant. Clara joined the massive rally in Trafalgar Square headed by J. B. Priestley on the last day of the four-day protest accompanied by Sarah Rackham aged eleven. They recognised familiar faces from Cambridge including the archaeologist, Jacquetta Hawkes, and were addressed by Michael Foot, Canon Collins, and Mervyn Stockwood, the Bishop of Southwark, formerly Canon of Great St Mary's Church in Cambridge. Clara took part in her last CND march in 1961 and was eighty-five when she walked the nine miles from Finchingfield to Braintree. She was defensive about not completing the full distances ('Well, Bertie Russell does an awful lot of sitting & not much walking').[47]

Clara was one of the Cambridge luminaries including James Cornford, Peter Laslett, the economic historian, Nicholas Kaldor, the economist, and Joseph Needham who signed a letter in *The Guardian* expressing support for Fidel Castro after the botched 'Bay of Pigs' invasion led by Cuban exiles from the United States in April 1961.[48] At its 1960 Conference in Brighton in October 1960 Labour voted for unilateral nuclear disarmament expressly against the wishes of its leader, Hugh Gaitskell. The decision was duly reversed at the Labour Party Conference in Blackpool in October 1961.

Whether through a fear that Gaitskell would resign as Party Leader, or because Bevan had come out against unilateral disarmament, or perhaps persuaded by Hugh Dalton's pragmatic argument that unilateralism might appeal to 'small groups of excited people, mostly middle class'[49] but would never be accepted by the Durham miners or any Working Men's Club he knew, Clara supported the majority.

On January 15, 1962 Clara heard that Tawney had died in his sleep in a nursing home in Bloomsbury, his last public act having been to sign a letter to *The Times* calling for the abolition of the death penalty.[50] On January 24 she heard her name had been mentioned by James Callaghan, MP, during a parliamentary debate on the Plowden Report on primary education: 'Margaret Bondfield told a very old lady, a friend of mine ... Clara Rackham, who was very active in political life: Always remember this: you are never doing anything in politics unless they describe you as "that intolerable woman"'.[51] She attended Tawney's Memorial Service held in St Martins in the Field in February. The address in the chapel of Highgate Cemetery given by Hugh Gaitskell.[52]

On July 19, Clara spoke at the Golden Jubilee of the National Council of Women at a dinner in the University Arms Hotel, as the sole survivor of those women in their bonnets and shawls who met in May 1912 to elect the committee of the Cambridge branch. The honorary guest was Dame Barbara Wootton. Clara remembered her own feelings on saying goodbye to Barbara in 1922 ('it was a great grief for me that she was leaving Cambridge. But I realised now that what Girton has lost the country has won').[53]

Replying to the toast, Clara reflected on how much the NCW had achieved: women magistrates, school managers, jurors, and councillors, nurses in the Great Eastern Hospital, improvements in conditions for college bed makers, better treatment of juvenile offenders and speed restrictions on motor cars. However, there was no room for complacency. The number of women on the town council was still only 6, only one more than in 1924.[54] The road to perdition, Clara, reminded her audience, was not so much paved with good intentions as littered with resolutions on which no action had been taken: 'I feel there is still a good deal to do. The numbers of women in the university are still 1 to 10 men and when you see the immense difficulty in getting money for our third women's college…'.[55]

Anne Hobbs had now become a student at Newnham College. 'We were very fond of each other, though I know she was a little sad that I was involved more with the arts and literature than with social and political causes'. They met for tea in the ivy-clad Garden House Hotel and watched the punts gliding slowly along the river: Anne had 'happy memories of swimming with Aunt Dorothea (in her mid-eighties) and my aunt Winifred Elisabeth Adams (in her early 50s) in the women's area of the Cam in 1962'[56] with the grassy river bank full of cow parsley, dandelions, buttercups, and daisies.

In October 1962 the world watched aghast as the Soviet Union and the United States came to the brink of nuclear war over the installation of nuclear-armed Soviet missiles on Cuba and the naval blockade of the island by the United States. The Cambridge Labour Party, always reliable in its anti-war ethos and its support for the United Nations, did what it usually did at moments of international crisis: it convened an emergency meeting and then organised a march and a protest meeting. This time the 'mass march' went from the Labour hall in Norfolk Street, renamed the Alex Wood Memorial Hall, distributing 'hands off Cuba' leaflets to spectators emerging from the football match on Milton Road, and culminated in a rally on Parker's Piece.

Clara is pictured in *The Cambridge Daily News*; a diminutive figure with an oversized handbag walking alone and unassisted with her eyes fixed on the horizon and dwarfed by lanky Robert Davies, the prospective Labour MP for Cambridge, a few steps behind[57] (see Figure 4.5). It would no more have crossed her mind to stay at home during a protest on war and peace than to refuse to brush her teeth. She was, as her friend, Lucy Munby, said approvingly, an 'activists' activist to the very end'.[58] But the Cuba demonstration was to be her last.

In 1963 the indoor swimming pool on the corner of Mill Road and Gonville Place, a bold rectilinear building with huge glass windows, for which Clara had battled long and hard, on behalf of the working people of Romsey Town which she had represented, was completed at a cost of 248,000 pounds and opened by Alderman Ridgeon. With its learner pool, café, and seating for 500 spectators, the light and airy Parkside Pool was lauded as one of the best in the country and would not have been out of place in any modern European capital. Had Clara still lived in Park Terrace she would have enjoyed a fine view of the imposing edifice to municipal modernism from her sitting room window.

Clara attended the gala opening but like many hardy swimmers disliked artificially heated water and 'silly' rubber swimming caps, although she did take a backward glance to admire the exotic fish in the aquarium. It was with great reluctance that she finally stopped swimming in the women's area of the river at Hodson's Folly and in the open air pool on Jesus Green. On a WEA coach trip to the sea side when she was over eighty she walked 3 miles along the coast and 3 miles back to enjoy a dip in the sea.[59] What did gain her approval, was a beautiful bronze sculpture 'Swimmers' by Betty Rea surrounded by mature trees behind the new swimming pool in Mortimer Road and completed in 1965 by John W. Mills after Betty's death.

Clara's ninetieth birthday was fast approaching and the mischievous side of her nature was delighting in her own status as a coelacanth; a fossil that amazed everyone by still being alive. The first and greatest man she met – she would tell awe-struck audiences – was Lord Shaftesbury. She was eight at the time, he two years short of eighty-five, and he was 'my mother's delight'.[60] Her memory sharp as ever, Clara was much in demand as a speaker; still relishing invitations to reminisce about the famous people she had known; still seizing every opportunity to see the great causes of the past were not forgotten; sparing no effort to ensure that the flame of reform was kept alight.

Clara's notes for her short talks are neatly penned in ink, sometimes on the back of a handy picture postcard, an invitation to an Open Day, or a grand civic reception. She was one of a frugal generation that never threw away a rubber band, a scrap of paper, or a used envelope if it could be reused. The cheap ball point pens that people handed her were always politely turned away. The writing is tiny but still firm and legible, betraying no sign of infirmity or of her having slowed down mentally, with very few smudges or tell-tale crossing-out. Written, in the main, to be read aloud to small voluntary organisations, clubs and community groups; Girl Guides, the Business and Professional Women, the Baptist Fireside Group, foreign students in Cambridge, the Soroptimists, the Round Table, etc., her talks are hardly sophisticated by today's standards. But they were expertly attuned to the needs of her listeners and when the occasion called for humour or lightness of touch, reliably entertaining.[61]

Clara had met Emily Davies when the latter was in her late seventies, dainty, delicate and precise with white lace cap and lace at her throat; her appearance suggesting a fairy godmother rather than the lifelong fighter for women's education and the parliamentary vote. The other subjects of her reminiscences; Sydney and Beatrice Webb, Millicent Fawcett, Octavia Hill, Eleanor Rathbone, Henrietta Barnett had one thing in common: they had left behind them a more humane and compassionate world. Clara spoke with some sadness about Margery Fry who had died in 1958; the 'sole originator of a Reform which is now before Parliament and will soon become law',[62] by which she meant the

Criminal Injuries Compensation Scheme which provided payment from public funds to the innocent victims of crimes of violence. Virtually all Clara's contemporaries were dead and she felt fortunate to have outlived them. But the dead were ever present in her octogenarian memory like flickering images in the lantern lectures she had watched as a child: 'I saw them, talked with them, stayed with them. All distinguished in their day and mine, not in yours, many forgotten, but we owe them a great deal and they should be remembered'.[63]

On October 15, 1965 the council voted to award Clara the Freedom of the City of Cambridge in anticipation of her ninetieth birthday. 'None of my arguments had any effect on her resistance to any form of honour', wrote Jack Warren, the Deputy Mayor, explaining that Clara asked for a wooden bench to be placed at the bus stop outside Meadowcroft instead. Two days later a fine teak specimen appeared and Clara rang Warren to express her thanks, noting that 'in her long experience, it was the fastest she had seen local government move'.[64] A feature entitled 'Freedom Fighters' written with Clara's consent by a local Labour Party activist, Sam Green, was published in *The Guardian* on October 25; Mary Stott, the editor of the *Women's Page* having requested a photograph of Clara 'in action'. Clara, mystified and annoyed in equal measure by the contemporary obsession with 'celebrity', sent an unprepossessing photograph which was rejected. The weeks before and after her ninetieth birthday on December 3 were hectic and exhilarating. Clara was overwhelmed under the weight of numerous greeting cards and presents: 'a scarf, two lovely bed jackets and bottled fruit', seventeen telegrams and quantities of flowers which the warden of Meadowcroft arranged as a showpiece in the entrance hall. Lucy thoughtfully sent the glorious golden brown chrysanthemums that Clara had always loved. Willie's son, Miles, a solicitor in Letchworth, came to visit as did Mary, Winifred, and Elizabeth, and Barbara arrived with some very superior writing paper. Jessie Stewart sent a book on Tutankhamun.

Sibyl Hutton collected Clara's used postage stamps, took them to the SOS Children's Village and helpfully arranged cars for Clara's friends who were too frail to travel on their own. Harold Shearman, newly appointed as Chair of the new Greater Council wrote to thank her for encouraging his early ventures in the WEA in Bedfordshire.[65] Lionel Elvin, Director of the Institute of Education at London University, and a member of the Robbins Committee on Higher Education, wrote to seek Clara's views on the report's findings and to renew their friendship of old.

Newnham College went to enormous trouble; Ruth Cohen, the Principal, and a small organising committee including Jean Salter, from the WEA, Sybil Hutton, and Barbara White, Registrar of the College Roll and a distant relative of Clara's by marriage, were determined to make Clara's ninetieth an unforgettable event (see Figure 4.6). One hundred people attended a sherry party in the Principal's Lodge including Alexander Todd (Baron Todd of Trumpington), Nobel Laureate and Master of Christ's College. Clara was sorry that Mary Cartwright, Mistress of Girton, had missed her twenty-minute speech as her garage door had been blocked by parked cars. Guests complimented Clara on an opal blue dress that perfectly matched the colour of her eyes.

The college had extended invitations to all the organisations with which Clara was known to be associated. Those accepting included the Playgrounds Association, the Humanists, the Nursery School Association, the Red Cross, the Medical Superintendent of Fulbourn Hospital, the Women's Co-operative Guild, the Federation of University Women, The Business and Professional Women's Association, the National Council of Women, the Women Citizens' Association, The United Nations Association and the Mental Welfare Association, as well numerous friends and former colleagues from local government and the city and county council. The numbers were constrained, as Jean Salter wrote to explain apologetically, only by the size of the Principal's rooms.

Clara was at her happiest when surrounded by old friends, activists, and comrades. Two hundred people from the Labour Party, the WCG and CND congregated in the Alex Wood Hall for a tea party and she was pleased to see Joseph and Dorothy Needham in their midst: 'He has just been made Master of Caius and is an old friend of mine'. Not to be outdone, the WEA organised a separate tea party in her honour at Christ's College with a cake with ninety birthday candles. The guests included the Master of Sydney Sussex College, David Thomson, author of *Europe Since Napoleon*.

Clara Rackham died peacefully on March 11, 1966 in Langdon House. She would have derived great satisfaction from, but did not live to see, Harold Wilson swept to power with a landslide majority of ninety seats in the General Election two weeks later on March 31. Miles organised a quiet family funeral with 'the usual short C of E service' at the Crematorium in Huntingdon Road. A memorial meeting organised by Helen Pease was held in the Society of Friends Meeting House in Jesus Lane. Clara's estate was valued at £9,749 pounds, the equivalent of 155,845 pounds today. She left small bequests to the Cambridge branch of the RSPCA, the RSPB, and the Howard League for Penal Reform. The essence of a life lived selflessly in the service of others was captured by Isabel Quigly, the writer, translator and film critic in her obituary in the Newnham College Roll.

> Anyone who studies the social reforms of the century in Cambridge will see how much they owe to Mrs Rackham's devoted and unstinting championship of the under-privileged. Her aim was to give them a better way of life. Her success is her memorial.[66]

Afterwards: Remembering Clara Rackham

Rackham Place on the Arbury Estate was named in Clara Rackham's honour after her death and more recently Clara Rackham Street as part of the new building developments in Romsey. Two meeting rooms were also named after her. The first is in the Alex Wood Hall in Norfolk Street, the headquarters of the Cambridge Constituency Labour Party, and the second in the renovated Public Library in Milton Road. In 1972 a large modern building with 'state of the art' teaching rooms and science laboratories was named the Rackham Building at what was formerly the Cambridgeshire College of Arts and Technology and is now Anglia Ruskin University. The Rackham building was demolished in 2009. On October 4, 1980 Joyce Bellamy wrote to *The Cambridge Evening News* requesting readers with information about Clara to contact her and was overwhelmed by the correspondence she received much of which was used in the entry in *The Dictionary of Labour Biography* written by Joyce Bellamy and Eileen Price.

At a commemorative event in Leeds in 2018 organised by the Women's Local Government Society Clara Rackham and Leah Manning were both fêted as two of a hundred 'suffrage pioneers' nominated by villages and towns across the country whose lives had inspired women to become active in their communities. A Blue Plaque to Clara Rackham was paid for by public subscription and erected at her home at 9 Park Terrace in January 2019 and an informal reception in the college organised by Dame Fiona Reynolds, Master of Emmanuel College in her rooms. Dame Stella Manzies officially unveiled the Blue Plaque at a ceremony held in Newnham College in November 2018. In the same month, I organised a celebration of Clara's life and work in music, words, theatre, and dance at Anglia Ruskin University. This included a play, 'Clara Rackham and the General Strike' which was specially commissioned from local author, Ros Connelly, and performed in the Mumford Theatre with Grainne Kennedy in the leading role.

Notes

1 *Labour's Plan for Cambridge* (Cambridge Labour Party, April 1945), 3.
2 Mary Tabor, letter to Joyce Bellamy dated August 17, 1990 (TFP).
3 Clara Rackham, 'Old People', *The Economic Journal* 57, no 226 (June 1947), 218-20, 219.
4 As one example, Nan Youngman's own painting, 'Morning in Dieppe', signed by the artist, dated 1947, and marked 'London Pictures for Schools, 1949', was sold by the auctioneers, Cheffins in Cambridge for the sum of 3,200 pounds in 2019. My thanks to Carolyn Ferguson for this information.
5 Anne Stevenson Wright in conversation with the author, c. November 11, 2018.
6 Clara Rackham, 'Thirty Years on the Bench', typescript (n.d.) (TFP).
7 Mary Tabor, letter to Joyce Bellamy (TFP).

8 Helen Pease, letter to Joyce Bellamy, dated December 4, 1980 (CDR, U DLB/9/55), Hull History Centre Archive.
9 Anne Stevenson Hobbs (n.d.) (ASH).
10 Sara Rackham, conversation with the author, November 20, 2018.
11 Lucy Munby, conversation with Mary Joannou, c. April 6, 2016.
12 Clara Rackham, handwritten notes, King's Lynn School, May 9, 1951; Sawston Village College, May 15, 1955; Bottisham Village College, July 22, 1954; Burwell School, July 28, 1954; Orton Hall School Peterborough; July 7, 1956; Ely High School, October 22, 1957; Impington Village College, November 8, 1957 (TFP).
13 William A. Robson, ed., *Social Security* (London: Allen and Unwin, 1943), 11.
14 Ibid., 37.
15 International Committee of the Howard League for Penal Reform, *Lawless Youth: A Challenge to the New Europe (A Policy for the Juvenile Courts)* (London: Allen and Unwin, 1947).
16 Clara Rackham, 'Susan Lawrence', *Fabian Quarterly*, no 57 (spring 1948), 20–3, 23.
17 Brian Harrison interviews, Miss Lucy Tabor, 8SUF/BO65, January, 6, 1976, Women's Library, LSE.
18 Mark Clapson, 'The English New Towns Since 1946', *Histoire Urbaine* 3, no 50 (2017), 93–111, 93.
19 Quoted by Anthony Alexander, in *Britain's New Towns: Garden Cities to Sustainable Communities* (London: Routledge, 2009), 102.
20 Margaret Tabor, 'My Reminiscences', 58 (TFP).
21 Ben Pimlott, *Hugh Dalton* (London: Jonathan Cape, 1985), 605.
22 Jack Warren, letter to Joyce Bellamy dated October 16, 1980 (CDR, U DLB/9/55), Hull History Centre Archive.
23 Clara Rackham, letter to Helen Pease dated December 9, 1953 (c.525, Pease, H.B., letters to Helen Bowen chiefly from C. D. Rackham, 1949–1964), Cambridgeshire Collection, Cambridge Central Library.
24 J. G. Leary, letter to Clara Rackham, dated February 8, 1954 (TFP).
25 H. H. Pease, 'In Memoriam Margaret Emma Tabor, 1867-1954 (N.C. 1887–I891)', Newnham College Roll, (January, 1955), 34–35, 35.
26 Margery Fry, letter to Clara Rackham, dated May 18, 1957 (TFP).
27 C. D. Rackham, 'Comprehensive Schools', *The Political Quarterly* xxiii, no 2 (April–June 1952), 134–46, 135.
28 Ibid., 139.
29 *Cambridge Daily News*, November 8, 1956, 8.
30 Letter from C. M. Courtney to Joyce Bellamy, dated October 30, 1980 (CDR, U DLB/9/55), Hull.
31 *Cambridge Independent Press and Chronicle*, November 5, 1956, 8.
32 Clara Rackham, *Cambridge Adventure Playground, Holiday Experiment: A Report*, 1957, no publisher (TFP).
33 *Cambridge Daily News*, October 30, 1902, 3.
34 All quotations from individuals responding to Clara's retirement are from an exercise book marked 'Letters, January, 1957' into which Clara pasted letters and press cuttings (TFP).
35 A systematic search of the deposits of both the Guildhall and Shire Hall was undertaken by council officers in 2018 to locate the bust for exhibition purposes but it was never found and may be assumed to have been destroyed.
36 G. D. Edwards, letter to Mary Tabor, dated April 1, 1966.
37 Letter from Helen Pease to Joyce Bellamy, dated December 4, 1980 (CDR, U DLB/9/55), Hull Archive.

38 Written tributes were received from *inter alia*, Mrs D. Simmons, HMI; G. D. Edwards, Chief Education Officer; B. W. Downs, Master of Christ's College; C. P. Thorn, County Treasurer; T. V. Burrows, City Surveyor; W. Wingate, County Architect; E. Purvis, Head of Engineering at the 'Tech'; M. K. Ross, Warden of Sawston Village College; the Head Teachers' Association, Miss Weir, a head teacher; Miss Walker, a high school teacher, the head of Soham Grammar School and B. Bacon, Chair of the governors; the headmistress of the Cambridgeshire Girls' School, the staff in the Open Air School in Ascham Road, Miss Smith, a High School teacher; Miss Hall, an art teacher; the headmaster of St George's School, Miss Howlett, headmistress of Coleridge School; Phyllis Clarke, HMI; Miss Wallman, a headmistress; Harry Walston; Stan Edwards, Chair of the Labour Party; Howard Mallett; Councillor F. H. Fry; Miss Rounds, Children's Officer; the staff of the Planning Department and Cambridge NALGO.
39 Mary Hobbes (n.d.) quoted Anne Stevenson Hobbs (ASH).
40 Letter from Helen Pease to Joyce Bellamy, December 4, 1980.
41 Winifred Adams, letter to Joyce Bellamy dated October 21, 1980 and from Frederick Poole to Joyce Bellamy dated October 30, 1980 (CDR, U DLB/9/55), Hull History Centre Archive.
42 Janet Walters, letter to Clara Rackham dated December 12, 1960 (TFP).
43 Anne Stevenson Hobbs (n.d.) (ASH).
44 Winifred Adams, letter to Joyce Bellamy dated October 21 (CDR, U DLB/9/55), Hull History Centre Archive.
45 Sarah Rackham, conversation with the author, November 10, 2018.
46 Anne Stevenson Hobbs, letter home, April 21, 1964 (ASH).
47 Ibid.
48 *The Guardian*, April 29, 1961, 6.
49 Pimlott, *Hugh Dalton*, 629.
50 Lawrence Goldman, *The Life of R. H. Tawney: Socialism and History*. London: Bloomsbury, 2013, 292.
51 Hansard, vol. 652, January 24, 1962, Select Committee Report on Control of Public Expenditure.
52 Goldman, *Life of Tawney*, 293.
53 Transcript of speeches by Baroness Wootton and C. D. Rackham at Jubilee Dinner of Cambridge NCW, July 9, 1962 (789/Q105), 1–12, 7, Cambridgeshire County Archive, Ely.
54 Ibid., 10.
55 Ibid., 12. The third women's foundation in Cambridge University was New Hall started in Silver Street in 1954 and moved to Huntingdon Road in 1964 when the Darwin family donated their family home, the Orchard. It is now Murray Edwards College.
56 Anne Stevenson Hobbs (n.d.) (ASH).
57 *Cambridge Daily News*, October 29, 1962, 9.
58 Conversation with Mary Joannou, September 16, 2015.
59 I. H. Quigly, Clara Dorothea Rackham (née Tabor) 1975–1966 (Newnham, 1895-1898), Newnham College Roll, (January 1967), 48–51, 49.
60 'Clara Rackham, 'Some Distinguished People I Have Met', handwritten notes for a talk to the Hard of Hearing Club, June 10, 1964, 1–13, 2.
61 The local groups that Clara addressed, even after her formal retirement from the council, are legion. They include the Victoria Road Chapel Women's Friendship Circle, Sawston British Legion, Histon Round Table, Dry Drayton Women's Institute, After School Clubs, Congregational Women, Mill Road Baptists, and the Trumpington Old Folks. We have her brief notes

for talks to WEA groups, the Fabian Society, and numerous meetings of women's sections of the Labour Party, Women's Institutes, Townswomen's Guilds, and branches of the Women's Co-operative Guild much further afield (TFP).

62 'Some Distinguished People', 3.

63 Ibid, 1.

64 Jack Warren, letter to Joyce Bellamy dated October 16, 1980 (CDR, U DLB/9/55), Hull History Centre Archive.

65 Letter from Sir Harold Shearman to Clara Rackham dated September 11, 1965 (TFP).

66 I. H. Quigly, Clara Dorothea Rackham, Newnham College Roll Letter (January 1967), 48–51, 51.

Bibliography

Clara Rackham (Own Publications)

'Banishing the Basement Bogey', *Good Housekeeping* 1927, 54, 166, 168.

Cambridge Adventure Playground, Holiday Experiment: A Report, 1957, 1957, no publisher.

'Cambridge' in Helen Bosanquet, ed. *Social Conditions in Provincial Towns* (London: Macmillan, 1912), 23–36.

'Comprehensive Schools', *The Political Quarterly* xxiii, no. 2 (April–June 1952), 134–46.

'Employment and Leisure', in Eglantyne Jebb, *Cambridge: A Brief Study in Social Questions* (Cambridge: Macmillan and Bowes, 1906), 139–42.

'England's Climbing Boys', *The Economic Journal* 60, no. 238 (June 1950), 381–2.

Factory Law (London: Nelson, 1938).

'From Tolpuddle to T.U.C.', *The Economics Journal* 59, no. 233 (March 1949), 108–10.

'Hungary', *Howard Journal* 5, no. 1 (January 1938), 17–20.

International Committee, Howard League for Penal Reform, *Lawless Youth: A Challenge to the New Europe (A Policy for the Juvenile Courts* (London: Allen and Unwin, 1947).

'Ninety Years' Work for Suffrage and Socialism', *Labour Woman*, March 1966, 56.

'Old People', *The Economic Journal* 57, no. 226 (June 1947), 218–20.

'Old Students and Local Government', Newnham Roll letter, 1958, 18–21.

'One Hundred Years Ago', Cambridge Public Library Record, vol. v, no. 18, March 31st, 1933, 43–6.

'Matrimonial Jurisdiction of Justices', *Probation*, 2, no. 6 (October 1936), 63–84.

'Susan Lawrence', *Fabian Quarterly*, no. 57, spring 1948, 20–3.

'Sussex Branch: Autumn School at Haywards Heath', *Probation* 2, no. 7 (June 1937), 101–2.

'The Cambridgeshire Village Colleges', *Fabian Quarterly*, no. 47, October 1945, 12–13.

'Thrift', in Eglantyne Jebb, *Cambridge: A Brief Study in Social Questions* (Cambridge: Macmillan and Bowes, 1906), 120–2.

'Unemployment', *Outpost: Journal of the Northern Ireland District Council of the Union of Post Office Workers* 4, no. 10 (October 1934).

'Unemployment Insurance', in William Robson, ed. *Social Security* (London: Allen and Unwin, 1943), 125–37.
'When I am M.P., *The Vote XX1X*, no. 973, June 15, 1928, 185.
'William Morris 1834–1876', Cambridge Public Library Record, vol. vi, no. 24, September 29, 1934, 119–24.

Books and Book Chapters

Addison, Paul. *The Road to 1945: British Politics and the Second World War*. London: Jonathan Cape, 1975.
Alberti, Johanna. *Beyond Suffrage: Feminism in War and Peace, 1914–28*. Basingstoke: Macmillan, 1989.
Alexander, Anthony. *Britain's New Towns: Garden Cities to Sustainable Communities*. London: Routledge, 2009.
Anderson, Adelaide, Mary, *Women in the Factory: an Administrative Adventure, 1893-1921* (London: John Murray, 1922).
Barton, Ruth. 'Sunday Lecture Societies, Naturalistic Scientists, Unitarians and Secularists Unite against Sabbatarian Legislation'. In *Victorian Scientific Naturalism: Community, Identity*, edited by Gowan Dawson and Bernard Lightman, 189–219. Chicago, IL: Chicago University Press, 2014.
Beard, Mary. *The Invention of Jane Harrison*. Cambridge, MA: Harvard University Press, 2000.
Beard, Mary, Gillian King, and Christopher Stray. *The Birds and the Bees: Women in Classics*, Cambridge 1871–1948. Cambridge: Faculty of Classics, 1998.
Beaumont, Catriona. *Housewives and Citizens: Domesticity and the Women's Movement, 1926–1964*. Manchester: Manchester University Press, 2013.
Beers, Laura. *Red Ellen: The Life of Ellen Wilkinson, Socialist, Feminist, Internationalist*. Cambridge: Harvard University Press, 2016.
Bell, Adrian. *Only for Three Months: The Basque Children in Exile*. Norwich: Mousehold Press, 1996.
Bill, Ron, and Stan Newens. *Leah Manning*. Harlow: Leah Manning Trust, 1991.
Blaszak, Barbara J. *The Matriarchs of England's Co-operative Movement. A Study in Gender Politics and Female Leadership, 1883–1921*. Westport, CT: Greenwood Press, 2000.
Bosanquet, Helen (ed.). Social Conditions in Provincial Towns. London: Macmillian, 1912.
Brendon, Piers. *The Dark Valley: A Panorama of the 1930s*. London: Pimlico, 2001.
Brigham, Allan. *A Brush with the Past: Cambridge Local History*. Cambridge: Cambridge Place Publishing, 2021.
Brown, Henry. *Co-operation in a University Town*. London: Co-operative Printing Society, 1939.
Calder, Angus. *The People's War: Britain, 1939–1945*. London: Jonathan Cape, 1969.
Cohen, Ruth. *Margaret Llewelyn Davies: With Women for a New World*. London: Merlin, 2020.
Cole, Margaret. *Growing Up into* Revolution. London: Longmans, Green, 1949.

Crawford, Elizabeth. *The Women's Suffrage Movement: Reference Guide 1860–1928*. 2nd ed. London: Routledge, 1999.

Dalton, Hugh, *Call Back Yesterday: Memoirs 1887-1931*. London: Muller, 1953.

Davies, Margaret Llewelyn. 'Foreword' to Catherine Webb, *The Woman with the Basket*, 9–14. Manchester: Co-operative Wholesale Society, 1927.

Davies, Margaret Llewelyn ed. *Life as We Have Known It by Co-operative Working Women*. London: The Hogarth Press, 1931.

Dubrovsky, Gertrude. *Six from Leipzig*. London: Valentine Mitchell, 2003.

Dyhouse, Carol, *Feminism and the Family in England 1880–1939*. Oxford: Basil Blackwell, 1989.

Dyhouse, Carol, *Girls Growing Up in Late Victorian and Edwardian England*. London: Routledge, 2014.

Elvin, Lionel. 'Socialism in the University'. In *Silver Jubilee, 1912–1937: Twenty Five Years in the History of the Cambridge Labour Party*, 26–27. Cambridge: Cambridge Labour Party, 1937.

Fawcett, Millicent, Garrett. *What I Remember*. London: Fisher Unwin, 1924.

Fawcett, Millicent, Garrett, *Women's Suffrage: A Short History of a Great Movement*. London: T.C. and E.C. Jack, 1911.

Fawcett, Millicent, Garrett. *The Women's Victory – and After: Personal Reminiscences 1911–1918*. London: Sidgwick and Jackson, 1920.

Fowler, Helen. 'Eleanor Mildred Sidgwick 1845–1936'. In *Cambridge Women: Twelve Portraits*, edited by Shils, Edward and Blacker, Carmen, 7–28. Cambridge: Cambridge University Press, 1996.

Gaffin, Jean and Thoms, David. *Caring and Sharing: The Centenary of the Co-operative Women's Guild*. Manchester: Holyoake, 1983.

Gardner, Alice. *A Short History of Newnham College*. Cambridge: Newnham College, 1921.

Gloyn, Liz. 'This Is Not a Chapter about Jane Harrison: Teaching Classics at Newnham College, 1882–1922'. In *Women Classical Scholars: Unsealing the Fountain From the Renaissance to Jacqueline de Romilly*, edited by Rosie Wyles and Edith Hall, 153–175. Oxford: Oxford University Press, 2015.

Goldman, Lawrence. *The Life of R. H. Tawney: Socialism and History*. London: Bloomsbury, 2013.

Graves, Pamela, M. *Labour Women: Women in British Working Class Politics 1918–1936*. Cambridge: Cambridge University Press, 1994.

Hamilton, Cicely. *A Pageant of Great Women*. London: Marian Lawson, 1948.

Hamilton, James. *Arthur Rackham: A Life with Illustration*. London: Pavilion, 1990.

Hamilton, Mary, Agnes. *Remembering my Good Friends*. London: Jonathan Cape, 1944.

Hardman, David, ed. *Silver Jubilee, 1912–1937: Twenty Five Years in the History of the Cambridge Labour Party*. Cambridge: Cambridge Labour Party, 1937.

Harrison, Brian. *Prudent Revolutionaries: Portraits of British Feminists between the Wars*. Oxford: Oxford University Press, 1987.

Harrison, Jane, Ellen. *Reminiscences of a Student's Life*. London: Hogarth, 1925.

Helmore, Roy. *CCAT: A Brief History* (Cambridge: Cambridgeshire College of Arts and Technology, 1989).

Hinton, James. *Nine Wartime Lives: Mass-Observation and the Making of the Modern Self.* Oxford: Oxford University Press, 2010.

Hinton, James. *Protests and Visions: Peace Politics in Twentieth-Century Britain.* London: Hutchinson Radius, 1989.

Hollis, Patricia. *Jennie Lee: A Life.* London: Faber, 2014.

Holtby, Winifred. *South Riding* (1936). 3rd ed. London: Fontana, 1974.

Hudson, Derek. *Arthur Rackham: His Life and Work.* London: Heinemann, 1960.

Humphreys, Robert. *Sin, Organised Charity and the Poor Law in Victorian England.* Basingstoke: Macmillan, 1995.

Jackson, Louise, A. *Child Sexual Abuse in Victorian England.* London: Routledge, 2000.

Jebb, Eglantyne, ed. *Cambridge: A Brief Study in Social Questions.* Cambridge: Macmillan and Bowes, 1906.

John, Angela, V., *Turning the Tide: The Life of Lady Rhondda.* Cardigan: Parthian, 2003.

Johnson, Richard and Walsh, Ashley. *Camaraderie: One Hundred Years of Cambridge Labour Party 1912–2012.* Cambridge: Cambridge Labour Party, 2012.

Jones, Enid Huws. *Margery Fry: The Essential Amateur.* Oxford: Oxford University Press, 1966.

Keynes, Florence Ada. *By-ways of Cambridge History.* Cambridge: Cambridge University Press, 1947.

Koven, Seth. *Slumming: Sexual and Social Politics in Victorian London.* Princeton, NJ and Oxford: Princeton University Press, 2004.

Law, Cheryl. *Suffrage and Power: The Women's Movement 1918–1928.* London: I. B. Taurus, 1997.

Lester, Markham,V. H. *Asquith: Last of the Romans.* London: Rowan and Littlefield, 2019.

Lewis, Jane. *The Voluntary Sector, the State and Social Work in Britain: The Charity Organisation Society/Family Welfare Association Since 1869.* Aldershot: Edward Elgar, 1995.

Lewis, Jane. *Women and Social Action in Victorian and Edwardian Britain.* Aldershot: Edward Elgar, 1993.

Lloyd-Jones, Hugh. 'Jane Ellen Harrison 1850–1928'. In *Cambridge Women: Twelve Portraits*, edited by Shils, Edward and Blacker, Carmen, 29–72. Cambridge: Cambridge University Press, 1996.

Logan, Anne. *Feminism and Criminal Justice: A Historical Perspective.* Basingstoke: Palgrave, 2008.

Logan, Anne. *The Politics of Penal Reform: Margery Fry and the Howard League.* London: Routledge, 2018.

Lonsdale, Sarah. *Rebel Women between the Wars.* Manchester: Manchester University Press, 2020.

Marshall, Mary, Paley. *What I Remember.* Cambridge: Cambridge University Press, 1947.

McFeely, Mary, Drake. *Lady Inspectors: The Campaign for a Better Workplace 1893–1921.* Oxford: Blackwell, 1988.

Mahood, Linda. *Feminism and Voluntary Action: Eglantyne Jebb and Save the Children, 1876–1928.* Basingstoke: Palgrave Macmillan, 2009.

Manning, Leah. *A Life for Education: An Autobiography*. London: Gollancz, 1970.

Meacham, Standish. *Toynbee Hall and Social Reform 1880–1914: The Search for Community*. New Haven, CT: Yale University Press, 1987.

McCarthy, Helen. *Double Lives: A History of Working Motherhood*. London: Bloomsbury, 2020.

McDonough, Frank. *Neville Chamberlain, Appeasement and the British Road to War*. Manchester: Manchester University Press, 1998.

McFeely, Mary, Drake. *Lady Inspectors: The Campaign for a Better Workplace 1893-1921*. Oxford: Basil Blackwell, 1988.

Middleton, Lucy, ed. *Women in the Labour Movement: The British Experience*. London: Croom Helm, 1977.

Mitchell, Hannah. *The Hard Way Up: The Autobiography of Hannah Mitchell, Suffragette and Rebel*. London: Virago, 1984.

Needham, Joseph. *History is on Our Side: A Contribution to Political Religion and Scientific Faith*. London: Allen and Unwin, 1946.

Oakley, Anne. *Barbara Wootton, Social Science and Public Policy in the Twentieth Century*. London: Bloomsbury, 2011.

Oldfield, Sibyl. *Spinsters of This Parish: The Life and Times of F.M. Mayor and Mary Sheepshanks*. London: Virago, 1984.

Searby, Peter, ed. *Cambridge at War: The Diary of Jack Overhill 1939–1945*. Cambridge: Cambridgeshire Records Society, 2010.

Parkes, Susan, M. *A Danger to the Men? A History of Women in Trinity College Dublin 1904–2004*. Dublin: Liliput Press, 2004.

Pedersen, Susan. *Eleanor Rathbone and the Politics of Conscience*. New Haven, CT and London: Yale University Press, 2004.

Pederson, Susan. *Family Dependence, and the Origins of the Welfare State, Britain and France 1914–1945*. Cambridge: Cambridge University Press, 1993.

Pevsner, Nicolaus. *The Buildings of England: Cambridgeshire*. Harmondsworth: Penguin, 1954.

Phillips, Ann, ed. *A Newnham Anthology*. Cambridge: Newnham College, 1979.

Pimlott, Ben, ed. *The Political Diary of Hugh Dalton*. London: Cape, 1986.

Poovey, Mary. *Making a Social Body: British Cultural Formation 1830–64*. Chicago, IL: University of Chicago Press, 1995.

Raverat, Gwen. *Period Piece: A Victorian Childhood*. Cambridge: Faber and Faber, 1952.

Rée, Harry. *Educator Extraordinary: The Life and Achievement of Henry Morris 1889–1961*. London: Longman, 1973.

Rée, Harry, ed. *The Henry Morris Collection*. Cambridge: Cambridge University Press, 1984.

Robinson, Jane. *Hearts and Minds: The Untold Story of the Great Pilgrimage and How Women Won the Vote*. London: Doubleday, 2018.

Robinson, Sydney W. *The Last Victorians: A Daring Reassessment of Four Twentieth-Century Eccentrics: Sir William Joynson-Hicks, Dean Inge, Lord Reith, and Sir Arthur Bryant*. London: Robson Press, 2014.

Robson, William, ed. *Social Security*. 3rd ed. London: Allen and Unwin, 1948.

Rosen, Andrew. *Rise Up Women: The Militant Campaign of the Women's Social and Political Union 1903–1914*. London: Routledge and Kegan Paul, 1974.

Ross, Ellen, ed. *Slum Travelers: Ladies and London Poverty 1860–1920*. Berkeley: University of California Press, 2007.
Rubinstein, David. *A Different World for Women: The Life of Millicent Garrett Fawcett*. Columbus: Ohio University Press, 1991.
Russell, Dora. *The Tamarisk Tree: My Quest for Liberty and Love*. London: Elek/Pemberton, 1975.
Ryan, Mick. *The Acceptable Pressure Group: Inequality in the Penal Lobby: A Case Study of the Howard League for Penal Reform*. Farnborough: Saxon House, 1978.
Schaffer, Talia. '"Nothing but Foolscap and Ink": Inventing the New Woman'. In *New Woman in Fiction and in Fact: Fin-de Siècle Feminisms*, edited by Richardson, Angelique and Willis, Chris, 39–52. London: Palgrave, 2002.
Scott, Gillian. *Feminism and the Politics of Working Women: The Women's Co-operative Guild, 1880 to the Second World War*. London: UCL Press, 1998.
Searby, Peter, ed. *Cambridge at War: The Diary of Jack Overhill 1939–1945*. Cambridge: Cambridgeshire Records Society, 2010.
Slack, Sue. *Cambridge Women and the Struggle for the Vote*. Stroud: Amberley, 2018.
Stevenson, John. *British Society 1914–45*. London: Penguin, 1984.
Stevenson, John and Cook, Chris. *Britain in the Depression: Society and Politics 1929–39*. London: Longman, 1994.
Stewart, Jessie. *Recuerdos – The Basque Hostel at Cambridge*. Cambridge, distributed by *Cambridge Daily News*, 1939.
Strachey, Ray. *Millicent Garrett Fawcett*. London: John Murray, 1931.
Dupree, Marguerite, ed. *Lancashire and Whitehall: The Diary of Sir Raymond Street 1931–1939*. Vol. 1. Manchester: Manchester University Press, 1977.
Stocks, Mary. *My Commonplace Book*. London: Peter Davies, 1970.
Sutherland, Gillian. *Faith, Duty and the Power of the Mind: The Cloughs and Their Circle 1820–1960*. Cambridge: Cambridge University Press, 2006.
Sutherland, Gillian. *In Search of the New Woman: Middle-Class Women and Work in Britain 1870–1914*. Cambridge: Cambridge University Press, 2015.
Swindells, Julia. *Victorian Writing and Working Women: The Other Side of Silence*. Cambridge: Cambridge University Press, 1985.
Thane, Pat. *Divided Kingdom: A History of Britain, 1900 to the Present*, 103. Cambridge: Cambridge University Press, 2018.
Thane, Pat. 'What Difference Did the Vote Make?' In *Women, Privilege and Power: British Politics 1750 to the Present*, edited by Vickery, Amanda, 253–88. Palo Alto: University of Stanford Press, 2001.
Thane, Pat. 'Women, Liberalism and Citizenship, 1918–30'. In *Citizenship and Community: Liberals, Radicals and Collective Identities in the British Isles, 1865–1931'*, edited by Biagini, Eugenio, F., 66–92. Cambridge: Cambridge University Press, 1996.
Thom, Deborah. *Nice Girls and Rude Girls: Women Workers in World War One*. London: I. B. Taurus, 1998.
Thorpe, Andrew. *A History of the British Labour Party* (1997). London: Palgrave, 2015.
Tullberg, Rita Mcwilliams. *Women at Cambridge: A Men's University – Though of a Mixed Type*. London: Gollancz, 1975.

Vellacott, Jo. *Pacifists, Patriots and the Vote: The Erosion of Democratic Suffragism in Britain during the First World War.* Basingstoke: Palgrave, 2007.
Wade, Francesca. *Square Haunting: Five Women, Freedom and London between the Wars*. London: Faber and Faber, 2020.
Ward, Stephanie. *Unemployment and the State in Britain: The Means Test and Protest in 1930s South Wales and North-East England.* Manchester: Manchester University Press, 2013.
Williams, Raymond. *What I Came to Say*. London: Hutchinson, 1989.
Williams, V. and White, G.J. *Adult Education and Social Purpose: A History of the WEA Eastern District 1913–1988*. Cambridge: Graham Cameron Publishing, 1988.
Women's Co-operative Guild. *Working Women and Divorce: An Account of Evidence Given on Behalf of the Women's Co-operative Guild before the Royal Commission on Divorce*. London: David Nutt, 1911.

Journal Articles

Chitty, Clyde. 'David Rooney, *The Cambridgeshire Village Colleges and Community Education*'. *Forum* 56, no. 2 (2014): 319–21.
Clapson, Mark. 'The English New Towns since 1946'. *Histoire Urbaine* 3, no. 50 (2002): 93–111.
Freeman Mark. 'The Provincial Social Survey in Edwardian Britain'. *Historical Research* 75, no. 187 (2002): 73–89.
Fry, Margery. 'General Survey'. *Howard Journal* 5, no. 1 (January 1938): 8.
Fry, Margery. 'Roumania'. *Howard Journal* 5, no. 1 (January 1938): 20–7.
Hannam, June. 'Women as Paid Organisers and Propagandists for the British Labour Party Between the Wars'. *International and Working-Class History vol* 77, issue 1, (spring 2010): 69–88.
Jones, Helen. 'Women Health Workers: The Case of the First Women Factory Inspectors in Britain'. *Social History of Medicine* 1, no. 2 (1988): 165–81.
Laybourn, Keith. '"Waking Up to the Fact That There Are Any Unemployed": Women, Unemployment and the Domestic Solution in Britain, 1918–1939'. *History* 88, no. 4 (292) (October 2003): 606–23.
Livesey, Ruth. 'The Politics of Work: Feminism, Professionalisation and Women Inspectors of Factories and Workshops 1890–1906'. *Women's History Review* 13, no. 2 (2004): 233–61.
Logan, Anne. 'In Search of Equal Citizenship: The Campaign for Women Magistrates in England and Wales, 1910–1939'. *Women's History Review* 16, no. 2 (2007): 501-18.
Logan, Anne. 'Political Life in the Shadows: The Post Suffrage Life of S. Margery Fry (1874–1958)'. *Women's History Review* 23, no. 3 (2014): 365–80.
Logan, Anne. 'Professionalism and the Impact of England's First Women Justices, 1920–1950'. *Historical Journal* 49, no. 3 (2006): 833–50.
Logan, Anne. *'The International Work of Margery Fry in the 1930s and '40s'. Women's History* 2, no. 3 (2016): 23–9.
Myers, Kevin, 'National Identity, Citizenship and Education for Displacement: Spanish Refugee Children in Cambridge, 1937'. *History of Education* 28, no. 3 (1999): 313–25.
Steedman, Carolyn. 'Prisonhouses'. *Feminist Review* 20 (Summer 1985): 7–21.

Winter, J.M., and Joslin, D.M. (eds). *R. H. Tawney's Commonplace Book, Economic History Review Supplement*, no. 5 (Cambridge) (1972): i–xxiv.

Archive Sources

Rackham Family Papers, Anne Stevenson Wright (ASH).
Tabor Family Papers, Lucy Tabor and Helen Bloxsome (TFP).
Marie Thompson, personal papers.

Archives Consulted

Cambridge University Library Department of Manuscripts and University Archives; Cambridgeshire Collection, Cambridge Central Library; Cambridgeshire County Council Archives, Ely; Christ's College, Cambridge; Churchill College, Cambridge; Hull History Centre Archive; Needham Research Institute, Cambridge; National Archives at Kew; Newnham College, Cambridge; People's History Museum, Manchester; Women's Library at the LSE.

Newspapers and Periodicals

Chelmsford Chronicle, Common Cause, Essex Newsman, Guardian, Cambridge Daily News, Cambridge Independent Press, Cambridge Weekly News, Daily Herald, Daily Mirror, Good Housekeeping, Manchester Guardian, New Statesman, Times, Vote, Woman's Leader.

Unpublished Dissertations and Theses

Breay, Claire, 'A Gentleman's Education? Women and the Classical Tripos 1869–1914', unpublished dissertation, Newnham College, 1990.
Debenham, Claire, 'Grass roots Feminism: A Study of the Campaigns of the Society for the Provision of Birth Control Clinics, 1924–1938', unpublished Ph.D. thesis, University of Manchester, 2010.
Lee, Chi-Hao, 'The Workers' Educational Association and the Pursuit of Oxford Idealism, 1909–1949', unpublished Ph.D. thesis, University of Cambridge, 2018.
Purkiss, Sallie, 'Over the Bridge: Another Cambridge between Two Wars: Communal Responses to Political, Economic and Social Changes, 1919–1938', unpublished MA dissertation, University of Essex, 1982.
Williams, Vivian, 'The Eastern District of the Workers' Educational Association: Growth and Development, 1913–1940', unpublished Ph.D. thesis, University of London, 1979.

Bibliographical Entries

Bellamy, Joyce and Price, Eileen, *Rackham, Clara Dorothea (1875–1966) Labour Alderman, Social Reformer and Educationalist*, in Joyce Bellamy and John Saville, eds, *Dictionary of Labour Biography*, vol. ix (1993), 232–8.

Harrison, Brian, 'Rackham [née Tabor], Clara Dorothea' (1875–1966), *Oxford Dictionary of National Biography*, 2004, 722–3.

Hartley, Cathy, 'Clara Dorothea Rackham' (1865–1965), [sic] *A Historical Dictionary of British Women* (London: Taylor and Francis, 1983) revised, 2003, 364.

Hodgkin, Thomas L., 'Fry (Sara) Margery' (1874–1958), *Oxford Dictionary of National Biography* 2004, 101–4, revised Mark Pottle, 2007.

Pease, Helen, 'Margaret Emma Tabor' (1867–1954) (N.C. 1887–1891), Newnham College Roll, 1935, 24–35.

Quigly, I. H., 'Clara Dorothea Rackham (née Tabor)' (1975–1966) (Newnham, 1895–1898), Newnham Roll, January 1967, 48–51.

Official Reports

Report of the Royal Commission on the Poor Laws and Relief of Distress, 1909: Appendix vol. xvii [Cmd.4690].

Annual Report of the Chief Inspector of Factories and Workshops for the years 1915, May, 1916, [Cd.8276], and 1919, May, 1920 [Cmd.941].

Report of the War Cabinet Committee on Women in Industry, 1919 [Cmd.135].

Report of the Departmental Committee on Medical Examination of Young Persons for Factory Employment, 1924 [Cmd.2135].

Report of the Departmental Committee on Sexual Offences against Young Persons, 1925 [Cmd.2561].

Report of the Royal Commission on Unemployment Insurance, 1931, First Report [Cmd.3872).

Report of the Royal Commission on Unemployment Insurance, 1931–1932, Final Report [Cmd.4185].

Report of the Royal Commission on Tithe Rentcharge, 1934–1934 [Cmd.5693, 1936].

Online and Digital Sources

Brigham, Allan, A Community in Transition – Romsey Town, Cambridge 1966–2006, https://capturingcambridge.org/wp-content/uploads/2015/10/A-Community-in-Transition.pdf, accessed June 20, 2020.

Harrison, Brian, Interviews with Mary Tabor, interviewed, November 25, 1975, Ref 8SUF/BO62, Women's Library at the LSE and Lucy Tabor, 8SUF/BO65, January 6, 1976, Women's Library at the LSE. https://www.lse.ac.uk/library/-collection-highlights/the-suffrage-interviews, accessed February 6, 2019.

Logan, Anne, https://first100years.org.uk/gertrude-tuckwell-londons-first-woman-magistrate/, accessed July 10, 2018.

Smith, Ann, Kennedy, 'The Cambridge Ladies' Dining Society (*act* 1890–1914)', *Oxford Dictionary of National Biography*, https://doi.org10.93/odnb/9780198614128.013.109658, accessed October 20, 2019.

Ingram, William, Mill Road History Project, Building Report, Romsey Town Labour Club, 2015, https://www.capturingcambridge.org/wp-content/uploads/2014/05/Romsey_Labour_Club_2nd_edn-rev.pdf, accessed June 1, 2020.

Sawston Village College, https://cambsvc.org.uk/category/sawston/, accessed July 5, 2021.

Stevenage Museum, Mary Tabor, Housing Officer, https://www.stevenage.gov.uk/stevenage-museum/blog/mary-tabor-housing-officer, accessed March 16, 2021.

Thompsett, Marjorie, 'The Tabor Diaries 1868–70: Some Aspects of the Mid-Victorian Scene', 2012, https://commons.wikimedia.org/wiki/File:Henry_Tabor_Diaries.pdf, accessed October 22, 2018.

Index

Note: *Italic* page numbers refer to figures.

For Product Safety Concerns and Information please contact our EU
representative GPSR@taylorandfrancis.com
Taylor & Francis Verlag GmbH, Kaufingerstraße 24, 80331 München, Germany

www.ingramcontent.com/pod-product-compliance
Ingram Content Group UK Ltd.
Pitfield, Milton Keynes, MK11 3LW, UK
UKHW022313250926
475702UK00046B/753
9780367373924